# KEATS, HERMETICISM, AND THE
# SECRET SOCIETIES

*For Rabbits and Monkeys*

# Keats, Hermeticism, and the Secret Societies

JENNIFER N. WUNDER
*Georgia Gwinnett College, USA*

ASHGATE

Published by
Ashgate Publishing Limited
Gower House
Croft Road
Aldershot
Hampshire GU11 3HR
England

Ashgate Publishing Company
Suite 420
101 Cherry Street
Burlington, VT 05401-4405
USA

Ashgate website: http://www.ashgate.com

**British Library Cataloguing in Publication Data**
Wunder, Jennifer N.
  Keats, hermeticism, and the secret societies. – (The nineteenth century series)
  1. Keats, John, 1795–1821 – Philosophy 2. Keats, John, 1795–1821 – Criticism and interpretation 3. Hermeticism in literature
  I. Title
  821.7

**Library of Congress Cataloging-in-Publication Data**
Wunder, Jennifer N., 1970–
  Keats, hermeticism, and the secret societies / by Jennifer N. Wunder.
    p. cm.
  Includes bibliographical references.
  ISBN 978-0-7546-6186-3 (alk. paper)
  1. Keats, John, 1795–1821—Philosophy. 2. Keats, John, 1795–1821—Criticism and interpretation. 3. English poetry—19th century—History and criticism. 4. Hermeticism in literature. 5. Secret societies in literature. 6. Romanticism. I. Title.

  PR4838.P5W86 2007
  821'.709—dc22

2007023676

ISBN 978-0-7546-6186-3

Printed and bound in Great Britain by MPG Books Ltd, Bodmin, Cornwall.

# Contents

# The Nineteenth Century Series
## General Editors' Preface

The aim of the series is to reflect, develop and extend the great burgeoning of interest in the nineteenth century that has been an inevitable feature of recent years, as that former epoch has come more sharply into focus as a locus for our understanding not only of the past but of the contours of our modernity. It centres primarily upon major authors and subjects within Romantic and Victorian literature. It also includes studies of other British writers and issues, where these are matters of current debate: for example, biography and autobiography, journalism, periodical literature, travel writing, book production, gender, non-canonical writing. We are dedicated principally to publishing original monographs and symposia; our policy is to embrace a broad scope in chronology, approach and range of concern, and both to recognize and cut innovatively across such parameters as those suggested by the designations 'Romantic' and 'Victorian'. We welcome new ideas and theories, while valuing traditional scholarship. It is hoped that the world which predates yet so forcibly predicts and engages our own will emerge in parts, in the wider sweep, and in the lively streams of disputation and change that are so manifest an aspect of its intellectual, artistic and social landscape.

Vincent Newey
Joanne Shattock
University of Leicester

# Acknowledgements

Many friends and colleagues provided open minds and sound advice as this book took form, but I owe special thanks to Christine Gallant who read and re-read variations of this manuscript over many stages and always offered valuable comments. I could not have wished for a better mentor.

I also owe a debt of gratitude to the gentlemen of the Atlanta-Peachtree Masonic Lodge, and particularly Richard S. Sagar, the former librarian and curator of the Atlanta Masonic Library and Museum, who welcomed me and allowed me free access to their remarkable collection of Masonic texts housed in the Ray Denslow and Greenfield-Blackwell Libraries. I am very grateful for their generous spirit.

# Introduction

# Correspondences

In late 1815, a newly matriculated medical student named John Spurgin wrote a long, intensely personal letter to John Keats. By chance or intent, the letter escaped Keats's occasional fits of housekeeping in which he burned old letters and notes that no longer held his interest. Instead, it passed quietly through history, its existence unknown to scholars. In 1958, the letter appeared at a Sotheby's auction where it was purchased by Arthur A. Houghton, Jr. and placed in the Keats Collection at Harvard's Houghton Library. Where the letter came from, who had possession of it after Keats, who jotted a note in its margin about religion, and who placed the letter for sale at Sotheby's are unknown.

Today, the letter remains almost equally unknown. It has been published in its entirety only once, when Edward B. Hinckley provided readers with a transcription of it and a short biography of John Spurgin in the Winter 1960 issue of the *Keats–Shelley Journal*.[1] Brief phrases from the letter have occasionally resurfaced over the decades, such as a comment Spurgin makes indicating that Keats once described religion to him as a "mazy Mist," but most of the letter's four pages have been largely forgotten as though they had never been found.[2] Several details about the letter, however, beg for greater notice.

Dated 5 December 1815, Spurgin's letter is the earliest existing letter to Keats, written only one month after the earliest letter we have from Keats himself. The letter also contains a long discourse on religion – a scarce enough topic in letters to or from Keats – and in it, Spurgin directly ties spiritual philosophies to Keats's love of poetry and his desire to become a poet even as he was embarking upon his medical studies at Guy's Hospital. Spurgin begins his letter with a request and a warning: "Dear Keats. – read slow if you please I write very queerly."[3] He then offers Keats a complex, personal profession and explanation of Emanuel Swedenborg's philosophies. His writing style suggests that he is specifically responding to previous questions posed by Keats, and this impression is reinforced by the final passages of the letter in which he turns to other, more conventional topics, but does so while referencing remarks that Keats made previously.

---

1 John Spurgin, letter to John Keats, 5 December 1815, Edward B. Hinckley, "On First Looking into Swedenborg's Philosophy: A New Keats-Circle Letter," *Keats–Shelley Journal* 9.1 (Winter 1960): 15–25.

2 Spurgin 24. See, for example, Walter Jackson Bate, *John Keats* (Cambridge, Mass.: The Belknap Press of Harvard University, 1963) 46; and Robert Ryan, *Keats the Religious Sense* (Princeton: Princeton UP, 1973) 53; 72.

3 Spurgin 20.

Throughout, Spurgin explicitly ties aspects of his faith to Keats's own poetic goals, and his comments correspond closely to remarks Keats himself would later make about both poetry and his continually developing philosophies of life. In the midst of his arguments, Spurgin takes care to stress that his belief is one felt in the heart first, and as such, one he trusts implicitly. While he can provide many logical proofs for his belief in Swedenborg's doctrines, Spurgin tells Keats that the greatest proof he can offer is that, "I feel, perceive, and acknowledge thereby the Truth and Sanctity of those Writings."[4] He offers Keats heartfelt advice that he hopes will not only serve Keats's poetic aspirations but also will "disperse" the "mazy Mist" Keats has described to him.[5] He urges Keats to:

> ... cultivate a Knowledge of Things which concern the Life, which is eternal, and you will then see the Life which actuates and animates Nature, which gives her Beauties, which are still subservient to Mankind and you will and can judge then of what can give the brightest and most lucid Flame to the Fire of Poetry even, and wander in Paths amid the Geniuses of old which I know you so much admire, and crop and make choice of the most delicate Fruits and Flowers strewed on both Sides of you, your Contemplations will ascend from Earth to Heaven, by making the former the conveying Medium, and as may be plainly seen in the Face of Man by his Features, the State of his Soul which actuates them, within, so may you judge of the Correspondence of earthly Things with heavenly, as they exist even in the same Manner as the Body does from the Soul.[6]

If readers familiar with Keats's poetry and letters were presented Spurgin's words without attribution, it would be understandable if many suspected Keats as the author. Like Spurgin, Keats will later claim in his letters to friends that truth may lie in what the heart feels and man perceives rather than in consecutive reasoning, and he will assert that knowledge of the heart, human nature, and the world, may lead to a "Mist" and "the 'burden of the Mystery'" man must face as well as the wisdom needed to lighten it.[7] During the year following Spurgin's letter, Keats also will formulate and put into verse a plan of poetic development that bears a striking resemblance to the course of action suggested by Spurgin.

In the 1816 poems *Sleep and Poetry* and *I stood tiptoe upon a little hill*, Keats emphasizes the concepts of wandering and selection as vital to the poet's education as he immerses himself in Nature and Poesy through which he will pass like a traveler in various realms, reading "an ever-changing tale" of "human life," sipping from pastoral fountains, tasting the fruits of Flora's and Pan's worlds, and plucking and choosing "each pleasure that [his] fancy sees" (*Sleep and Poetry* 91–104). In both poems, Nature acts quite clearly as the conveying medium that Spurgin has urged Keats to explore. The poet of *Sleep and Poetry* describes his contemplations as ascending from the beauties of Nature and its earthly pleasures and delights to

---

4  Spurgin 23.
5  Spurgin 24.
6  Spurgin 24.
7  John Keats, letter to John Reynolds, 3 May 1818, *The Letters of John Keats, 1814–1821*, ed. Hyder Rollins, vol. 1 (Cambridge, Mass.: Harvard UP, 1958) 281. Hereafter, this work will be referred to as *Letters I*.

thoughts of "the Framer of all things," of Poesy's "wide heaven," and of a nobler life and aim in which poetry is "a friend / To soothe the cares, and lift the thoughts of man" (39; 49; 246–47). Nature inspires the poet-speaker's "wand'ring spirit" to "soar" in *I stood tiptoe* as well, and leads the poet who first tells Endymion's tale to a contemplation of heaven, literally and figuratively; we are told "surely he had burst our mortal bars; / Into some wond'rous region he had gone" (242; 190–91).

Both *Sleep and Poetry* and *I stood tiptoe* have been identified by scholars as preludes to Keats's first extended poem, *Endymion*, and similarities also exist between Spurgin's advice and comments Keats makes to Benjamin Bailey in letters discussing *Endymion*'s length and its form as a romantic tale that creates "a little Region to wander in" from which lovers of poetry "may pick and choose."[8] Still more significant parallels appear when one considers Keats's letters to Bailey discussing *Endymion* in conjunction with his philosophical musings. In the letters, Keats describes an interchange between Nature and the poet as the medium through which mankind may ascend "from Earth to Heaven," and finds that "we shall enjoy ourselves here after by having what we called happiness on Earth repeated in a finer tone and so repeated," because "Imagination and its empyreal reflection is the same as human Life and its spiritual repetition."[9]

Given the dating and context of Spurgin's letter, its contents, and the highly suggestive connections that exist between Spurgin's thoughts and those later expressed by Keats, it may seem unusual that scholars have passed over the letter. Yet, several reasons exist to explain the situation. Unfortunately, the letter appeared after the publication of Hyder Rollins's *The Letters of John Keats* and thus was not included in the volumes that long constituted the authoritative source for Keats's letters. The letter also is not from Keats but rather to him, and until it appeared, scholars had no idea that Spurgin and Keats were acquainted. Although the contents of the letter indicate they were friends, and that after Spurgin left medical school, he returned to visit, lent Keats books, and carried on a correspondence with Keats of which the December letter is only a portion, Spurgin was not a regular member of Keats's circle during his most active years writing poetry.

Then, too, by most standards, the letter might be called highly unusual considering the nature of its contents. Despite marked similarities between Spurgin's advice to Keats and Keats's own writings, Spurgin's recommendations exhibit one, crucial characteristic most scholars today would not attribute to Keats. Spurgin's arguments bear all the markings of the hermeticism underpinning Swedenborgian philosophies. His views seem too uncommon, too esoteric, and hermeticism is not a topic scholars associate with Keats. Traditional views of Keats's education and exposure to such concepts have made it seem unlikely that he would be aware of Swedenborgian, much less, hermetic philosophies.

But, what if much of the language and many of the philosophical concepts contained in Spurgin's letter were not exclusive to Swedenborgism, and what if the hermetic language and philosophies were in far more common use than we suspected? What if they were contained within one of the most widespread cultural movements

---

8    Keats, letter to Benjamin Bailey, 8 October 1817, *Letters I* 170.
9    Keats, letter to Bailey, 22 November 1817, *Letters I* 184–86.

of the eighteenth and nineteenth centuries? If this were true, there would be good reason to re-evaluate our perspectives of not only Keats's exposure to hermeticism and its presence in his writings but also much of our own scholarship during the last century.

Like those of other popular mystics such as Jacob Boehme, Swedenborg's teachings included a mix of ideas contained in a number of alchemical and philosophical texts loosely designated hermetic. The texts varied widely and included older works such as the *Tabula Smaragdina*, or *Emerald Table*, Plato's *Timaeus*, and various texts about the Eleusinian Mysteries as well as more recent Renaissance writings by famous authors and physicians such as Ficino and Paracelsus. The writings served as the basis for exoteric and esoteric Neo-Platonic alchemical philosophies and theories of a system of correspondences between heaven and earth and the spiritual and the physical. Spurgin discusses these concepts in the context of Swedenborgism, but hermetic philosophies were espoused by and associated with a wide range of societies during the Romantic period.

During the eighteenth century and well into the nineteenth, beginning with the Freemasons and the establishment of multiple Masonic lodges and degrees, there was an explosion of "secret" societies, many of which were associated in the public mind with hermetic philosophies in general and alchemical philosophies in particular. The Swedenborg Society represented only one variation of an extremely popular movement, and the extent of this movement and its repercussions in Romantic society are suggested in Spurgin's letter. It contains more than his testimony, and Spurgin's comments as the letter draws to a close provide readers with a brief glimpse of the influence that secret societies had during the Romantic period.

Spurgin tells Keats that he is "very silent respecting Swedenborg, as it might perhaps cause Something disagreeable I keep all under <u>Lock</u> and <u>Key</u> – your Suggestions respecting Canning &c are unfounded, as I have made Enquiries, and no one seems to know any Thing about it; Your Allusion to Joanna &c told me the Extent of your Feeling."[10] Notwithstanding his devotion to Swedenborg's doctrines and his trust in Keats, Spurgin's caution was well founded. During the Romantic period, esoteric societies such as Swedenborg's proliferated rapidly, and their spread as well as their teachings evoked both fear and fascination. In the aftermath of the French Revolution, many books were published blaming the Revolution on a conspiracy between the French *philosophes* and the secret societies, and bestselling authors often highlighted Swedenborg's society, identifying it as a branch of higher degree Freemasonry and claiming that it and the other esoteric degrees of Freemasonry disseminated philosophies encouraging the overthrow of the monarchies and Christianity itself.[11]

---

10  Spurgin 24.

11  The Abbé Barruel's *Mémoires Pour Servir à l'Histoire du Jacobinisme* (London, 1798) and John Robison's *Proofs of a Conspiracy against all Religions and Governments of Europe, Carried on in the Secret Meetings of Freemasons, Illuminati, and Reading Societies* (Edinburgh, 1797) related Swedenborgian societies to those of higher degree Freemasonry and the Illuminati throughout. W. K. Firminger, "The Romance of Robison and Barruel,"

Keats appears to have discussed at least some of these issues with Spurgin. Spurgin's reference to Canning, grouped in the same sentence as his confession of silence and the allusion to the prophetess Joanna Southcott, suggests that Keats was wondering if Canning was somehow associated with the Swedenborgians. The reference puzzled Hinckley, but its import becomes clearer when we realize that Canning was not only a well known Freemason but also one who engaged in public, poetic disputes about Masonic politics and philosophies with another Freemason fond of the Mysteries and hermeticism – Erasmus Darwin. Like so many others of the period, Keats seems to have conflated Swedenborg's doctrines with those of the Freemasons, and Spurgin is "setting the record straight." Keats's impulse, however, is entirely understandable.

Bestsellers such as the Abbé Barruel's *Mémoires Pour Servir à l'Histoire du Jacobinisme* and John Robison's *Proofs of a Conspiracy against all Religions and Governments of Europe, Carried on in the Secret Meetings of Freemasons, Illuminati, and Reading Societies* insisted that societies such as Swedenborg's were variations derived from alchemical, philosophical Rosicrucianism adopted and promoted by the Freemasons, and Masons were known to have founded the Swedenborg Society of London. Although the "official" Masonic lodges of England disavowed it in response to accusations by conspiracy theorists, the Society inevitably bore marked similarities to Freemasonry. In addition, because Swedenborg's doctrines were derived from the same alchemical, philosophical hermeticism that had been publicized as the basis for popular higher degrees of Freemasonry, and Freemasonry was widely assumed to be a modern version of Rosicrucianism, it was inevitable that those not initiated in the societies would group them together as did so many authors writing about them during the Romantic period.[12]

Spurgin's letter indicates interest on Keats's part, and Keats's comments imply he possessed at least some general knowledge of these cultural issues, but that too is not unusual. Public fascination with groups such as the Rosicrucians and Freemasons had resulted in a flood of publications about the societies discussing their influence, goals, and hermetic philosophies and drawing upon their mythologies for literary purposes. Debates about the nature of the secret societies and their hermeticism during the Romantic period, what Thomas De Quincey would eventually summarize as "*what* they do," and "what they do it *for*," ranged across all fields of study and figured in arguments about politics, class, religion, philosophy, literature, science, and more.[13] It would have been virtually impossible for Keats to have been unaware of the secret societies. The societies were so well known that references to them appeared in the writings of virtually all the major authors of the period, and Keats's writings are no exception.

---

*Ars Quatuor Coronatum: Transactions of the Quatuor Coronati Lodge No. 2076* 50 (1937): 31–69.

12 Robert Rix, "William Blake and the Radical Swedenborgians," *Esoterica* 5 (2003) <http://www.esoteric.msu.edu/VolumeV/Blake.htm>.

13 Thomas De Quincey, "Secret Societies," *De Quincey's Collected Writings: Historical Essays and Researches*, ed. David Masson (London: A. & C. Black, 1897) 173. The essay appeared in the August and October 1847 editions of *Tait's Magazine*.

In his letters and poetry, Keats consistently uses the language and imagery of groups such as the Rosicrucians and Freemasons to express views that correspond with philosophies promoted by the secret societies. But, much in the same way that Spurgin's letter has been missed over the years, I believe scholars also have overlooked the hermeticism in Keats's writings because they have been unaware of the influence that secret societies exercised on the culture of the Romantic period. This study recovers the common knowledge once available about the societies, their rituals, and their philosophies and considers that knowledge as a possible source for the religious and philosophical concepts that Keats examined and developed throughout his career. Once the hermetic philosophies and linguistics that appear in Keats's writings are properly understood, their presence significantly alters our analysis of both his poetry and what Keats called his "metaphysical speculations" about the relationships amongst poetry, life, and the possibility of some form of transcendence. They reveal a serious attempt on Keats's part to fully explore what he believed might be "a better system of salvation" for mankind that was substantially influenced by views associated with the secret societies.[14]

Recovering knowledge about the secret societies and the hermeticism associated with them, and re-examining the concepts Keats puts forth and the language he uses in his letters and poems with that knowledge in mind, allows us to offer richer and more accurate interpretations of both Keats's poetry and his speculations. By adding popular culture to Keats's sources for the philosophical concepts he considered and developed throughout his career, we can place his writings within a wider context, and while expanding the interpretative range, we can rejuvenate debates about Keats's religious views and re-evaluate both his writings and our own from new perspectives.

The most recent book-length studies that fully examine Keats's metaphysical and philosophical speculations, Robert Ryan's *Keats: The Religious Sense* and Ronald Sharp's *Keats, Skepticism, and the Religion of Beauty*, date back to the 1970s.[15] Meanwhile, although recent authors have touched upon Keats's speculations in the course of their studies, for almost four decades, there has been a dichotomy in the criticism surrounding Keats's philosophical writings. Over the last four decades, the majority of the scholarship discussing Keats's speculations has maintained a polarizing shift that began in the 1960s and disallowed the validity of older, alternative views. Studies before and during the mid-century tended towards what scholars now identify as an excessive spiritualization of Keats in which Neo-Platonism and various forms of transcendentalism figured prominently and effectively took Keats out of time and disallowed the very qualities many of us now find so attractive in him.[16]

---

14  John Keats, letter to George and Georgianna Keats, 21 April 1819, *The Letters of John Keats, 1814–1821*, ed. Hyder Rollins, vol. 2 (Cambridge, Mass.: Harvard UP, 1958) 102. Hereafter, this work will be referred to as *Letters II*.

15  Robert M. Ryan's *Keats: The Religious Sense* (Princeton: Princeton UP, 1976) and Ronald A. Sharp's *Keats, Skepticism, and the Religion of Beauty* (Athens: University of Georgia Press, 1979).

16  See, for example, Sir Sidney Colvin, *John Keats: His Life and Poetry, His Friends, Critics and After-Fame* (1917; New York: Octagon Books, 1970); Clarence DeWitt Thorpe, *The Mind of John Keats* (New York: Oxford UP, 1926); Claude Lee Finney, *The Evolution*

Many studies posited the poet as engaged in forms of a Platonic quest in the name of beauty and art and portrayed Keats as an aesthete dreamer with escapist tendencies. More often than not, they stripped Keats of his practicality and his keen engagement with the realities of his time. These multiple studies resulted in a backlash on the part of scholars, and the theories were countered by others intended to place Keats more firmly in the real world.

Response to Bernard Blackstone's 1959 study *The Consecrated Urn, an Interpretation of Keats in Terms of Growth and Form* illustrates the decisive shift that occurred in Keats criticism. By 1959, the critical currents already were turning against the sort of Neo-Platonic and essentially mystical interpretation of Keats's poetry that Blackstone offered, and his study became an example other scholars cited to illustrate the vast difference they perceived between the spiritual and material poles in interpretation. Concerned more with possibilities than actual sources, Blackstone provided readers with an analysis of Keats's poetry based on what he saw as points of contact between Keats's philosophies and those of Neo-Platonism, Eastern spiritual texts, the hermeticism of Cornelius Agrippa, and the more mystically inclined Romantic poets such as Blake and Coleridge.

He argued that Keats viewed the poet as a "wizard" practicing a "natural magic," and he highlighted hermetic elements in Keats's writings as part of a mystical view of the natural, biological world of growth, decay, and rebirth.[17] Keats's use of hermetic language and concepts indicated to Blackstone a belief in the literal role of the magus, Apollo, and the magical elements of hermeticism that granted an "all-embracing" wisdom to the "poet-magus."[18] Unaware of the influence secret societies exercised on popular views of hermeticism during the Romantic period, Blackstone based much of his theorizing on surmises that seemed to lead him to an untenable stance in terms of proof, and because he lacked proof of Keats's reading or general knowledge, some scholars, while acknowledging that his ideas appeared intriguing, remained largely unconvinced. Others rejected his theories not only because his sources seemed too obscure for Keats's knowledge but also because the conclusions Blackstone reached seemed too extreme.

It was just such an approach as Blackstone's that led scholars like Newell Ford to offer correctives and argue against transcendental interpretations of Keats's writings. In *The Prefigurative Imagination of John Keats*, Ford attempted to reground the poet by explicitly materializing Keatsian phrases such as "fellowship with essence," that previously had been used to argue poems like *Endymion* as "an allegory of the poet-soul in quest of transcendental Beauty" or "a wedding of finite mind with Infinite Being."[19] Other scholars followed suit and increasingly portrayed Keats as

---

*of Keats's Poetry*, 2 vols. (Cambridge: Harvard UP, 1936); and Bernard Blackstone, *The Consecrated Urn, an Interpretation of Keats in Terms of Growth and Form* (London: Longmans, Green and Co., 1959).

17 Blackstone 75. Although I disagree with many of Blackstone's premises and conclusions, I am indebted to him for his steadfast assertions that Keats was a hermetic writer and for his intriguing speculations that sparked my own research.

18 Blackstone 104.

19 Newell F. Ford, *The Prefigurative Imagination of John Keats* (Stanford: Stanford UP, 1951) 14–15.

either disinterested in or distrustful of religious and philosophical speculations; they rejected interpretations suggesting that he intentionally included elements of Neo-Platonism or mysticism in his writings. The trend gathered momentum, and in 1973, Stuart Sperry published *Keats the Poet* and contended that specific language Keats used to elucidate his theories about poetry, life, and religion did not reflect Neo-Platonic philosophies as once supposed, but rather, the science Keats learned in his chemistry classes at Guy's Hospital.

Sperry's chapter entitled "The Chemistry of the Poetic Process," carefully linked Keats's use of many terms previously described as Neo-Platonic, and in Blackstone's case, as hermetic as well, to Keats's chemistry studies at Guy's Hospital instead. Faced with strong opposition to spiritual readings, and concrete proof that Keats could have encountered some of his terminology in his medical studies, critics soon discarded spiritual and philosophical interpretations of Keats's writings in favor of scientific ones. Later, critics such as Donald Goellnicht and Hermione De Almeida argued the role that Keats's medical training played in his poetry, and they linked the medicine and the philosophies of the Romantic period, but they continued the tradition begun by Sperry of ascribing Keats's terminology solely to his education in chemistry.[20] The materialist reading became almost a given that encouraged scholars to consider the subject closed.

M. H. Abrams's 1998 Keats Bicentennial lecture and essay "Keats's Poems: The Material Dimensions" is illustrative of the overall effect this has had. While asserting the importance of "the material qualities" of Keats's writings, Abrams warned of the dangers of "philosophizing" Keats.[21] He reminded readers that many commentators once believed that Keats was a Neo-Platonist because of Keats's tendency to describe the imagination and the imaginative process with terms such as "ethereal," "spirit," "spiritual," "empyreal," and "essence."[22] He then noted that Sperry and others had proved this notion false. Chemistry, he stressed, was the key to a better reading of Keats's texts in which the imagination and the products of the imagination were understood to be entirely material. Abrams argued that Keats's technical knowledge of chemistry supplied him with "unprecedented metaphors for poetry" in which the imagination was portrayed as refining and purifying concepts to create an ideal, a "material sublime," but not an ideal that included a more spiritual aspect or led to transcendence, and most certainly not an ideal that should be viewed in light of Neo-Platonism.[23] Abrams concluded that to read Keats's metaphors as

---

20  Donald C. Goellnicht, *The Poet-Physician: Keats and Medical Science* (Pittsburgh: University of Pittsburgh Press, 1984). Donald C. Goellnicht, "Keats's Chemical Composition," *Critical Essays on John Keats*, ed. Hermione De Almeida (Boston: G. K. Hall & Co., 1990) 143–56. Hermione De Almeida, *Romantic Medicine and John Keats* (New York: Oxford UP, 1991).

21  M. H. Abrams "Keats's Poems: The Material Dimensions," *The Persistence of Poetry: Bicentennial Essays on Keats*, eds. Robert M. Ryan and Ronald A. Sharp (Amherst: University of Massachusetts Press, 1998) 44.

22  Abrams 42.

23  Abrams 43.

anything other than chemical would "disembody" him and "eliminate what is most Keatsian in his poems."[24]

Like many recent critics, Abrams wished to stress Keats's full awareness of the world in which he lived and to emphasize that Keats's poetry is not an attempt to escape the world but to engage it. However, these attempts by Abrams and others have resulted in narrowed interpretations of Keats's terminology and a perspective of Keats that is in many ways as extreme as the one scholars rejected. This study proposes a more balanced view and re-opens the discussion by providing scholars with the proof needed to acknowledge a previously unknown connection between the spiritual and material poles they have created. If we allow Keats an awareness of the widespread information about the secret societies, several points in opposing interpretations of his writings actually can co-exist, just as they co-existed in the philosophies promoted by the societies. By recovering the hermetic elements during the Romantic period and placing Keats's writings in context, I illustrate how scholars can mix older interpretations with those of the last decades without disembodying Keats in any way.

For example, the chemical terms that Keats uses when he describes the processes of the imagination are derived from alchemical hermetic studies that were infused with elements of Neo-Platonism. Although also used in chemistry, the same terms originally were used to describe alchemical processes, and there is a very good reason why Keats's use of these terms appears to be "a perfect metaphor for the workings of the imagination, which draws together various thoughts and feelings into a new creative whole."[25] This was exactly the way in which the alchemical terms had been used to express the operations of the imagination for centuries and most notably by Paracelsus, the Renaissance alchemist-philosopher and physician whose theories the Romantics viewed as the foundations for not only chemistry but also the Rosicrucian and later Swedenborgian and higher degree Masonic movements.

For the Rosicrucians, the products at the end of the process were not only material. Rather, the material resulting from chemical interactions was secondary, something which represented a mental and spiritual achievement that took place in an atmosphere of "fellowship divine," not only with mankind but also with God and Nature, the contemplation of which yielded wisdom and power as well as the ability to heal both body and soul. In this sense, Keats's "material sublime" was, quite literally, sublime – not only a finer material but also a spiritual one of great worth. Far from being unprecedented, Keats's metaphors draw upon a rich and full tradition of spiritual philosophy that blended hermeticism and Neo-Platonism with science, a tradition that was widely known during Keats's time thanks to the popularity of the Rosicrucian mythologies that had been adapted and extended in both the Gothic literature of the period and the rituals and publications surrounding Freemasonry. Once this is understood, it becomes possible that Keats had both the material *and* the spiritual in mind, and the analysis of previous scholars as well as more recent ones may be in some sense correct, because both the spiritual and material were part of the cultural context of hermeticism during the Romantic period.

---

24 Abrams 44.
25 Donald Goellnicht, *The Poet-Physician: Keats and Medical Science* 56.

During the Romantic period, mysticism and secularization existed side by side in Masonic organizations, and the same language and concepts in Keats's writings that scholars have designated as strictly Neo-Platonic or purely scientific were more often considered a modified fusion of both. The syncretic societies deliberately offered men a mixture of philosophy and science and were famous for their rituals, lectures, and mythologies that merged hermeticism and elements of Neo-Platonism with developing theories in the fields of medicine and chemistry in particular. Keats's blend of science and myth, facts and philosophy, and skepticism and mysticism reflects not only a regular tendency during the period but also one that was highly common amongst the same medical community that scholars have relied upon to argue a strictly materialist analysis of his writings.

If we take into account the popular hermeticism associated with the secret societies, we can see why there is validity to both sides of polarized debates regarding Keats's religious and philosophical views, and we can acknowledge the possibility that Keats's stances embraced what seem at first glance to be contradictory perspectives. Although much of the earlier Keats scholarship like Blackstone's is now considered dated, if we examine it within the context of the popular hermeticism of the period, we may be able to reset a balance that for several decades has tilted heavily towards the materialistic side, and do so without disallowing the validity of the more recent stances.

Critics today generally acknowledge a ritualistic aspect in Keats's poetry and mystical overtones in his terminology and in their own analyses of his works often resort to the same language, but they discourage viewing Keats's references as hermetic, much less as guides to his philosophic or religious leanings. They do this in part because they have been unable to find evidence that Keats may have been interested in hermetic doctrines or even aware of them. But with the approach I am suggesting, scholars may discover the proof they need to accept portions of arguments such as Blackstone's. The popular knowledge and debates about the secret societies can provide us with a way to connect much of the Keats criticism of the past with current analyses of the cultural, political and social issues of the Romantic period. We can mitigate the tendency in some older studies to isolate Keats from the times in which he lived while still retaining the interpretive value of those studies that suggest Keats had strong philosophic leanings. There is no need to wholly discard older studies or adopt polarized stances, and there is good reason to draw upon past studies once again, especially in reference to Keats's religious and philosophical views because this focus has been absent from the scholarship for so long.

One reason for the lack of focus in recent decades on Keats's religious and philosophical views may well be the sheer difficulty of pinning them down. Some critics such as Robert Ryan and Ronald Sharp have attempted to define Keats's opinions, but no consensus has been reached. Ryan, for example, argues that Keats subscribed to a modified form of natural religion, but believes Keats's system offered scant satisfaction and was neither "a way of life, offering encouragement to the spirit and nourishment to the imagination," nor a particularly "satisfying faith to live by," because natural religion lacked the emotional, supernatural, and mysterious elements of traditional religions that offered inspiration and comfort.[26]

As an alternative, Sharp writes that Keats was a humanist who "maintained a deep and abiding skepticism about the possibility of knowing with any certainty any kind of transcendent or higher reality."[27] Sharp contends that Keats's skepticism was so strong that it precluded a system of metaphysics or even a sustained interest in creating one. He suggests that Keats faced a specific problem: how to derive solace from this world without resorting to belief in a higher power or a transcendent spirituality that would give meaning to pain and sorrow. He concludes that Keats's solution was to view the imagination as "an exclusively human agency serving purely human ends" and to create a religion of Beauty to provide solace in this life with no concern for the life thereafter.[28]

Other scholars agree with Robert Gittings that Keats was a Deist and eschew further examination, and some believe he was agnostic or a Neo-Platonist.[29] Still others argue that Keats seems disinterested in any definable religion or philosophy, and in the absence of a clearly identifiable faith, some critics assume Keats had none. Yet, while it is clear that Keats distrusted the established church, his refusal to ally himself with the standard, accepted faith of his time does not mean he lacked interest. Although it may be impossible to arrive at a definitive conclusion about Keats's religious or philosophical views, by analyzing the milieu in which he attempted to formulate his philosophies and by examining the parallels that exist between his speculations and major cultural currents of his time, we can find much that is meaningful. Keats's use of hermetic terminology may not indicate clear allegiance to any established religion, but it does indicate a sustained interest in religious questions on his part, and when his poetry and letters are examined in the context of hermetic references, a pattern emerges of a man searching for a better system of faith and a better philosophy of life.

Examining Keats's speculations in this fashion does not require, however, that we settle on one system at the expense of others. In his 1817 letters discussing religion and philosophy with Benjamin Bailey, Keats claims that he can be "certain of nothing but of the holiness of the Heart's affections and the truth of Imagination."[30] His statement highlights the fact that during his poetic career he was open to and

---

26 Ryan, *Keats: The Religious Sense* 208.

27 Sharp 5.

28 Sharp 5; 5–12.

29 Robert Gittings, "Sparks of the Divinity," *John Keats* (Boston: Little, Brown and Co., 1968) 305–21. David Perkins discusses his view of Keats's agnostic perspective of "uncertainty," particularly in regards to the capacities of visionary and transcendental states in *The Quest for Permanence: The Symbolism of Wordsworth, Shelley and Keats* (Cambridge, Mass.: Harvard UP, 1965). Walter Jackson Bate describes Keats's perspective as an "almost absent-minded agnosticism" in *John Keats* (Cambridge, Mass.: The Belknap Press of Harvard University, 1963) 133. Colvin's, Finney's and Blackstone's works already noted are fairly representative of the Neo-Platonic perspective.

30 Keats, letter to Bailey, 22 November 1817, *Letters I* 184. While some have interpreted this statement as proof of a skepticism that precludes metaphysics on Keats's part, the authenticity of the Imagination gives enormous latitude.

exploring a great many different ideas about poetry, life, and even the existence of an afterlife. In keeping with Keats's open spirit of inquiry, the intent of this study is not to exclude other possible influences, but rather, to include in the mix a new option that enables us to work with many possibilities at once. If we will allow Keats an awareness of one of the more prominent movements of his time, we can find many points of contact in our opposing interpretations of his writings.

If Blackstone's theories represent the extreme spiritualizing pole of the debate about Keats's philosophic and religious leanings, Ronald Sharp's *Keats, Skepticism, and the Religion of Beauty* represents in large part the materializing pole, but Sharp's approach resembles Blackstone's in several ways. Both men stress that Keats's religious views were consistent throughout his adult life, and that these views alter how we interpret his body of work, and both argue extremes of interpretation that eliminate the possibility of the other's stance. Blackstone argues that Keats's views, as part of an ancient tradition, establish a literal role for the poet as magus and that Keats believed literally in the magical potential of hermeticism. Sharp insists that Keats's views represent an entirely new perspective and a radical break with the philosophies of the Romantic period and that Keats's skepticism extends beyond a rejection of a higher power to include an active repudiation of a visionary imagination that might lead to spiritual wisdom or metaphysical truths. He concludes that Keats lacked interest in developing a system of metaphysics and held instead "a conception of spirituality that does not depend on – that in fact denies – transcendent reality."[31]

But, Sharp makes a mistake similar to Blackstone's. To argue his stance, he must narrow his analysis and not take into account a great deal of evidence in Keats's writings indicating that he did place some trust in the visionary imagination as a means to garner truth, did believe in a higher power, and did display a sustained and serious interest in developing a system of metaphysics that included the possibility of transcendence. That Keats did not believe he could ever know for certain if he was in the right does not preclude his willingness to search for a better philosophy that could include more than the concrete world. It also does not mean that his humanism must be sacrificed to his desire for something more. Just as Sharp believes Keats's questioning mind made it impossible for him to embrace a dogmatic religious perspective, we must accept that Keats's mind made it possible for him to examine and make use of the entire spectrum of metaphysical concepts available to him.

The philosophical concepts promoted by Rosicrucianism and Freemasonry provide for readings in which Blackstone's analysis of Keats's visionary tendencies as well as Sharp's insistence on Keats's "humanized religion" both play roles. Furthermore, other scholars' analyses of Keats's views, such as Robert Ryan's contention that Keats operated within the context of natural religion, and Sperry's opinion that Keats's mystical language reflects instead the materialistic aspects of science and chemistry also find their places within such an approach. These perspectives scholars oftentimes consider incompatible in their studies of Keats actually functioned as points of contact in the secret societies that not only contained all these views, but actively promoted their intermingling.

---

31   Sharp 4.

In *Keats: The Religious Sense*, Ryan argues that discussions of Keats's possible religious views often fall into either/or categories because scholars interpret Keats's writings without a full appreciation of the theological trends during the Romantic period. Ryan suggests that spiritualized characterizations by authors such as John Middleton Murray and Clarence Thorpe presenting Keats as an inspired and almost prophetic thinker engaged in a "Platonic quest for and worship of beauty," pose just as many interpretive problems as arguments positing Keats as a secular humanist.[32] Analysis tending towards Neo-Platonism requires that Keats reject much of the world around him, but materialist versions necessitate another form of rejection, as scholars such as Sperry must claim that Keats's references to a "great Power" describe not a Deity but rather "an endless potential for creation of an ideal of beauty latent amid the elements of human perception."[33]

Yet, if scholars consider Freemasonry's history, they will discover that the texts surrounding the society included all of these aspects. In the context of the Romantic period, Freemasonry presented the public with an eclectic mix that drew upon so many religions and philosophies that many people felt free to interpret it as advancing all the religious views scholars suggest Keats may have espoused. One of the most frequent charges leveled against the secret societies was that they promoted natural religion, and in fact, groups such as the Freemasons offered not only the most well known versions of natural religion but also the most popular ones. Furthermore, the type of natural religion advanced by the secret societies was designed to include the emotional, supernatural, and mysterious aspects of faith that Ryan believes the philosophies lacked and does not factor into his analysis of Keats's writings. The teachings of the secret societies combined the rational and the mystical, engaged both the head and the heart, and placed a high significance on the visionary imagination and spiritual growth.

The societies appeared radical to those such as John Robison and the Abbé Barruel, both of whom emphasized the Neo-Platonic elements in the societies, traced Freemasonry's rituals back to the Mystery societies, accused the Masons of promoting natural religion, and labeled Freemasonry a new version of the same ancient, insidious heresy. To others such as Gotthold Lessing, Freemasonry contained within it such potential that, if realized, it could be regarded as a holy revelation and gift from God.[34] Significantly, Masonic texts also regularly made use of language in reference to "the great Power" that was understood to mean *both* the Deity and the "endless potential ... amid the elements of human perception." William Preston, a particularly popular and well known Masonic author, made exactly this sort of

---

32 Ryan, *Keats: The Religious Sense* 5.

33 Sperry 135.

34 See Lessing's dialogues *Ernst and Falk* in *Lessing's Masonic Dialogues*, trans. *The Builder* 1915–1929, ed. Robin L. Carr (1778; Bloomington, IL: The Masonic Book Club, 1991). Although Lessing fully recognized Freemasonry's shortcomings, he also saw within Freemasonry an enormous potential to realize an idealistic, world-wide society that could lessen the ills of the world caused by religious and nationalistic disputes, and he regarded this potential with clear reverence.

connection in his *Illustrations of Masonry*, first published in London in 1772 and running to 12 editions in England by 1812.[35]

The syncretic society deliberately contained within it elements of the traditional and the radical, and its diversity was intended to offer something for any man who might seek to join and to encourage men to find points of compromise with each other rather than points of difference. Moreover, it did this by creating a series of lectures and rituals by which men of varying modes of faith might form a union around not only principles but also a series of allegorical modes steeped in the mythological forms of what Walter Evert, yet another critic with yet another perspective, saw as classical antiquity.

In *Aesthetic and Myth in the Poetry of Keats*, Evert argued that while Keats did not reject religion entirely, he did reject the prevailing forms of religious experience during the period and turned instead to the classical mythologies to find a new system. But, there was already a system in place employing many of the mythologies Keats incorporated into his poetry and containing within it a flexibility that enabled men to view its teachings as elements of natural religion, pantheism, Neo-Platonism and a humanist pursuit of beauty. The mystical rituals and publications of Masonry stressed lessons garnered from the study of Pythagorean and Neo-Platonic principles as well as reverence for the three pillars of wisdom, strength, and beauty. The hermetic philosophies of the societies included a reverence for beauty and its purpose in life remarkably similar to what Sharp describes; at the same time, however, the societies emphasized a practical humanism that many critics would have little trouble identifying as secular.

If Keats's religious and philosophical speculations are placed in this context, it appears that when various scholars see all these differing viewpoints in his writings it may well be because one of the most popular movements of the Romantic period contained all these elements, created connections between them, and encouraged men to tolerate them all as part of a system that fused the mystical and the rational, much like the alchemical language, philosophies, and allegories the secret societies used to convey many of their teachings. Moreover, Keats himself uses these same elements to convey his thoughts.

Hermetic language, imagery, and ideas appear throughout Keats's letters and poetry, and his use of such concepts offers not only new perspectives on his views of religion and philosophy and the role poetry plays in society but also his engagement in the political and social issues of his time. Aside from general correspondences between his philosophies and those represented to the public as Rosicrucian or Masonic, Keats makes many highly specific hermetic allusions in his letters and poetry as he develops his philosophies, and they are too strong to be mere coincidences. Several of Keats's most famous letters discussing spiritual truths, religion, and the possibility of an afterlife contain extended passages in which he demonstrates a strong understanding of hermetic philosophies. Keats draws upon

---

35  See for example his discussion of the moral advantages of geometry and architecture in relation to the senses: William Preston, Part IV, "Remarks on the Second Lecture," *Illustrations of Masonry* (1772; Louisville: American Masonic Publishing Association, 1858) 40–45.

the hermetic language and philosophies associated with the secret societies in his important letters to Benjamin Bailey in 1817, his "Pleasure Thermometer" letter to his publisher John Taylor in 1818, and his famous "Vale of Soul-making" letter to his brother George and sister-in-law Georgianna in 1819.

Likewise, many of his poems written at the same time as those letters appear to be active and explicit examinations of hermetic philosophies, and some like *Endymion* take the philosophies as their very basis. *Endymion*, Keats's first extended verse narrative, functions as an allegorical version of well known initiation rituals intended to convey Rosicrucian and Masonic values and beliefs, and many of Keats's later poems such as *Lamia* and the *Hyperion* fragments express variations and refinements of the same themes and philosophies. The concepts Keats advances in these letters and poems, the terminology he uses, and even the examples he offers to reinforce his arguments match those found in multiple popular texts associated with the secret societies. Because scholars have lacked information about the secret societies, however, they have been unaware of these correlations and have not factored the hermetic philosophies into their analyses.

Rosicrucian and Masonic texts consistently stressed the struggles man must face to gain wisdom and reach a higher state of spirituality, and both societies maintained that the search itself, the process, was the key. The issue of the co-existence of good and evil and joy and sorrow in this world, and how man might create a richer life from both, was one central not only to Keats's speculations but also those of the alchemically inclined Rosicrucians and the Masonic groups assumed to have sprung from them. These secret societies symbolized their philosophies and the processes that they taught of gradual advancement in knowledge and spiritual growth with alchemically based allegories and rituals. The same processes also appear and are described in strikingly similar terms in Keats's 1818 letter to his publisher about "a kind of Pleasure Thermometer," the understanding of the "gradations" of which Keats saw as a "first Step towards ... the playing of different Natures with Joy and Sorrow."[36]

Those who advance along Keats's "Pleasure Thermometer" discover a true "Happiness" that exists

> ... In that which becks
> Our ready Minds to fellowship divine;
> A fellowship with essence, till we shine
> Full alchymized and free of space. Behold
> The clear Religion of heaven—[37]

Keats's words echo both Rosicrucian philosophy and ritual elements of the secret societies whose goals were commonly understood during the Romantic period to include not only fellowship with man but also "fellowship with divinity," that was expressed in the same alchemical language that Keats uses.[38] Keats's processes or

---

36  Keats, letter to Taylor, 30 January 1818, *Letters I* 218–19.

37  Keats, *Letters I* 218.

38  Thomas Taylor, *Thomas Taylor the Platonist: Selected Writings*, eds. Kathleen Raine and George Mills Harper (Princeton: Princeton University Press, 1969) 367.

"gradations" of increasing intensity that integrate the "Minds" with a pure "essence," thereby transforming men to a shining, higher state, coincide precisely with the language of alchemy and its esoteric goals advanced in the texts associated with the secret societies. The terms are literally alchemical, and Keats uses them correctly.

Multiple alchemical texts related to Rosicrucianism described a union with "essence" and presented the "shining," joyful result of the union as a true religion that "freed" the soul and allowed it to range through space. The famous hermetic text *The Divine Pymander*, first reintroduced to the Western world by the Neo-Platonist Ficino and later popularized during the Rosicrucian mania, asserted that "the Mind being made Free and pure ... rangeth abroad in every place" and that the soul put on a "shining," "Fiery Coat."[39] Basil Valentine, a famous alchemist-physician, also presented esoteric alchemy as "the fire of Divine Love" that by "gradations" resulted in a "Heavenly Quintessence" that "tinctured" the soul thereby liberating it through spiritual regeneration, clothing it in "splendour," and granting it "everlasting joy."[40] And Paracelsus, the most famous alchemist-physician of all, also used the same terms that Keats does to describe the exoteric and esoteric processes of alchemy throughout his works, and his philosophies formed the basis for Boehme's and Swedenborg's both of whom did so as well.[41] And while it is certainly true that these goals played a role in many religions, given the precise correspondence to alchemy of the concepts and language Keats uses, including the term "alchymized," it seems only reasonable that when Keats writes "alchymized," we should take him at his word and allow the hermetic connotations as well as others.

Masonic texts also stressed the value of the same fellowship and used many of the same terms within their rituals and teachings. Masons taught "Five Points of Fellowship," they described alchemically at times as the way to gain the "quintessence," and Masonic initiation rites offered to their brethren a process by which they moved in stages called "grades" to what initiates were told was a purer "approximation of spiritual essence" and union with the "Divine," but always with the pre-requisite that initiates dedicate themselves to improving society as well as themselves.[42] A key component of this process was a growing self-awareness combined with a knowledge of the world that insisted the physical, mental, and spiritual aspects of life were inextricably linked.

---

39 "The Key," Book Four, *The Divine Pymander in XVII Books*, trans. John Everard (London: 1650): <http://www.levity.com/alchemy/ch4.html>. See also Thomas Vaughan's alchemical, Rosicrucian work published under the pseudonym Eugenius Philalethes, *Magia Adamica: or the antiquitie of magic, and the descent thereof from Adam downwards, proved.* (London: T.W. for H.B, 1650): <http://www.levity.com/alchemy/vaughan1.html>. Vaughan enters into extended discussion on the goal of merging with the spiritual essence and makes use of the same terms.

40 Basil Valentine, *His Triumphant Chariot of Antimony, with Annotations of Theodore Kirkringus*, transc. Ben Fairweather (London: 1678) <http://www.levity.com/alchemy/antimony.html>.

41 Desiree Hirst, *Hidden Riches: Traditional Symbolism from the Renaissance to Blake* (New York: Barnes & Noble, Inc., 1964) 81–91.

42 Alexander Piatigorsky, *Who's Afraid of Freemasons? The Phenomenon of Freemasonry* (London: The Harvill Press, 1997) 132.

The same concepts appear in Keats's letters and poetry. In his extended Vale of Soul-making letter composed during the spring of 1819, Keats asks his brother George, "Give me this credit – Do you not think I strive – to know myself?" and ties his question to thoughts throughout the letter about the ways in which knowledge, philosophy, and poetry might help mankind arrive at a "system of salvation" that did not "philosophise" away the troubles of the world, but rather, turned them to nourishment for the spirit.[43] He perceived what he wished George to understand – that the world is

> "The Vale of Soul-making" … I say "*Soul making*" Soul as distinguished from an Intelligence – There may be intelligences or spark of the divinity in millions – but they are not Souls till they acquire identities, till each one is personally itself. I[n]telligences are atoms of perception – they know and they see and they are pure, in short they are God – how then are Souls to be made? How then are these sparks which are God to have identity given them – so as ever to possess a bliss peculiar to each ones individual existence? How, but by the medium of a world like this? … it is a system of Spirit-creation – This is effected by three grand materials acting the one upon the other for a series of years – These three Materials are the *Intelligence* – the *human heart* (as distinguished from intelligence or Mind) and the *World* or *Elemental space* suited for the proper action of *Mind and Heart* on each other for the purpose of forming the *Soul* or *Intelligence destined to possess the sense of Identity.*[44]

His sense of the truth of these words lay behind his belief that ultimately sorrow cannot be separated from joy nor good from evil and that a man must be more than a dreamer and a poet do more than vex. Keats's continual effort, expressed throughout his letters and poems, was to move from human passions to knowledge and transmute that knowledge to poetry that might provide physic to men. He wished to be "one who pours out a balm upon the world," and he recognized that to do so required an engagement with the world in all its contradictory states (*Fall of Hyperion* I, 201).[45]

Keats's convictions resemble those taught by societies such as the Freemasons and the society the Romantics considered its precursor, the Rosicrucians. For example, widely published tracing boards illustrating Masonic values and aspects of initiation ceremonies included depictions of checkered floors in alternating black and white specifically to remind initiates that "the steps of man tread in the various and uncertain incidents of life; as our days are chequered with strange contrariety of events, and our passage through this existence, though sometimes attended with prosperous circumstances, is often beset by a multitude of evils."[46] Masons were told, however, that they must nonetheless persevere in their work and goals for the same reasons Keats declares the necessity of a "World of Pains and troubles" to

---

43  Keats, *Letters II* 81; 101–102.

44  Keats, *Letters II* 102.

45  John Keats, "The Fall of Hyperion," *John Keats: Complete Poems*, ed. Jack Stillinger (Cambridge, Mass.: The Belknap Press of Harvard UP, 1982). Unless otherwise noted all citations of Keats's poems are taken from this volume.

46  William Hutchinson, *The Spirit of Masonry* (1775; New York: Bell Publishing Co., 1982) 123.

his brother George.[47] Indeed, the very perspective put forth parallels the bulk of Keats's analysis of the world as a "Vale of Soul-making" in which the "sparks of the divinity" are individualized and refined till they become souls, and the terminology Keats uses to describe the process resembles still more the hermetic, alchemical language associated with the Freemasons and the Rosicrucians before them.

As Keats explains further to his brother, he like the Freemasons locates the process within the "circumstances" of the world and writes ...

> I began by seeing how man was formed by circumstances – and what are circumstances?
> – but touchstones of his heart –? and what are touchstones? – but proovings of his heart?
> – and what are proovings of his heart but fortifiers or alterers of his nature? and what is his altered nature but his soul? – and what was his soul before it came into the world and had These proovings and alterations and perfectionings? – An intelligence – without Identity – and how is this Identity to be made? Through the medium of the Heart? And how is the heart to become this Medium but in a world of Circumstances?

Keats's "touchstones" of the heart that alter the "intelligences or sparks of the divinity" in a process of "perfectionings" till they become souls occur in the midst of contraries, of "three grand materials acting the one upon the other," and thereby mimic the Philosopher's Stone of alchemy that transmutes and "perfects" the soul via interactions of the same materials. Touchstones appear frequently in hermetic texts both because these stones were used to assay the purity of gold or silver and because the quintessence or Philosopher's Stone of alchemy was also known as the great touchstone. As Francis Barrett explained in his 1801 abridgement *The Magus, or Celestial Intelligencer* of the alchemist-philosopher Agrippa's *De Occulta Philosophia*, alchemy was considered "of divine origin" and "the grand touchstone of natural wisdom," that purified and transformed the souls of men who lived by principles of fellowship to others.[48]

Like the Rosicrucians he referenced, Barrett maintained that this salvationist, esoteric transformation was made within a man and only could be achieved through self-knowledge and engagement with the contraries ever present in life. He also exhorted the adept to "look into thyself, and endeavour to find out in what part of thy composition is the *prima material*," and claimed that from this process men would find the means by which "the soul or essence was extracted."[49] Thus, Keats uses the term "touchstones" correctly in an alchemical philosophical sense when he explains to George that a man's interaction with the world and examination of his own life creates "touchstones of his heart," "touchstones" are "proovings of his heart ... fortifiers and alterers of his nature," and "his altered nature" is his soul after the "alterations and perfectionings" have taken place.

In addition, the three "Materials" Keats describes as "acting the one upon the other," to produce a fourth that he designates as the "*Soul* or *Intelligence destined*

---

47  Keats, *Letters II* 102.

48  Francis Barrett, "Of Alchymy, Its Divine Origin, &c.," *The Magus, or Celestial Intelligencer*, vol. 1, (London: 1801): <http://www.sacred-texts.com/grim/magus> 56.

49  Francis Barrett, "Of the Preparation of a Man to Qualify Him for the Search of This Treasure" *The Magus, or Celestial Intelligencer*, vol. 1, 67–68.

*to possess the sense of Identity*," match the three elements that the alchemist-philosophers also called "materials" and whose mixture within the world and in man acted to individuate and purify his soul.[50] Just as Keats's "Intelligence[s]" are "sparks of the divinity" that "know ... see ... and are pure" but are not yet in their destined state, Rosicrucian works such as the *Clavis Philosophiae et Alchymiae Fludanae* informed readers that every man possessed a "divine spark" that was "continuous and eternal," but that it was each man's task to nurture and refine this spark by acting well within the world and seeking within himself till it became transformed into "living fire" that resulted in proper conjunction with the divine essence.[51]

In a similar vein, the alchemist-philosopher and physician Paracelsus, revered by the Rosicrucians, used the term "Intelligence" to describe in his writings a Neo-Platonic "Intelligence" that transcended the understanding or reasoning faculty and was capable of knowing truth intuitively and instinctively because it was of divine origin but was nonetheless in need of individualization. In his hermetic systems, Paracelsus described the "Intelligence" as interacting with man's will or intellect, that included his passions and imagination, and with the elemental aspects of Nature. The three, in combination, resulted in individualization and spiritualization.[52] The "*human heart*" that Keats takes care to distinguish from the "intelligence or Mind," also parallels the Paracelsian conception of the intellect, passions and imagination, and Keats's definition of the world as "*Elemental space*" is a particularly apt description of Paracelsus's four elements that comprise the world of Nature that serves as man's alchemical alembic and his place of learning. Just as Keats emphasizes that knowledge of the world is necessary if each "Soul" is to "possess a bliss peculiar to each ones individual existence," Paracelsus did so as well, arguing that by living within the world and exploring both himself and Nature, "man also explores the heaven and its essence, namely God and his realm," and that "there are many mansions in God's house and each one will find his mansion according to his learning."[53]

While these concepts and terms were adopted by others, including mystics such as Boehme and Swedenborg, they were widely understood as hermetic. As Keats himself notes, they also were applicable to the philosophies advanced by "the ancient persian and greek Philosophers" and the Zoroastrians and Oromanes, but these too had long been associated with alchemy and more recently in Keats's time with the

---

50 I use the term "individuate" deliberately. Paracelsus's alchemical philosophical system included the "Archeus" or "individualizing principle" and the "Vulcan" that created "the individual being from the reservoir of raw material available ... not strictly material but rather a principle of matter" (Hirst 64).

51 *Clavis Philosophiae et Alchymiae Fluddanae* as quoted by Herbert Silberer, *Hidden Symbolism of Alchemy and the Occult Arts*, prev. *Problems of Mysticism and Its Symbolism*, trans. Smith Ely Jelliffe (New York: Dover Publications, Inc., 1971) 180–81.

52 These arguments appeared throughout his works. Readers may consult Hirst 59–68 or E. J. Holmyard, *Alchemy* (1957; Baltimore: Penguin Books, 1968) 165–76.

53 Paracelsus (Theophrastus Philippus Aureolus Bombastus von), prologue, "Liber de Nymphis, Sylphis, Pygmaeis et Salamandris et de Caeteris Spiritibus Theophrasti Hohenheimensis," *Paracelsus: Four Treatises*, trans. and ed. Henry E. Sigerist (Baltimore: Johns Hopkins UP, 1996) 223–25.

esoteric degrees of Freemasonry.[54] Moreover, these references in Keats's letters, appearing from January 1818 to April 1819, and spanning his work on *Endymion* as well as *Hyperion*, and in the case of the Soul-making letter, written in conjunction with the Rosicrucian *Song of the Four Fairies* and only a few months before Keats turned to *The Fall of Hyperion* and *Lamia*, suggest such terminology and the concepts related to it were not a passing, youthful fancy.[55] All of the works I have mentioned, as well as others Keats wrote, contain not only alchemical allusions but also elements of the various initiation rituals related to Masonic groups of the period. As in the Vale of Soul-making letter, Keats uses terms that match exactly ones found in multiple hermetic texts and he uses these terms in passages that correlate correctly with hermetic concepts.

While these elements and points of contact exist throughout Keats's poetry and letters, *Endymion* may best illustrate the ways in which hermetic allusions and their relationship to Keats's philosophies coalesce in his poetry. The correspondences between Keats's writings and the secret societies are most evident in his first extended attempt at poetry, and the criticism both of Keats's time and our own highlights the very elements of the poem that most clearly reveal its underlying hermeticism. The charges against *Endymion* based on its obscurity, its dream-like quality, its surreal digressions and authorial intrusions, its recursive narrative elements, and its continual assertion of what appear to be irreconcilable values were the same as those leveled against the texts and rituals associated with the secret societies. The reviews of the poem published during Keats's time suggest that his critics were well aware of the connections, but the poem's biggest fault may be that it draws so heavily upon the mix of philosophies, hermetic details, and rituals of the period that it presents as many opportunities for misunderstanding today as the texts surrounding the societies.

---

54  Keats, *Letters II* 103. In yet another link, Keats tells George "I think it probable that this System of Soul-making – may have been the Parent of all the more palpable Schemes of Redemption." This too was a claim and charge often associated with the Freemasons. Masonic writers claimed Freemasonry was the oldest and truest of religions while detractors posited it as a mixed bag of all the deluded philosophies of the past.

55  Scholars often relate the *Song of the Four Fairies* sylph-like elementals to those in Pope's *Rape of the Lock*. The term "sylph" was coined by Paracelsus to describe these elemental spirits and popularized by Rosicrucian texts. Pope notes this in his preface. In addition, Erasmus Darwin explained the origins of the elementals, and their relationship to alchemy and esoteric philosophy in his Apology for "Economy of Vegetation," in *The Botanic Garden*. Robert Burton also described them as Rosicrucian, explained that Paracelsus believed fairies were in fact these spirits, and used the terms interchangeably. We know Keats was reading Burton around the time he wrote *Song of the Four Fairies*, and Burton's "A Digression on the Nature of Spirits …," provides a useful example of not only the connection between hermetic elements and, in this case, fairies, but also Keats's exposure to hermetic concepts. The section is 12 pages long and on every page Burton references at least one commonly known hermetic writer and oftentimes two or three. Paracelsus is referenced on all but three pages. Robert Burton, "Cure of Melancholy," *The Anatomy of Melancholy… By Democritus Junior…* (Philadelphia: J. W. Moore; New York: J. Wiley, 1850) 115–27. University of Michigan, "Making of America Books" <http://name.umdl.umich.edu/ACM8939.0001.001>.

Once the sources and the cultural context are properly understood, however, the hermetic elements and their exposition in *Endymion* provide readers with an early and extensive view of the speculations and philosophies Keats would refine and espouse throughout his career. Keats was searching for a life philosophy or religion in which he could believe and attempting to devise "a system of Salvation which does not affront our reason and humanity."[56] Early to late, throughout his career, he explored one of the most basic tenets of the hermeticism popularized by the secret societies and described in Spurgin's letter: the belief that the materials of this world served both humanist *and* spiritual ends. The belief that by living in full engagement with the world, in the interplay of joy and sorrow, a man could gain the wisdom necessary to transmute the materials of the world to greater spiritual purpose and become "a sage; / A humanist, a physician to all men," providing solace to the heart, nourishment to the imagination, and physic to both soul and body (*Fall of Hyperion* 189–90).

---

56 Keats, *Letters II* 103.

# Chapter One

# Historical Hermeticism and the Secret Societies

The number of avenues by which Keats could have been exposed to hermeticism is higher than many suspect, and this is true even if we take only the general atmosphere of the period into account. Roughly thirty years ago, M. H. Abrams discussed the influence of hermetic views on various authors of the Romantic period in his work *Natural Supernaturalism*, and although he did not include Keats in his assessments, the general atmosphere that he described is one other scholars have acknowledged in their own studies of authors such as Blake, Coleridge, Wordsworth, and the Shelleys.[1] Abrams argued that the heavy emphasis during the Enlightenment upon a mechanistic and analytic worldview had resulted in a divided perspective that disallowed the hermetic vitalism of the Renaissance. He suggested that many Romantic authors were seeking a means to reconnect man with nature, so they embraced Renaissance allegorical modes of thought and analogical ways of thinking of the world and man in terms of correspondences, macrocosm and microcosm. These modes of thought included hermetic and Neo-Platonic philosophies as well as variations of both later created by mystical theosophists and philosophers such as Jacob Boehme, the Cambridge Platonists, and Emanuel Swedenborg who permeated their writings with hermetic thought and symbolism.

Abrams posited the Romantics who drew upon these writings as representative of a more general trend during the period in which those reacting to the strictures of Enlightenment thought began to formulate new systems more adequate to their needs, systems in which the "mythical elements" of the previous doctrines were "translated into philosophical concepts," and "ordered into a 'scientific,' that is, a coherent conceptual system."[2] The same needs and systems, however, also formed the basis and impetus for the popularity of secret societies during the Romantic period.[3] When the popular history of secret societies such as the Rosicrucians and the Freemasons is taken into account, it seems the esoteric, mythical elements were *already* translated into philosophical concepts and offered to men in a complex blend that contained within it both reason and mysticism. What is more, many of the Romantic authors Abrams cited had been exposed to the previously existing systems

---

1    M. H. Abrams, *Natural Supernaturalism: Tradition and Revolution in Romantic Literature* (New York: W. W. Norton & Co., 1971) 11.

2    Abrams 170–71.

3    Alexander Piatigorsky makes this argument throughout *Who's Afraid of Freemasons? The Phenomenon of Freemasonry* (London: The Harvill Press, 1997).

by means of their membership in Freemasonry or knowledge of publications about the society and its precursor Rosicrucianism.

The Romantics had a blueprint to work from, albeit a much more diverse one than Abrams proposed. Their "reaction" was not so much a reaction as it was an amplification of currents of thought that had remained active throughout the Enlightenment, though not in the most commonly recognized channels today. Attempting to syncretize a century's worth of science with a human need to believe in something more, something that acknowledged man as a "mixed essence," but that also placed some faith in a spark of divinity that might enable man to arrive at a truth without relying solely on reason, many men of the period turned to the blend of reason and mysticism offered by the secret societies (*Manfred*, I.ii.40).[4] Secret societies provided Romantic readers and writers with both the materials and the system itself, updated to reflect the needs and issues of their time.

Analyzing Freemasonry's remarkably strong and widespread influence in Britain during the eighteenth and nineteenth centuries does present difficulties, however. Its very popularity resulted in a profusion of published material that mingled fact and fiction and presented so many polarized opinions that unified conclusions about the society were and still are virtually impossible to come by. In addition, Freemasonry's rise during the eighteenth century was accompanied by the rapid growth of many, many mystical societies and clubs that were either offshoots of Masonic lodges or explicitly modeled after Freemasonry but that often espoused varying ideas. Freemasonry itself, which initially had possessed only three degrees of initiation, also began to accumulate multiple higher degrees that contained increasingly hermetic philosophies and ceremonies and frequently incorporated Renaissance Rosicrucianism into their names, rites, and publications.

Enthusiastic Masons often supported the concept that the society shared an ancient history and wisdom with the Rosicrucians, and when Masons began to innovate by expanding the number of degrees in Freemasonry, the two societies became even more intertwined, whether by official Masonic choice or not. Indeed, the variety and number of Masonic degrees men could take on the Continent and in Britain proliferated so rapidly during the eighteenth century even Masonic historians had trouble distinguishing which was what and where. The situation became no clearer as the Freemasons drew for their rituals upon the "mysteries" of societies discussed in Neo-Platonic texts as well as Rosicrucian works, and societies outside Masonry adopted wholesale much of Freemasonry's forms and tenets. The headlong growth resulted in a blend of mysterious sounding names incorporating terms such as Rose-Croix, or references to knights, the sun, moon, or true light, mystical orders, sepulchers, and temples, most of which the general public could not differentiate amongst. By Keats's time, the heterogeneity and confusion surrounding the societies

---

4    Byron, too, was not exempt from this trend. He drew upon the popular elements of hermeticism, via Goethe's writings, although frequently turned to very different purposes than those Goethe espoused. In addition, Byron's association with the Carbonari, a secret society explicitly modeled after Freemasonry is well known today. See Jonathon Gross, "Byron, Freemasonry, and the Carbonari," *Freemasonry in Enlightenment Europe*, ed. William Weisberger (New York: Columbia University Press, 2002) 347–74.

had become so pronounced that, as Spurgin's letter suggests, most of the societies and the more esoteric ones in particular were often grouped under the under the header of Freemasonry.[5]

But despite the confusion, and while acknowledging that the "facts" presented to the public during the period were oftentimes pure fiction, it is possible to trace some common public views of Freemasonry's origins and its association with Rosicrucianism and hermetic alchemical philosophies. In Britain, many considered Freemasonry and Rosicrucianism to be essentially two forms of the same society, and those who wrote about them during the Romantic period frequently tracked the philosophical origins of both back to the ancient Mystery societies and the teachings contained in the *Hermetica*.[6] The general public recognized a common strain running through all the societies – what one scholar has referred to as a creative, "religion-making mysticism" – and hermeticism and alchemical philosophies, Neo-Platonism, Behmenism, Swedenborgism, Pietism, Martinism, and Mesmerism, as well as links to the Knights Templar and Cagliostro's famous Egyptian Masonry became intermingled in the public's mind.[7]

In Britain, the dominant society became Freemasonry, but the society itself contained an extraordinary number of degrees and variations. The very range, however, ensured that the basic hermetic elements underpinning the different groups' philosophies and rituals were widely disseminated, and many of the elements already had been presented to the public before, most notably via the revivals of Neo-Platonism and the creation of Rosicrucianism. These ideas so common during the period, however, are less familiar today. To fully understand why authors as well as the general public of the Romantic period grouped such concepts together, and often conflated the secret societies of the time, it is necessary to first discuss the popular hermeticism and philosophies of the Renaissance that led to the creation of such societies.

The Rosicrucian manifestos appearing in the first decades of the seventeenth century represented a synthesis of ideas contained in the works of not only the Neo-

---

5    While the majority of new degrees appeared on the Continent, the international nature of Masonry made it inevitable they would spread, even if only by word of mouth or by published texts. One of the more curious aspects of Masonry during the eighteenth century is the number of Masonic exposés printed in England revealing Masonic practices on the Continent. The exposures often were offered to the English public as though there was no difference between Masonry from one lodge or even one country to the next. To make matters more confusing, names often made their way through translation only to have their English version thought to be a separate entity from the French or German. Thus, there were any number of titles to contend with such as: Scottish Degrees, Scottish Rites, Ancient Rites, Rosea Crucis Knights, London Rose-Croix, Knights of the Gold and Rose Cross, Harodim Templars of Clermont, Knights of the Sun, Illustrious Knights Templar and Sepulchre, Knights and Companions of the Mystic Crown, the Mystical Order of the Knights of the True Light, the Illuminati, the Order of the Temple, and the Royal Arch, to name only some.

6    John M. Roberts, *The Mythology of the Secret Societies* (London: Secker & Warburg, 1972) 90–154.

7    Lance S. Owens, "Joseph Smith and the Kabbalah: The Occult Connection," *Dialogue: A Journal of Mormon Thought*, 27.3 (Fall 1994) 134: 117–94.

Platonists but also the *Hermetica* and the writings of their Renaissance interpreters. When Renaissance Neo-Platonism began to spread from the Medici court in Florence and the Platonic Academy founded by Marsilio Ficino and Giovanni Pico della Mirandola, the movement included a renewed interest in the texts of the *Hermetica* and an acknowledgement that hermetic and Renaissance worldviews shared a similar perspective. Both shared a belief in a universe bound by correspondences above and below and activated by vitalist principles – a notion the Florentine Neo-Platonists derived in part from their study of the *Hermetica*.[8]

The term *Hermetica* was used to designate a wide range of alchemical, astrological, medical, and philosophical treatises such as *The Emerald Table*, Plato's *Timaeus*, and Apuleius's *The Golden Ass*. The *Hermetica* also included a collection of works ascribed to a divinely inspired sage named Hermes Trismegistus and those attributed to the god known to the Egyptians as Thoth and to the Greeks as Hermes. As the patron of literature and music, the god of learning and medicine, and the one to whom men turned for divine revelation, Thoth-Hermes played many roles, and the breadth of his associations with the sciences and arts led very early on to the practice of attaching his name to multiple works. Many authors, appealing to the authority of ancient texts, also stressed that Plato and Pythagoras had been students of Hermes and referenced Hermes as a manner of course, and as early as the time of Plotinus, Porphyry and Iamblichus, such hermetic texts figured prominently in any discussion of the Mysteries and the divine wisdom communicated to initiates of the higher degrees. From very early on, hermeticism, Platonism, and Neo-Platonism intermingled and existed in a state of symbiosis in the minds of philosophers and writers; hermetic concepts typically embodied by alchemy often were put forth to illustrate and support Platonic and Neo-Platonic philosophies and vice versa.[9]

The connections between the texts were maintained when they were reintroduced during the Renaissance, and the fusion of the hermetic and the Neo-Platonic created a ripple effect as the concepts put forth by Ficino and Pico della Mirandola affected those of famous authors such as Francesco Giorgi, Cornelius Agrippa, and Paracelsus. The men merged the philosophies, and in doing so, they introduced to Europe and Britain a blend that combined medicine and natural philosophy with theology and the exoteric and esoteric practices of alchemy. As prominent writers adopted and modified the concepts, their own modifications were expanded upon in turn by men such as Jacob Boehme, Robert Fludd, and Robert Burton. Later, the range of influence expanded even further as the views were amplified by the Cambridge Platonists who made extensive use of hermetic symbolism and quoted freely from Pythagoras, Hermes Trismegistus, Plato, Plotinus, Giorgi, Agrippa, and Paracelsus, and the hermetic authors and concepts found their way into literary

---

8   Stanton J. Linden, *Darke Hierogliphicks: Alchemy in English Literature from Chaucer to the Restoration* (Lexington, Kentucky: The University of Kentucky Press, 1996) 23.

9   Kathleen Raine, "Thomas Taylor in England," *Thomas Taylor the Platonist: Selected Writings*, eds. Kathleen Raine and George Mills Harper (Princeton: Princeton University Press, 1969) 5.

productions where they acted as inspiration for poets such as Sidney and Milton and those who followed.[10]

Paracelsus was one author whose works would later prove to be extremely influential; his fusion of alchemical and Neo-Platonic concepts designed to give physic to both man's soul and body and his exhortations to gain wisdom through direct experimentation and study of the natural world had such an impact on medicine, chemistry, philosophy, and theology that he and his followers eventually were credited with the creation of iatrochemistry as well as the framework for the Rosicrucian and Behmenist movements.[11] He was declared the Luther of physicians because he was among the earliest and most vocal advocates of reforming scientific methods, and he insisted that medical theories be based on experimentation and practice rather than tradition. He gave alchemy a practical application that revolutionized medicine, and because of his efforts, chemistry became an integral part of men like Keats's medical training, but he also remained famous for his metaphysics centuries after his death.

For Paracelsus, the Rosicrucians and many of the Freemasons who followed him, Pythagorean theories, Platonism, Neo-Platonism and exoteric and esoteric alchemy were considered interlocking aspects of the same philosophy. Most Paracelsian texts mingled practical details with the speculative and combined material science and experimentation with philosophies exploring the possibilities of an animistic, analogical universe filled with spirits and various esoteric elements.[12] Paracelsus refined Agrippa's expositions on the four temperaments of man, the interchange of influence between the planets and stars and man's humors, and the three elements of the world – the elementary, intellectual and celestial – to argue that the four temperaments were linked to alchemical metaphorical concepts of earth, air, fire, and water, which in turn corresponded to the humors determining man's disposition and health.[13] He emphasized the imaginative faculty and its interplay with the four

---

10  Desiree Hirst, "The Cambridge Scholars," *Hidden Riches: Traditional Symbolism from the Renaissance to Blake* (New York: Barnes & Noble, Inc., 1964) 144–61. Hermetic concepts also were often re-introduced to the reading public in the form of translations, new editions, and in some cases, thinly veiled plagiarism. One work by Agrippa, *De Occulta Philosophia,* that blended hermeticism and Neo-Platonism throughout and drew heavily upon Ficino's translations of Plato and various Neo-Platonic and hermetic sources, enjoyed an extended life when in 1801 Frances Barrett published as his own in London essentially an abridged version of the multi-volume work and entitled it *The Magus, or Celestial Intelligencer.*

11  Francis Yates discusses this throughout *The Rosicrucian Enlightenment* (Saint Albans: Paladin, 1975).

12  Gareth Roberts, *The Mirror of Alchemy: Alchemical Ideas and Images in manuscripts and Books from Antiquity to the Seventeenth Century* (Toronto: University of Toronto Press, 1994).

13  Paracelsus rejected Galen's theory that illness was due to an imbalance in the humors. Rather, he argued that illness was caused by disease and specific imbalances in isolated organs. He theorized that when one organ became diseased the imbalance affected the entire body. The distinction may seem small today, but it was a radically different perspective then. In addition, while others theorized that too much of one humor led to a certain temperament, and treated the temperament by altering the physical, Paracelsus argued the opposite. He believed that imbalances in temperament – in the mental aspects – could lead to illness, and he designed his medicines to treat both spirit and body.

temperaments and their link to the four elements as central to his belief in a World Soul with which man interacted and received inspiration.

For Paracelsus, the invisible spirit existed within the physical body of man. Because of its strength, the spirit determined the health, and as a vital portion of the spirit, the imagination acted as a primary means of enabling man to attain stronger and purer spiritual, mental, and physical states. Similarly, he argued that an alternate, invisible world of the spirit existed, mirroring the visible world and that man might discover traces or "signatures" of it by engaging the imagination and studying Nature, and his belief in a system of correspondences enabled him to envision a specific use for such signatures.[14] By studying these traces, he believed physicians might discover the means by which diseases could be countered, and they might use alchemy to create cures.

Man's physical health depended upon a harmony amongst man, Nature, and the spirit, and Paracelsus argued that alchemy helped the physician identify and encourage the conjunctions in all three. Heaven and earth, the spiritual and the material, the macrocosm and the microcosm, Nature and man, were linked – though often out of joint – and alchemy was the means by which they could be joined together in beneficial interaction.[15] At the same time, the alchemist's physical experiments and preparations acted as a microcosmic representation of man's own struggles to attain a purer state. Inherent in this concept was the belief that man possessed an element or spark of the divine and could achieve a higher state by allowing that element to interact with the imperfect world. Like the physical matter contained in the alchemist's flask, the spiritual matter, a man's soul, could only be transmuted, individualized, and purified through a reaction between dissimilar materials representative of the contraries of life that continually interacted and defined the universe. In other words, the presence of good and evil in the world was necessary to achieve the philosopher's gold of spiritual knowledge and learning.[16]

It was Paracelsus who drew together the Neo-Platonic conception of the World Soul, the integral role of the imagination and psychology in health, and the hermetic language of alchemy to actively promote the ideal of the priest-physician. He broadened the practical conception of exoteric alchemy to encompass far more than gold, all the while stressing that alchemy's esoteric doctrines held the key to spiritual, mental, and physical health, and his philosophies formed the foundation for the precepts of the Rosicrucian society's supposed physicians whose primary goal was not gold-making, but rather, healing of both the mind and body.[17]

---

14  Paracelsus (Philippus Aureolus Theophrastus Bombastus von Hohenheim) "Sickness and Health," *Paracelsus Selected Writings*, ed. Jolande Jacobi, trans. Norbert Guterman, 2nd edn (Princeton: Princeton UP/ Bollingen Foundation, 1951; 1988) 61–64. See also Hirst, "The Tradition in Action," *Hidden Riches: Traditional Symbolism from the Renaissance to Blake* 44–75.

15  Paracelsus, "Alchemy, Art of Transformation," *Paracelsus Selected Writings* 141–49.

16  Paracelsus, "Alchemy, Art of Transformation," *Paracelsus Selected Writings* 141–49.

17  E. J. Holmyard, "Paracelsus," *Alchemy* (1957; Mineola, NY: Dover Publications, Inc. 1990) 165–76. Hirst 60–63.

The same mix of hermetic and Neo-Platonic philosophies that led to a surge in alchemical studies such as Paracelsus's also resulted in the popularization of the Rosicrucian fraternity. In 1614 and 1615, the Rosicrucian manifestos the *Fama Fraternitatis* and *Confessio Fraternitatis* were published in Germany and sparked both a furor and a cultural movement. The texts announced the existence of the Order of the Rosy Cross and described the brotherhood's laws and goals while also declaring that, although the brothers would remain invisible to the public, the fraternity was open to new members should the proper men seek them out. The *Fama* and *Confessio* told the tale of Christian Rosenkreutz, an "illuminated man" who journeyed to the East, learned all the secrets of the *Hermetica* and the "heavenly and human mysteries," and founded a secret brotherhood of men who dedicated themselves to healing the sick and effecting the reformation and enlightenment of society and the sciences to "partly renew and reduce all Arts ... to perfection; so that finally Man might thereby understand his own Nobleness and Worth, and why he is called Microcosmus, and how far his knowledge extendeth in Nature."[18] The *Fama* and *Confessio* declared that the brotherhood possessed all the wisdom of the magi and the secrets of alchemy, and the texts were soon followed by *The Chymical Wedding*, an alchemical allegory containing elements of initiation into a society.

The manifestos inspired a slew of writings in response, and those who published Rosicrucian texts and claimed to be or were assumed to be members of the fraternity were widely known as experts in the hermetic art of alchemy. The Rosicrucian appropriation of hermeticism was clear to readers of the period. The *Fama* and *Confessio* included not only the story of Rosenkreutz's adventures in the East but also the tale of the discovery of his tomb in a hidden vault by brothers of the fraternity, and both ensured that links to the *Hermetica* could not be mistaken. Readers were told that Rosenkreutz had faithfully recorded his knowledge of the Mysteries of Nature in a book, and that when the brothers discovered his miraculously preserved body, they found the book in his arms. The story echoed in all points the legend surrounding the discovery of the *Emerald Table* in Hermes Trismegistus's tomb.

In addition, the emphasis the Rosicrucian texts placed on social and scientific reforms, particularly in regards to medicine, their charge to provide physic to those in need for free, and their claims to have mastered the art of alchemy, even while they stressed that as "true Philosophers," Rosicrucians thought little of "making of Gold, which is but a parergon; for besides that they have a thousand better things," by which to "honor God and help mankind," all offered clear parallels to the teachings of Paracelsus.[19] And to make sure the connection could not be missed, Paracelsus was explicitly mentioned in the *Fama* as one whose works were revered and preserved in Rosenkreutz's secret vault.[20]

---

18 *Fama Fraternitatis*, trans. Thomas Vaughan (1652), transcriber, Kevin Day (Sept. 2002) <http://www.levity.com/alchemy/fama.html>. *Confessio Fraternitatis*, trans. Thomas Vaughan (1652), transcriber, Kevin Day (Sept. 2002) <http://www.levity.com/alchemy/confessi.html>.

19 *Fama Fraternitatis*.

20 Following the publication of the *Fama* and *Confessio*, Paracelsus's influence grew. By the late seventeenth century, over 24 new English editions and translations of his works

As the Rosicrucian society captured the public imagination, these connections inevitably became stronger when writers influenced by Paracelsus published works defending the fraternity, seeking membership in it, and offering their own interpretations of its mysterious texts. Philosophers, scientists, physicians, writers, and the general public as well speculated about the fraternity's existence, means, and motives. Charlatans traded on the name and the Rosicrucians's reputation as accomplished alchemists and doctors, while men of high repute and learning such as Michael Maier, Robert Fludd, Francis Bacon, Thomas Vaughan, Elias Ashmole and Robert Molay defended the society and published Rosicrucian related works. Bacon's *New Atlantis* published in 1627 resembled so strongly the Rosicrucian calls for reformation in the sciences and the creation of an ideal college for study and dissemination of knowledge that it resulted in a common belief that Bacon was a Rosicrucian, and both Maier's and Fludd's works inspired similar assumptions about them.

For more than a century after the Rosicrucians and their mythology raised a furor both on the Continent and in Britain, philosophers such as Descartes, Leibniz and Kant discussed the fraternity's existence and its humanistic goals. The knowledge was so common, *The Spectator* blithely assumed its readers were so familiar with the society that they need not be informed of particulars.[21] In response to a 1712 article in *The Spectator* relating a Rosicrucian anecdote, "Emilia Lovetruth" sent a letter noting that she recalled reading the same story "a great while ago" and had "just done reading the Rosicrucian story in the Fame and Confession, a book published by the fraternity."[22] Two years later, Pope was revising *The Rape of the Lock* to take advantage of the society's popularity and adding a note for ladies to explain the Rosicrucian "machinery," and the Abbé De Montfaucon De Villars's *Comte de Gabalis: Discourses on the Secret Sciences and Mysteries, in Accordance with the Principles of the Ancient Magi and the Wisdom of the Kabalistic Philosophers* was being re-issued to mark the anniversary of the initial Rosicrucian publications. The society's popularity remained strong throughout the century and well into the next. During the Romantic period, elements of Rosicrucian lore appeared in texts by many of the major writers and were a standard component in gothic novels.

In addition, just as writers were adapting the Rosicrucian concepts to suit their own views and needs, the general public was as well. As Rosicrucian ideas spread throughout the Continent and England, they were increasingly associated with Freemasonry, and by 1824, when Thomas De Quincey discussed Freemasonry's origins in *London Magazine* in a series of essays titled "Historico-Critical Inquiry into the Origins of the Rosicrucians and the Free-Masons," the Masonic societies

---

had appeared as well as multiple reprints of his treatises in collections and commentaries, and a great many apothecaries and physicians had become adherents of his theories (Linden 211–15).

21  See, for example, Eustace Budgell, No. 379, 15 May 1712, *The Spectator*, ed. Donald F. Bond, vol. III (Oxford: Clarendon Press, 1965) 422–25. Joseph Addison, No. 574, 30 July 1714, *The Spectator*, ed. Donald F. Bond, vol. IV (Oxford: Clarendon Press, 1965) 561–65.

22  *The Spectator*, vol. III, 422–25.

were assumed by many to have originated with Rosicrucianism.[23] Indeed, the public had linked Rosicrucian and Masonic concepts for at least a century, oftentimes following the same logic De Quincey did when he wrote that, "FREE-MASONRY IS NEITHER MORE NOR LESS THAN ROSICRUCIANISM AS MODIFIED BY THOSE WHO TRANSPLANTED IT INTO ENGLAND," and:

> The original Free-masons were a society that arose out of the Rosicrucian mania, certainly within the thirteen years from 1633 to 1646, and probably between 1633 and 1640. Their object was *magic* in the cabbalistic sense, *i.e.*, the *occult wisdom* transmitted from the beginning of the world, and matured by Christ; to communicate this when they had it, to search for it when they had it not; and both under an oath of secrecy. ... Hence it is that all the Masonic symbols either refer to Solomon's Temple, or are figurative modes of expressing the ideas and doctrines of *magic* in the sense of the Rosicrucians, and their mystical predecessors in general.[24]

To De Quincey as well as others, the links between the societies seemed obvious. He argued that men such as the alchemist-physicians Michael Maier and Robert Fludd, both famous supporters of Rosicrucianism, introduced the society to the English, and because of the furor surrounding the Rosicrucians, they gave the society a new name – Freemasonry. In its modified and Englished form, Freemasonry was then exported back to the Continent, and soon thereafter new versions and grades of the society began to appear. As the public was aware, the common thread between the societies was what De Quincey termed "the ideas and doctrines of *magic* in the sense of the Rosicrucians, and their mystical predecessors in general," and that thread included the old ties to hermeticism, Neo-Platonism, the Mystery societies.

The average reader such as Keats would have easily caught both the hermetic allusions and their relationship to Freemasonry, in large part because the magazines and newspapers of the Romantic period such as *The Courier, The Gentleman's Magazine, European Magazine, London Magazine, The British Critic, The London Review and Literary Journal, The Anti-Jacobin Review, The Monthly Review, The Critical Review,* and *The Free-Masons' Magazine* consistently published reviews of Masonic publications and articles about Freemasonry discussing rituals and philosophies and oftentimes relating them to political and religious issues. Articles about Freemasonry linking its hermetic elements and secrets to those contained in both Rosicrucianism and ancient Mystery societies also appeared in encyclopedias including the *Encyclopaedia Brittanica*, the infamous *French Encyclopédie, ou Dictionnaire raisonné des sciences, des arts et des métiers*, and even the popular *Every Young Man's Companion* which contained a chapter entitled "Mystery of Free Masonry Explained." In addition, dozens of pamphlets called "exposures"

---

23 De Quincey's essays translated and paraphrased J. G. Buhle's 1804 essay written in Latin. They appeared in the January, February, March and June editions of *London Magazine*. Thomas De Quincey, "Historico-Critical Inquiry into the Origins of the Rosicrucians and the Free-Masons," *De Quincey's Collected Writings: Tales and Prose Phantasies*, ed. David Masson, vol. 13 (Edinburgh: Adam & Charles Black, 1890) 384–448.

24 De Quincey 420–21 and 426, respectively.

that revealed Masonic initiation rituals appeared throughout the period, most ran to multiple editions, and some were reissued year after year for decades.

Although De Quincey discounted the more fabulous Masonic histories tracing the society back to Adam, he stressed it was widely accepted that, philosophically, Freemasonry and Rosicrucianism shared common goals. Both were ostensibly dedicated to aiding man in his quest for earthly knowledge and spiritual wisdom. Both emphasized the importance of studying the liberal arts and Nature itself as the means to advance the wisdom necessary for brotherhood, harmony, happiness on earth, and the spiritual growth that was the key to happiness in the afterlife. Both advocated *"Entire equality of personal rights among their members in relation to their final object,"* thereby removing "all distinctions of social rank," and perhaps most strongly, both societies shared a religious mysticism implicit as a prerequisite to reach their final object.[25] Just as Rosicrucian texts claimed that study and contemplation ultimately led one closer to communion with God, the "lessons" and "grades" of the speculative Masonic degrees were "designed to bring the candidate nearer to a true interpretation of the will of the Great Architect and his submission to it."[26]

De Quincey's conclusion that the "Work" of both the Rosicrucians and the Freemasons entailed a "striving after hidden knowledge" also was reinforced by frequent references in the popular Masonic *Monitors* and rituals to hermetic emblems such as the sun and moon that had long played prominent symbolic roles in the exoteric and esoteric alchemical work of the Rosicrucians.[27] There were more direct links as well. Mozart's well known Masonic opera *The Magic Flute* contained alchemical and initiatory elements in action and word. The chorale warned, "He who commits himself to this dangerous route will be purified by Fire, Water, Air, and Earth. If he can surmount the terror of death, he will soar upward from the earth toward the sky" and the characters proceeded through an initiation publicly associated with Freemasonry at the time.[28] Meanwhile, Goethe, also a Freemason, included alchemical allusions in his own works, and many of the French and English descriptions of rituals published during the period and made infamous by their inclusion in works such as Barruel's and Robison's drew explicit connections between alchemy and initiation rites. The work *Francs-Maçons Parisiens du Grand-Orient de France* explained the initiation rite as alchemical transformation:

> The first element is the Earth, the subterranean domain where germination and seeding develop. It is represented by the Cabinet of Reflection in which the Member-Elect is

---

25  De Quincey 389.

26  A. C. F. Jackson, "Rosicrucianism and Its Effect on Craft Masonry," *Ars Quatuor Coronatum: Transactions of the Quatuor Coronati Lodge No. 2076*, 97 (1984) 116.

27  See William Hutchinson's "Lecture VII, The Temple at Jerusalem," *The Spirit of Freemasonry* (London: J. Wilkie and W. Goldsmith, 1775; New York: Bell Publishing Co., 1982) 145–46. De Quincey, "Historico-Critical Inquiry," 392.

28  Jacques Chailley, *The Magic Flute, Masonic Opera*, trans. Herbert Weinstock (New York: Alfred A. Knopf, 1971) 137. In Part One of his study, "Preliminary Circumvolutions," Chailley provides extensive documentation of how *The Magic Flute* was received and viewed as Masonic during the Romantic period.

confined. The first journey is related to Air, … the first journey is the emblem of human life, the tumult of the passions, the collision of diverse interests, the difficulty of undertakings, the obstacles that are multiplied in our path by rivals eager to harm us … . To give the Member-Elect assurance, he is made to undergo the purification by water, … . In order to contemplate the Queen of Hell – that is, the truth hidden within himself – the Initiate must pass through a triple enclosure of flames. This is the trial by Fire. The initiate remains amid the flames (circumambient passions) without being burned, but must allow himself to be penetrated by the beneficent warmth that they emit.[29]

And, in England, De Quincey told his audience, "Masonic readers will remember a ceremony used on the introduction of a new member which turns upon [the] distinction between lead and gold as the symbol of transition from the lost state of Adam to the original condition of innocence and perfection."[30]

In addition, like most mystery societies, Freemasonry taught a legend of ritual death of the body, disintegration and reintegration, in this case embodied in the murder of Hiram, the Master builder of Solomon's temple and original "Master Mason." Hermetic associations in the story included the symbolic number of days passed after the murder, the dismemberment or decomposition of the body, the loss of a "Key-Word" or secret knowledge with Hiram's death and the attempt to rediscover the same, the "raising" of Hiram by "the Five Points of Fellowship," and his ritual recomposition and burial in the "Sanctum Sanctorum" of the temple.[31] All of these reminded people of the allegorical, alchemical stories put forth in Rosicrucian texts where the same processes were understood as metaphors for "the reintegration of 'fallen man', man in general, as well as the man who had lost the 'Word – Soul – Self' and remained in the darkness of ignorance," as taken within the Platonic concept of the "eternal return."[32] Just as alchemical transformation effected by stages of decomposition, separation, purification and reintegration represented the greater spiritual transformation of man via physical toil, intellectual study, and divine revelation, the Masonic rituals and legends implied that reintegration could be achieved only through the physical and mental efforts of the Masons as well as "a *magical* act – an act of supernatural transformation" resembling nothing so much as the quintessence known both to alchemy and the ancient mystery societies.[33]

The goals of esoteric alchemy were understood to match those of not only Rosicrucianism but also Freemasonry, both of which advocated a philosophical path to reformation and regeneration of the spirit and body via a concerted effort to live within the world while acknowledging its relationship to that of the spiritual realm and the unifying series of correspondences that activated both.[34] The unity and harmony envisioned by alchemists such as Paracelsus and the Rosicrucians was

---

29  As translated in Chailley 137–38. The original quote may be found in Michel Brenet's *Francs-Maçons Parisiens du Grand-Orient de France (fin du XVIII siecle)* 308.

30  De Quincey 423.

31  *Jachin and Boaz* reprinted by A. C. F. Jackson in *English Masonic Exposures 1760–1769* (London: Lewis Masonic, 1986) 165–66.

32  Piatigorsky 305.

33  Piatigorsky 306.

34  Linden 8.

also sought after by the Masons and described in similar terms. For example, the concept of the quintessence, a pure form of air imbued with occult properties which could permeate a man and act as inspiration to guide him to wisdom or a purer state, grounded in Neo-Platonism and alchemical philosophy, took on yet another connotation when it became understood as a component of esoteric initiation rites in general and the Rosicrucian and Masonic rites in particular.[35]

Masonic goals and philosophies were often bound to those of Mystery societies, including the Eleusinian and Pythagorean, as authors grouped them together and various degrees claimed to offer a means to work towards the quintessence. In *Proofs of a Conspiracy*, Robison repeatedly accused the Freemasons and Illuminati of tying their own rituals to those of the Mystery societies as well as doctrines of natural religion, and he even went so far as to concede that he had "a notion that the Dionysiacs of Ionia … were really a Masonic Fraternity."[36] Similarly, a preface to an 1812 English extract of Barruel's *Mémoires* proclaimed: "The first part will treat of the GENERAL SECRET or LESSER MYSTERIES of FREE-MASONRY. The second part will show the GRAND MYSTERIES AND SECRETS OF THE OCCULT LODGES."[37] And, as Thomas Taylor explained to readers of his *On the Eleusinian and Bacchic Mysteries*, "the whole business of initiation was distributed into five parts, … 'and the fifth … is friendship with divinity … the fifth gradation is the most perfect felicity arising … and, according to Plato, an assimilation to divinity, as far as possible to mankind'," but it was only achieved after much study and spiritual labor.[38] Similarly, "The conjunction of rose and cross" for the Rosicrucian adept was perceived of as symbolic of the quintessence and "the transfiguring ecstasy … when the adept, after long pain and self-sacrifice of the quest in this world, a world in which opposites are forever quarrelling, [found] his cross – the symbol of that struggle and opposition – suddenly blossom with the rose of love, harmony and beauty."[39]

Ultimately, although the existence of the Rosicrucian order was never proved, its philosophies were widely known, and by the Romantic period, many considered the need for proof to be unnecessary. As writers such as De Quincey pointed out, the very story had taken on a life of its own and produced numerous secret societies that

---

35   Hirst 60–63.

36   John Robison, *Proofs of a Conspiracy Against All the Religions and Governments of Europe Carried on in the Secret Meetings of Freemasons, Illuminati and Reading Societies* (New York; London, 1798; Whitefish, MT: Kessinger Publishing, 2007) 268–69. During the Romantic period such wholesale assumptions and conflations of philosophies were quite common. Lempriere, for example, an author exceptionally well known to Keats, told his readers that Plato "followed the physics of Heraclitus, the metaphysical opinions of Pythagoras, and the morals of Socrates," and grouped the entirety with various mystery societies. Elizabeth Imlay, "Freemasonry, the Brontes, and the Hidden text of Jane Eyre," *Secret Texts: The Literature of Secret Societies*, 211: 210–27.

37   "Preface," *The AntiChristian and Antisocial Conspiracy. An Extract from the French of the Abbé Barruel, to which Is Prefixed Jachin and Boaz, or an Authentic Key to the Door of Free-Masonry Ancient and Modern* (Lancaster: Joseph Ehrenfried, 1812) i.

38   Thomas Taylor, *Thomas Taylor the Platonist: Selected Writings* 366–67.

39   Richard Ellmann, *The Identity of Yeats* (London: Faber Press, 1954) 64.

adopted the ideals of the Rosicrucian fraternity, the trappings, and even the name itself. What had begun as an allegory was transmuted by men into reality, and in England, one immensely popular version of that reality was Freemasonry.

The Masonic presence in society, both in Britain and on the Continent, was so widespread that when in 1797 the Abbé Barruel placed his estimate of Masonic followers at millions, many believed him. He overestimated, but more accurate estimates testify to the fraternity's appeal. Without taking into account its enormous popularity on the Continent or in Scotland and Ireland, by the beginning of the nineteenth century, lodges in England and Wales alone numbered over two thousand.[40] Masonic lodges were everyday features of life in virtually every city in Britain and many small towns as well.

A cursory list of influential cultural figures the public commonly assumed were Freemasons, or associated with Freemasonry, also suggests the scope of the society's appeal. The range of men, in terms of status, profession, and political or philosophical leanings, is startling. In addition to many of the contributors to the famous French *Encyclopédie*, including d'Alembert, Diderot, and Voltaire, the list includes not only the Prince Regent who would become King George IV but also: John Arbuthnot, Joseph Banks, Andrew Bell, Henry Brougham, Robert Burns, George Canning, Richard Carlile, Erasmus Darwin, Dr William Dodd, Henry Erskine, Edward Gibbon, Johann Wolfgang von Goethe, Franz Josef Haydn, David Hume, Johann Gottfried von Herder, William Hogarth, James Hogg, Henry Hunt, Dr Edward Jenner, Edmund Kean, Thaddeus Kosciusko, the Marquis de Lafayette, Johann Casper Lavater, Gotthold Lessing, John Gibson Lockhart, Henry Mackenzie, Franz Anton Mesmer, Charles Montesquieu, Wolfgang Amadeus Mozart, Thomas Paine, Joseph Priestly, Andrew Michael Ramsay, Frederic Schiller, Friedrich Schlegel, Sir Walter Scott, Joseph Spence, Dugald Stewart, Emanuel Swedenborg, John Toland, John Wilson, Horace Walpole, and John Wilkes.

Although this list is cursory, the majority of men listed were documented Masons. Others such as Diderot, Paine, and Priestly associated so closely and with so many Freemasons that they were grouped, *de facto*, with the Masons in publications of the period. Barruel's influential *Mémoires*, for example, linked the Freemasons and the French *philosophes* irrevocably in the public mind when he named them as co-conspirators, and though the association was never proved beyond doubt, from the Romantic period to today, writers both for and against Masonry still give the connection as fact. The situation is much the same with Paine and Priestly. Both men's personal connections as well as their radical philosophies, writings and politics made them prime targets for Robison. He denigrated the *Rights of Man* as a "whim of Free Masonry" and described Paine as one of the "most brilliant" and "choice" "Illuminators."[41] He blamed Priestly for "openly preach[ing]" "the detestable doctrines of Illuminatism," and wrote that Priestly, "has already given the most promising specimens of his own docility in the principles of Illuminatism, and has already passed through several degrees of initiation."[42]

---

40 Piatigorsky 154.
41 Robison 265.
42 Robison 277.

People often assume that because Freemasonry claimed secrets the society's membership was secret, but the opposite was true. Masons not only were highly visible but were so by their own choice. Men freely acknowledged their Masonic affiliations, and the names of famous Masons were frequently cited to promote the Craft, or as in the case of Priestly, to bind the society to ideas with which a writer disagreed. Burns and Voltaire, for whom Keats had great admiration, were both Freemasons whose memberships were widely publicized. Lodge members also often appeared in full Masonic regalia for ceremonial processions through the streets and the laying of cornerstones or dedications of new buildings; Masonic medals featuring emblems of the Craft were sold to the public, and Masonic symbols appeared as fashionable decoration in architecture as well. To give just one example of Freemasonry's popularity with the general public, Masonic historian Bernard Jones notes that in 1819 a new Freemasons' Hall was opened in Bath by the Duke of Sussex, and "for two days before the consecration of the hall upward of two thousand persons, chiefly ladies, paid for admission to view it and its contents."[43]

Places such as the Freemason's Tavern and Hall on Queen Street in London also were open to the public and served as popular gathering places for lectures and meetings by various non-Masonic societies as well as for Masonic sponsored lectures, theatrical or musical productions, and even balls. Lectures running the gamut from scientific to literary to historical to political topics, as well as those centered on Masonry itself, were a regular feature and frequently were sent to press and made available to the public at large. A few examples will suggest the range of groups that made use of the building. In 1807, the Geological Society of London, of which Keats's chemistry teacher, Babington, was a founding member, met there. In 1816 the Hampden Club did as well, and we can date the radical club's use of Freemason's Tavern to discuss "the Subject of Parliamentary Reform" thanks to William Hone's publication of the meeting.[44] As a more humorous example, earlier in 1783, Thomas Taylor nearly burnt the Tavern down when he started a fire while demonstrating a "Rosicrucian perpetual lamp" inspired by his reading of Bishop Wilkins's description of such a lamp in the *Confessio*.[45]

In addition, while the Freemasons were promoting their society and other groups were creating societies modeled after the Freemasons, the growing confusion surrounding them all added to the spread of information. Masonic membership was matched by the numerous publications about the fraternity, and throughout the eighteenth century well into the nineteenth century, information about Freemasonry was available to the public often and almost anywhere they might care to look. A steady stream of articles, pamphlets, and books continually were issued trying to sort

43 Bernard E. Jones, *Freemasons' Guide and Compendium* (1956; London: George G. Harrap & Company Ltd., 1971) 296.

44 *A Full Report of the Proceedings of the Meeting, Convened by the Hampden Club, which Took Place at the Freemason's Tavern, Great Queen-Street, Lincoln's Inn Fields, on Saturday, the 15th June, 1816, upon the Subject of Parliamentary Reform* (London: Published by Wm. Hone, Fleet-Street, 1816).

45 Thomas Taylor, "Mr. Taylor, the Platonist," *Thomas Taylor the Platonist: Selected Writings* 114. The entry is a reprint of from *Public Characters of 1798* (Dublin, 1798–99).

out the details, and these works found a continual audience. The popularity of the society resulted in an inexhaustible source of reading material for the general public. Beginning in 1723, even the *Book of Constitutions of the Antient and Honourable Fraternity of Free and Accepted Masons* could be purchased, and Masons were more than happy to educate the public about the society.

William Preston's *Illustrations of Freemasonry* was first published in London in 1772, and between 1772 and 1812 the work went through 12 editions in England. Other popular works by Masons included William Hutchinson's *Spirit of Freemasonry*, John Browne's *Masonic Master-Key*, Alex Lawrie's *History of Freemasonry*, Joshua Bradley's *Some of the Beauties of Freemasonry*, and George Oliver's *Antiquities of Freemasonry*.[46] In 1810, Thomas Paine's executrix Madame Bonneville published an edited version of his essay *The Origin of Freemasonry*, written between 1803 and 1805, in which Paine cited as his sources several general books on Masonry, the records of a French lodge, the exposures *Masonry Dissected* and *The Use and Abuse of Free-Masonry*, Dr Dodd's published oration on Masonry's history given at the dedication of Freemason's Hall in London, and the article "Freemasonry" in the French *Encyclopédie* by the famous astronomer and Freemason Lalande.[47] Richard Carlile republished Paine's essay, unexpurgated, in 1818. Alexander Fraser published *An Account of the Proceedings at the Festival of the Society of Freemasons at Their Hall, the 27th of January 1813*, and throughout the eighteenth and nineteenth centuries, Masonic *Pocket Companions*, *Miscellanies* containing songs, poems, and anecdotes, *Freemason's Monitors*, magazine and newspaper articles, tracing boards explaining Masonic symbols, and encyclopedia entries consistently appeared. There was even a *Free-Masons' Magazine or General and Complete Library* that published Masonic lectures and gave a positive review of Coleridge's 1796 *Poems on Various Subjects*.[48]

Oftentimes, articles about Freemasonry contained philosophic, religious or political overtones. A brief list of some of the titles appearing in the *Gentleman's Magazine* and the *European Magazine* at the turn of the century provides a useful glimpse into the topics discussed. In the *Gentleman's Magazine*, reviews of "John Bidlake's A Sermon preached ... before the Society of free and accepted Masons,"

---

46 William Preston, *Illustrations of Freemasonry* (London: G. Wilkie, 1772); William Hutchinson, *Spirit of Freemasonry* (London: G. Wilkie and W. Goldsmith, 1775); John Browne, *The Master Key through all the Degrees of a Freemason's Lodge, to which is added, Eullogiums and Illustrations upon Freemasonry* (London, 1798) and *Masonic Master-Key through the three degrees, by way of polyglot. Under the sanction of the Craft in general, containing the exact mode of working, initiation, passing and raising to the sublime Degree of a Master... with every requisite to render the accomplished Mason an explanation of all the hieroglyphics* (London, 1802); Alex Lawrie, *History of Freemasonry* (London: Longman and Rees, 1804); Alexander Fraser, *An Account of the Proceedings at the Festival of the Society of Freemasons at Their Hall, the 27th of January 1813* (London 1813); Joshua Bradley, *Some of the Beauties of Freemasonry* (London, 1816); George Oliver, *Antiquities of Freemasonry* (London: G. and W. B. Whittaker, 1823).

47 Thomas Paine, "The Origin of Freemasonry," *Writings of Thomas Paine*, ed. Moncure Daniels Conway, vol. 4 (New York: G. P. Putnam's Sons, 1896).

48 *Free-Masons' Magazine* 7 (1796): 52–53.

The Philosophy of Masons, "George Oliver's The Antiquities of Freemasonry," and "George Oliver's The Star in the East, shewing the Analogy which exists between the Lectures of Freemasonry, the Mechanism of Initiation into its Mysteries, and the Christian Religion" appeared, as did letters such as "The Revolution in France Ascribed to Free-Masonry," and "Priestley, Freemasonry, etc." and "J.M. on Free-Masonry."[49] The European Magazine reviewed Jethro Inwood's Sermons; in which are explained and enforced the Religious, Moral, and Political Virtues of Freemasonry, printed a letter entitled, "Address of the Antient Fraternity of Free and Accepted Masons to his Majesty, on his late Escape from Assassination," and provided readers with articles such as "Freemason's Hall and Tavern," a memoir of "William Preston, Esq." and "A Biographical Sketch of His Royal Highness the Duke of Sussex, K.G.," both of whose Masonic affiliations were discussed in the essays.[50]

In addition, pamphlets claiming to expose the brotherhood's secrets poured from the presses as did authorized Masonic works discussing elements of ritual, and these exposures almost always ran to multiple editions. In 1730, Samuel Prichard published Masonry Dissected in which he detailed the rituals of the first three degrees of Masonry and gave the legend of the Master Builder Hiram that functioned as a central allegory for Masonry's teachings. Thirty years later, the pamphlet had gone through 20 editions in England alone. Jachin and Boaz, another exposure, went through several editions when first printed in 1762, then was actually used in lodges and publicly re-issued almost every year until 1813 as both a stand-alone text and in combination with other works such as extracts of Barruel's Mémoires.[51] In the latter half of the eighteenth century, and well into the nineteenth, many more exposures appeared in English, often building upon Masonry Dissected, Jachin and Boaz, and various French exposures. Several of the titles ran to multiple editions for multiple years, including not only chapters in encyclopedias but also stand-alone editions such as Three Distinct Knocks, A Master Key to Free-Masonry; Hiram: The Grand-Master Key to the Door of both Ancient and Modern Free-Masonry; Ahiman Rezon; Shibboleth; Mahhabone or the Grand Lodge Door Open'd. Wherein is Discovered the Whole Secrets of Freemasonry, Both Ancient and Modern; Solomon in all His Glory; and The Free-Mason Stripped Naked.[52]

---

49 All found in Gentleman's Magazine 60-ii (1790): 1123; 66-ii (1796): 1017; 93-i (1823): 617–18; 95-ii (1825): 59–60; 64-i (1794): 491–93; 64-ii (1794): 617; and 64-ii (1794): 810, respectively.

50 All found in European Magazine 36 (July 1799): 38–39; 38 (July 1800): 6–7; 59 (May 1811): 329–32; 59 (May 1811): 323–27; and 61 (Apr. 1812): 243–46, respectively.

51 The Abbé Barruel, The AntiChristian and Antisocial Conspiracy. An Extract from the French of the Abbé Barruel, to which Is Prefixed Jachin and Boaz, or an Authentic Key to the Door of Free-Masonry Ancient and Modern (Lancaster: Joseph Ehrenfried, 1812).

52 A. C. F. Jackson, English Masonic Exposures 1760–1769 (London: Lewis Masonic, 1986) 1–19. Jackson provides reprints of the exposures and summaries of their publication histories after first issuance in the 1760s. For the publication history of Jachin and Boaz, see S. N. Smith "The So-Called 'Exposures' of Freemasonry of the Mid-Eighteenth Century," Ars Quatuor Coronatum: Transactions of the Quatuor Coronati Lodge No. 2076 56.1 (1943): 10–11.

The fact that most simply reprinted large chunks from previous works did not seem to hurt sales. When the pamphlet *The Free-Mason Stripped Naked* was initially reviewed in the *Gentleman's Magazine*, the reviewer noted "This absurd performance is entirely taken from two pamphlets; published a few years ago; the one entitled *Jachin and Boaz*, and the other *Three Distinct Knocks*; in which a number of ridiculous customs are described as the Secrets of Free-Masonry."[53] Such reviews were not unusual and indicate common knowledge of the exposures while also suggesting the sense that there was more to Freemasonry than the "ridiculous customs" being described.

Thomas De Quincey cited the abundance of opinions available when he published his series of essays in *London Magazine* in 1824 under the title "Historico-Critical Inquiry into the Origin of Rosicrucians and Freemasons," and declared with his usual flair that the subject was now closed, but his essays were themselves recycled from an 1804 work by German author J. G. Buhle. It is an indication of both De Quincey's interest and the popularity of the topic in general that his articles spanned four issues. Roughly twenty years later in 1847, De Quincey would write two more essays titled "Secret Societies" for the August and October editions of *Tait's Magazine* and would admit to a lifelong fascination with the topic. His articles did more than summarize origins though, and his attempts to understand the appeal organizations such as the Rosicrucians and Freemasons held neatly frame the debates of the period.

He opened "Secret Societies" by remarking:

> Generally speaking, a child may *not* – but every adult *will*, and *must*, if at all by nature meditative – regard with a feeling higher than vulgar curiosity small fraternities of men forming themselves as separate and inner vortices within the great vortex of society … and connected by the link of either purposes not safe to be avowed, or by the grander link of awful truths which, merely to shelter themselves from the hostility of an age unprepared for their reception, are forced to retire, possibly for generations, behind thick curtains of secrecy.[54]

Later in the same essay, he elaborated upon the mysterious purposes of such societies. Recalling the effect of two exceptionally well known works during the Romantic period, the Abbé Barruel's *Mémoires* and John Robison's *Proofs of a Conspiracy*, De Quincey wrote that although those men spoke of societies formed "if not always for a distinct purpose of evil, yet always in a spirit of malignant contradiction and hatred," he soon

> … read of other societies, even more secret, that watched over *truth* dangerous to publish or even to whisper, like the sleepless dragons that oriental fable associated with the subterraneous guardianship of regal treasures. The secrecy, and the reasons for the secrecy, were alike sublime. The very image, unveiling itself by unsteady glimpses, of men linked by brotherly love and perfect confidence, meeting … to shelter … some solitary lamp of truth … all this was superhumanly sublime. The fear of those men was sublime; the

---

53 "A Catalogue of New Books," *Gentleman's Magazine* 39 (1769): 406.

54 Thomas De Quincey, "Secret Societies," *De Quincey's Collected Writings: Historical Essays and Researches*, ed. David Masson (London: A. & C. Black, 1897) 173: 173–229.

courage was sublime; the stealthy, thief-like means were sublime; the audacious end – viz. to change the kingdoms of earth – was sublime.[55]

These are the images and terminology of the Romantic period, signals familiar to anyone who had read the novels, poetry, and philosophical or political prose of the time, and they reveal why the public found the societies so fascinating. Throughout the Romantic period, societies such as the Rosicrucians, the Freemasons and the Illuminati – those "malignant" groups that figured so prominently in Barruel's and Robison's works – had been linked to concepts of reformation and revolution. Their proclaimed truths of brotherhood, liberty, and equality hinted at broad political agendas, while their avowed possession of great secrets and their overlay of mystical rituals and hermetic symbols provided mysterious religious and philosophical overtones that captured the public's imagination. When in 1847 De Quincey wrote that his own interest in such societies sprang from an intense desire to know "*what* they do" and "*what they do it for*," he was summarizing a common preoccupation with these societies in general, and the Rosicrucians and Freemasons in particular, that had existed for centuries.[56]

When in 1797 and 1798 the Abbé Barruel and John Robison separately published their theories of a conspiracy between the *philosophes*, the Illuminati, and the "Occult" Freemasons to destroy not only the Christian religion but also the monarchies of the world and civilized society itself, all the aspects of Masonry that had provoked discussion throughout the century were gathered together like threads and woven into a dark tapestry telling a frightening tale. The two men wrote about a mysterious and dangerous cabal that orchestrated the French Revolution and was still at work in the shadows, attempting to unleash anarchy upon the civilized world. They named names, gave explicit details, quoted private letters they claimed authentic, and assured readers they wrote based on firsthand knowledge of the Freemasons.[57]

Both Barruel's and Robison's books sold exceptionally well and exercised substantial influence. The first two volumes of Barruel's four-volume work appeared in 1797 and the last two volumes were issued the next year. In between the publications, Robison's work was issued, and by the close of 1798 it had gone through three editions. Barruel's also rapidly ran into multiple editions, and both were covered extensively in the magazines, newspapers and journals.[58] The crisis in thought at the turn of the century and the burgeoning tensions in society in the decades following generated a need for answers, and those supplied by Barruel and Robison provoked extensive debate. Their works created such a sensation that when Pitt proposed the Unlawful Societies Act of 1799, Freemasonry in Britain was given particular notice and both men's works were used in the parliamentary debate. Years

---

55 De Quincey, "Secret Societies" 181.

56 De Quincey, "Secret Societies" 173.

57 Robison had been a Mason, and Barruel claimed to have been initiated into the society, though against his will and without taking the requisite oaths of secrecy.

58 W. K. Firminger, "The Romance of Robison and Barruel," *Ars Quatuor Coronatum: Transactions of the Quatuor Coronati Lodge No. 2076* 50 (1937): 33. For examples of reviews, see *European Magazine* 32 (1797): 104–108, 172–76; *The British Critic* 10 (1797): 156-57; and *The London Review and Literary Journal* (August 1797): 104–105.

later, long after fears of conspiracy had cooled, De Quincey would note in "Secret Societies" that his early interest in such societies was sparked in part by Barruel's and Robison's works which he had heard read aloud and discussed, it seemed, by everyone.[59] And, more than a decade following their initial publication, as Keats was entering adulthood, reprints and extracts of the books were still being issued, oftentimes with exposures of Masonic rituals attached, and they were still being read and discussed by authors such as the Shelleys.

Both Barruel and Robison featured prominently Freemasonry's supposed role in the French Revolution and the society's assumed ties to the occult and Rosicrucianism in particular. Their sensationalistic exposés consistently described the details of esoteric hermetic rituals they claimed were designed to promote natural religion and encourage the destruction of Christianity, and they linked such rituals and their underlying philosophies to Freemasonry throughout. Robison and Barruel considered Masonic societies to be primary conduits by which the pernicious philosophies of the Enlightenment were disseminated to the public. Although both stipulated that they considered many Masons to be of good character and merely unwitting "dupes" in the entire affair, they also made it clear that the heathen "secrets" of Freemasonry lay in the mysteries of its allegories and higher degrees, and those secrets could be read if only men would be willing to see what was plainly before them.

Even while absolving "official" English Masonry of censure, they made it clear, as Barruel puts it, that "We perfectly well know that many English are initiated in the occult mysteries of the Rosicrucian and Scotch degrees; but it is not their *Occult Science* which constitutes them English Masons; for the first three degrees are all that are acknowledged in England."[60] The wording was carefully chosen. A very public and somewhat acrimonious schism existed in Freemasonry in England during the period in question. While the "Antients" did practice higher degrees, the "Moderns" officially did not, and it was the "Moderns" who then boasted the greater patronage and membership of the Royal family. But, because a man could be a member of multiple lodges, take part in what Barruel designates as "official English" Masonry, and also be an initiate of higher degrees, the distinction did not exonerate English Freemasons. It even acted as an accusation against the many who were members of the Antient lodges. In Britain, these higher degrees were presented, both to Freemasons and to the public as explicitly holding hermetic significance, and the connections between Rosicrucian practices and the higher degrees existed not only in the more general similarities but also in the particulars as well.

Beginning with the 1756 edition of *Ahiman Rezon*, Lawrence Dermott publicly argued against the "Modern" version of Masonic *Constitutions* by stressing that the Antients understood what others did not – that the history of Masonry was one of mystical significance and the true "secret mysteries of the Craft" were such that only those of the higher degrees could comprehend them.[61] These mysteries, it was suggested, could be found in the Royal Arch degree, the very name of which was

---

59  De Quincey, "Secret Societies" 174.

60  Barruel 116–17.

61  Lawrence Dermott, *Ahiman Rezon* (1756; Bloomington, IL: Masonic Book Club, 1973) 17.

designed to call to mind "the imaginary arch made in the heavens by the course of King Osiris, the Sun, from the vernal to the autumnal equinox," and "the signs through which he passes ... being seven, the number of grades or steps required to be taken by the Mason to entitle him to the honours of this degree."[62]

The Royal Arch degrees were steeped in mysticism and symbolism that appeared both strongly hermetic and particularly Rosicrucian. A prayer spoken during Royal Arch rituals recorded by Dermott included the plea, "number us not among those that know not thy statutes, nor the divine mysteries of the secret Cabala," and the centerpiece of the ritual was the symbolic discovery of a secret vaulted crypt. The ritual reminded readers of the story in the Rosicrucian *Fama* which it matched in multiple particulars including the recovery/discovery of the sacred books symbolizing the physical and spiritual knowledge central to the fraternity. In symbolic terms, the discovery of the lost texts, or lost word, during the Royal Arch ceremonies, and the initiates' movements throughout the ceremonies from darkness to light, and ignorance to understanding, echoed the esoteric goals of the Rosicrucians allegorized in their alchemical studies in which the adepts moved from limited understanding of man, world, and God to a more perfect wisdom resulting in regeneration.[63]

In addition, by forming essentially seven steps – the three Craft degrees and the four grades – the Royal Arch drew upon hermetic associations with the number seven and the Rosicrucian emblem of the "House of the Holy Spirit" reached by seven steps representing the exoteric and esoteric alchemy of the four elements of earth, air, fire and water, and the three Paracelsian principles previously discussed. Likewise, the Royal Arch ceremonies contained a practice known as "Passing the Veils" with veils colored to represent the four elements.[64] The elements were also present within the vaulted crypt in the form of physical models of the Platonic Bodies used to represent the invisible and based on Plato's theory of the composition of the universe put forth in *Timaeus* and long since adopted by the alchemist philosophers.[65]

Replete with mysticism, the many higher degrees such as the Royal Arch available to Masons, and known by the public as the "Occult" or "Scotch" degrees, concerned and captivated not only Barruel and Robison but also the public in no small part because so many British Masons could in fact be considered members. Notwithstanding Barruel's qualified exception of the "official" first three degrees of English Freemasonry, his definition of the Lodges he considered a threat was broad. He wrote:

---

62  John Fellows, *The Mysteries of Freemasonry, or an exposition of the Religious Dogmas and Customs of the Ancient Egyptians, etc.* (London: Reeves and Turner, 1866) 297–98.

63  De Quincey noted the parallels in "Historico-Critical Inquiry" 402–404. The prayers, Royal Arch symbols, and symbolism are in Lawrence Dermott's *Ahiman Rezon* (18) as well as many *Freemason's Monitors*.

64  Roy A. Wells *Royal Arch Matters* (London: Lewis Masonic, 1984) 16.

65  Wells 16–17. As Wells explains, the elements and bodies corresponded as follows: "Tetrahedron = 1 Triple Tau – symbolizes Fire; Octahedron = 2 Triple Taus – symbolizes Air; Hexahedron = 3 Triple Taus – symbolizes Earth; Icosahedron = 5 Triple Taus – symbolizes Water; and Dodecahedron = 9 Triple Taus – symbol of the Universe" (17). The last, in alchemical terminology, was the quintessence.

We comprehend under the designation of Occult Lodges, or the higher degrees of Masonry, all Free-Masons, in general, who after having past the first three degrees of *Apprentice*, *Fellow-Craft*, and *Master*, show sufficient zeal to be admitted into the higher degrees, where the veil is rent asunder, where emblematical and allegorical figures are thrown aside, and where the principle of Liberty and Equality is unequivocally explained by *war against Christ and his Altars!*[66]

The sweeping statement is notable not only because of its dramatic conclusion but also because as early as the 1740s these higher degrees had begun spreading rapidly throughout England. Thus, even if Masons in Britain were not practicing the exact same blend of Freemasonry as their Continental counterparts, the public was informed that it did not matter. *Any* of the higher degrees posed a danger according to Barruel, and significantly, the higher degrees Barruel discussed in detail were not only those popular amongst English Masons but also those that seemed to provide the strongest links to Rosicrucianism.[67]

As Barruel made clear in his work, many of those Freemasons who practiced the "Occult" or "Scotch" degrees also dabbled in alchemy – what he called, "the hermetical part of the science, or the transmutation of metals," while also conceding that these Masons ascribed roles to exoteric and esoteric alchemy in their philosophies.[68] Barruel explained to his readers,

Masonic writers in general divide [occult or high degree] Free-masonry into three classes, the Hermetic, the Cabalistic … and the Eclectic Mason. … The Hermetic Masonry, or the Scotch degrees, who work in chemistry, have adopted *Pantheism or true Spinosism*. With them *every thing is God, and God is every thing*. That is their grand mystery … reducing the result of [the] whole doctrine to this famous text of Hermes Trismegistus, "All is part of God; if all is part, the whole must be God. Therefore every thing that is made made itself, and will never cease to act, for this agent cannot repose. And as God has no end, so can his works have neither beginning nor end." … "Such is the summary though expressive belief of the whole Hermetic System;" in a word the whole religious system of the Scotch degrees …[69]

Romantic readers familiar with Rosicrucian lore and its basis in both Neo-Platonism and alchemy would have understood precisely why Barruel linked "chemistry," "Pantheism or true Spinosism," and the premise taken from the *Emerald Table* attributed to Hermes Trismegistus. The "expressive belief" of a system of interlocking correspondences was considered the key to alchemical philosophies as well as the

---

66 Barruel 93.

67 The schism was not resolved until 1813, and so many Masons both Antient and Modern were members of higher degrees that the Royal Arch degree was formally adopted by all lodges in the 1813 Articles of Union, and Masons were specifically notified that they might practice other Orders as well.

68 Barruel 103.

69 Barruel 117–18. Barruel quotes from the "Preface to the Scotch Degrees" of a second edition from Stockholm published in 1782. He does not specify the work, but there were many Masonic texts to choose from – both authorized and unauthorized.

basis of the Rosicrucian physic designed to bring man's body and soul into harmony with Nature and the Deity.

Moreover, despite Barruel's separation of higher degree Masons into "classes," the same Rosicrucian elements appeared in all three of his classes. Thus, while the "Scotch" degrees were referred to as "Hermetic," the "Cabalistic" Freemasons also came under attack because of their views related in the allegories of alchemy, as well as their allusions to the Rosicrucian concepts of spirits and the ether acting as intermediaries between the Deity and man, and their recourse to the Cabala and the mysterious signs read in Nature. Barruel asserted that the "Cabalistic system" was to be found primarily in what he referred to as "Lodges of Rosicrucians," and lest anyone believe he was making up his information, he referred readers to the Masonic, "Cabalistic lectures lately printed under the title of *Telescope de Zoroastre*."[70]

Although he declined to examine the system in great depth, writing "It is not our object to give a dictionary of all their Hieroglyphics, much less to describe the circles, the triangles, the table, the urns, and the magic mirrors, in a word all the science of the Cabalistic Rosicrucian," all the objects listed in his summary were commonly known as part of the treasures the *Fama* described in Rosenkreutz's secret crypt.[71] Even the practices of the popular "Eclectic Masons" Barruel discussed most briefly were permeated with Rosicrucian concepts. These Masons, "who, after having passed through the different degrees of Masonry, attach themselves to no particular system into which they have been initiated, but adopt from them all whatever may best suit their views," appeared to Barruel to represent "an aggregate of all the errors of the Philosophism of the day," not least because, as he claimed, "these indeed should naturally predominate in an age when the Philosophism of the Atheists and Deists only succeeds to the ancient heresies in order to absorb them all."[72]

Because of works such as Barruel's and Robison's, which contained much the same charges and information, the assumed relationship between Rosicrucianism and Freemasonry was highlighted, and mystical occult aspects of the fraternities became titillating talk for all levels of British society. Both men, while emphasizing their distaste for such matters, nevertheless provided many details. The works served as clearinghouses of mystical information in terms of the myriad sources they compiled and cited to make their arguments. The end result of both the popularity and notoriety of the various Rosicrucian and Masonic societies was a blend of easily available information in which the philosophies, ideals and elements of Rosicrucianism and Freemasonry became interchangeable. In the process of denouncing the ideas supported by the *philosophes* and the many Masonic lodges, writers such as Barruel and Robison effectively created a broad platform for the very ideas they found most pernicious and bound together concepts of hermeticism with broader concepts of social reformation, politics and religion.

The secret societies became the focus of heated Romantic debates surrounding politics, philosophy and religion. In addition to esoteric alchemical philosophies, the concepts of reformation, revolution, liberty, equality and brotherhood integral

---

70  Barruel 119–20.

71  Barruel 121.

72  Barruel 134.

to Rosicrucianism were broadly claimed as the foundation for Freemasonry and presented to Romantic readers as either an unparalleled danger or incredible promise depending upon an author's political or religious leanings. For many conservatives during the turmoil of the late eighteenth and the early nineteenth centuries, the secret societies became the symbol of dissent, irreligion, revolution, and conspiracy. Authors attempted to provoke fear and discredit the societies by highlighting the hermeticism contained in the philosophies and rituals and yoking it to what they claimed were dark political and religious designs. Similarly, they often attempted to discredit liberal, freethinking authors by linking them to the societies either literally or metaphorically via hermetic language associated with the secret societies. In contrast, freethinkers and radicals often defiantly made use of the same hermetic terms and concepts to illustrate their differences, and as we will see, this was true not only amongst the authors at the turn of the century but also amongst the competing "schools" of writers and critics during Keats's career as well.

# Chapter Two

# The Secret Societies and the Romantic Cultural Context

By Keats's time, Freemasonry had become much more than a conduit of hermetic thought from previous centuries. In a reaction against the Enlightenment, many in the Romantic period found themselves unwilling to accept the old doctrines but also unwilling to forgo a sense of spirituality entirely. Freemasonry enjoyed widespread popularity in part because it was so closely associated with the Rosicrucianism considered the epitome of the Renaissance ideals and vitalism that M. H. Abrams posited as attractive to Romantic thinkers and writers but also because it was seen as embracing the advances made in the sciences during the Enlightenment. Freemasonry offered men a sense of spirituality and a place in a "Temple" encompassing all the natural world, while also maintaining a positive attitude towards reason and science. In essence, Freemasonry provided men with a middle way.

Freemasonry represented to many the "sublime" promised by the Rosicrucians and recalled by De Quincey. Essentially syncretic, immensely diversified, and inherently idealistic, it appeared to many to be an alternative to strict rationalism. Under the banner of liberty, equality, and brotherhood, and with the goal of bettering mankind through advances in wisdom and practical philanthropy, it blended science, mysticism, literature, philosophy, theology and politics, and provided men of all classes with a society in which they might meet as equals. For others, however, the society appeared as the malignant force so vividly painted by Barruel and Robison, and after the American and French Revolutions, Freemasonry became associated with not only social and religious reformation, and scientific and philosophical innovation, but also dissent, revolution and conspiracy.

The alternating views of Freemasonry put forth during the period were ones examined carefully not only by De Quincey but also other major authors. Direct or indirect references to the society appeared in the writings of virtually all the major authors of the Romantic period, including Godwin, Scott, Burns, Burke, Darwin, Canning, Blake, Wordsworth, Coleridge, Hunt, Hazlitt, Byron, the Shelleys and Keats. By examining some of the ways Freemasonry and its hermetic elements were portrayed in the discourse, we can begin to see why concepts associated with the society would have appealed to Keats.

The French Revolution served as a locus for much of the discussion at the close of the eighteenth century and well into the first decades of the nineteenth century. As previously noted, prominent authors accused the French *philosophes* and the Freemasons of a conspiracy in which the philosophies of men such as d'Alembert, Diderot, and Voltaire were adopted and propagated by Masonic lodges as an advancement of knowledge that was really a pernicious plan to destroy society.

Works such as Barruel's *Mémoires* and Robison's *Proofs of a Conspiracy* examined the hermetic elements in the rituals and publications of higher degree Masonic groups with names such as The Knights of the Sun, The Rose Croix, and The Rosicrucians, conflated the hermeticism with the writings of authors such as Voltaire, Paine, Priestley and an entire range of radicals and freethinkers, and then likened it all to the false gold of charlatan alchemists whose ungodly teachings threatened all government and true religion. Their theories were treated seriously, not least of all because d'Alembert, Diderot, and Voltaire were in fact Freemasons, and Paine and Priestley were assumed by many to be Masons as well.

As a result of such practices and assumptions, hermeticism and the secret societies became inextricably mixed with politics and religion, and the debates ranged across fields and genres. Their presence was so marked, Keats could have encountered hermetic concepts virtually anywhere, and because the same concepts had been tied to authors, philosophies and politics with which he agreed, it is difficult to believe he held no interest in such topics. Voltaire's discussions of politics and religion, and his initiation into Freemasonry shortly before he died, present one illustration of this. Voltaire was a skeptic but not an atheist and found enough to approve of in Freemasonry that he became a Mason, and those opposed to Freemasonry often cited his membership as support for their theories of a conspiracy between the French *philosophes* and the Masons. Authors such as Barruel and Robison argued that Voltaire's philosophies were practically synonymous with what they called the blasphemous teachings in higher degree Freemasonry and frequently cited passages from hermetic rituals alongside Voltaire's speculations about religion.

These interpretations of Masonry's religious implications are especially pertinent to discussions of Keats's own religious speculations and Voltaire's philosophies because Freemasonry, with its inclusive and syncretic religious nature, and its emphasis on both the practical and mystical aspects of religion, maintained a delicate balance offering the reason of the Enlightenment as well as an emphasis upon the liberal arts that critics such as Ryan and Sharp have argued as central to Keats's philosophies.[1] Charges of natural religion were levied regularly against the Freemasons, at whom Barruel thundered, "You are the children of Deism or Pantheism, and, replete with

---

1    In Masonic texts and lectures such William Preston's *Illustrations of Masonry*, these aspects were considered inter-related. Preston "earnestly recommended," "the study of the liberal arts (that valuable branch of education which tends so effectually to polish and adorn the mind)," and he emphasized that the "seven liberal Art and Sciences" were of a "divine and moral nature," that illustrated "the wonderful properties of Nature" and "more important truths of Morality." All tended to create "the most powerful incentives" to virtue, and study of "the symmetry, beauty, and order displayed in the various parts of animate and inanimate creation" naturally led men to "rapture and veneration of the Great Cause that produced the whole, and which continue[d] to govern the system." Poetry was included in this assessment and works like Preston's often included large portions devoted to Masonic poetry and songs. In *Illustrations of Masonry*, roughly thirty pages were devoted to Masonic odes, anthems and songs. This perspective towards the arts, philosophical and practical, is one Keats adopted at various times in his life. William Preston, *Illustrations of Masonry* (1772; Louisville: American Masonic Publishing Association, 1858) 39; 43–44.

the spirit of your forefathers, you wish to perpetuate it!"[2] Many Masonic texts, however, asserted that theirs was the "oldest" and most wholesome of "religions" requiring merely a belief in the Supreme Being and desire to serve Him and man to the best of their abilities "by whatever denomination or persuasion they may be distinguish'd."[3] Their acceptance of all religious views had implicit within it the very Keatsian belief that no man was "more in the right than other people" when it came to religion.[4] It was skepticism contained with a framework of possible belief, and Freemasonry came to represent a reformist alternative in which, as Masonic author Laurence Dermott claimed, "the welfare and good of mankind was the cause or motive of so grand an institution," that supplied men with both a liberal, common sense approach and a sense of the mysterious.[5]

Thus, Freemasonry was able to function as a system that did not, as Keats put it, "affront our reason and humanity," but did offer ample scope for men to exercise their emotions and enrich their imaginative faculties.[6] When Barruel argued that:

> … all their Lodges are but one temple representing the whole universe; the temple which extends from the *East to the West, from the South to the North*. They admit into this temple with equal indifference the Christian or the Jew, the Turk or the Idolater, in fine, without distinction of sect or religion. All equally behold the *light*, all learn the science of virtue, of real happiness, and all may remain members of the Craft, and rise in its degrees up to that where they are taught that all religious tenets are but errors and prejudices. Though many Masons may view this re-union in no other light than that of universal charity and benevolence … it is nevertheless much to be feared, that this re-union of error and falsehood only tends to infuse an indifference for all religious tenets into the minds of the adepts …

he presented in negative terms a perspective that would have appealed to Keats, who agreed wholeheartedly with Voltaire's analysis of religion and believed religious intolerance was the root of many evils.[7] Likewise, Barruel's analysis of a higher

---

2  The Abbé Barruel, *The AntiChristian and Antisocial Conspiracy. An Extract from the French of the Abbé Barruel, to which Is Prefixed Jachin and Boaz, or an Authentic Key to the Door of Free-Masonry Ancient and Modern* (Lancaster: Joseph Ehrenfried, 1812) 142.

3  James Anderson, *The Constitutions of the Free-Masons Containing the History, Charges, Regulations, &c. of that Most Ancient and Right Worshipful Fraternity* (London 1723; Philadelphia: Benjamin Franklin, 1734)*. An Online Electronic Edition*, ed. Paul Royster, University of Nebraska Lincoln Libraries, 14 February 2006 <http://digitalcommons.unl.edu/libraryscience/25> 48.

4  John Keats, letter to Bailey, 13 March 1818, *The Letters of John Keats, 1814–1821*, ed. Hyder Rollins, vol. 1 (Cambridge, Mass.: Harvard UP, 1958) 242. Hereafter, this work will be referred to as *Letters I*.

5  Laurence Dermott, *Ahiman Rezon* (1756; Bloomington, IL: Masonic Book Club, 1973) 17.

6  John Keats, letter to George and Georgianna Keats, 21 April 1819, *The Letters of John Keats, 1814–1821*, ed. Hyder Rollins, vol. 2 (Cambridge, Mass.: Harvard UP, 1958) 103. Hereafter, this work will be referred to as *Letters II*.

7  The Abbé Barruel, *The AntiChristian and Antisocial Conspiracy. An Extract from the French of the Abbé Barruel, to which Is Prefixed Jachin and Boaz, or an Authentic Key to the Door of Free-Masonry Ancient and Modern* (Lancaster: Joseph Ehrenfried, 1812) 94–95.

degree ceremony whose "secret object" was "to exhibit all men equally Priests and Pontiffs, to recall the brethren to natural religion, and to persuade them that the religion of Moses and of Christ had violated religious Liberty and equality by the distinction of Priests and Laity" would have been met with sympathy by Keats who, like Voltaire, decried the artificial separation of man from God by religion and class systems within religions.[8] Keats disapproved of the established church's tendency towards what he considered illegitimate rank. In a November 1817 letter commiserating with Benjamin Bailey over his difficulties finding a curacy, Keats railed against the "impudence" and "impertinence" of the Bishop of Lincoln who, undeservedly, sat in his "Palace" while men like Bailey and Keats "must bear ... the Proud Mans Contumely."[9]

Meanwhile, Keats certainly would have approved of the excerpt of a Masonic ritual Barruel provided in which a brother named *Veritas* taught the initiate:

> If you ask me what are the necessary qualities to enable a mason to arrive at the center of real perfection? I shall answer, that in order to attain it he must have crushed the head of the serpent of worldly ignorance and have *cast off* those prejudices of youth concerning the mysteries of the predominant religion of his native country. *All religions worship being only invented in hopes of acquiring power, and to gain precedency among men; and by a sloth which covets, under the falser pretence of piety, its neighbour's riches*; in fine, by Gluttony, the daughter of Hypocrisy ... This my dear brother, is what you have to combat, such is the monster you have to crush under the emblem of the serpent. *It is a faithful representation of that which the ignorant vulgar adore under the name of religion.*[10]

The very sins and evils attributed to religion in this passage are those Keats speaks against in his letters and his early poem *Written in Disgust of Vulgar Superstition* where he writes:

> The church bells toll a melancholy round,
> 　　Calling the people to some other prayers,
> 　　Some other gloominess, more dreadful cares,
> More heark'ning to the sermon's horrid sound.
> Surely the mind of man is closely bound
> 　　In some black spell ... (1–6)

Had Barruel read Keats's works, he might well have ranked Keats with the Rosicrucian Masonic sects he described that hoped for a general reformation, claimed Christ was not God incarnate, rejected the concept of hell, and maintained the current state of religion contained myriad corruptions and abuses.[11]

---

8　　Barruel 98–99.

9　　Keats, *Letters I* 178–79.

10　Barruel 101. Barruel quotes from the Abbé Le Franc's exposure of the Knights of the Sun.

11　Barruel condemns one Masonic group for suggesting, "'it is a most fallacious system to pretend to lead men in wisdom *by the frightful description of eternal flames in a life to come*. Such descriptions are of no avail when unfelt; therefore the blind teachers, who can only represent those torments to us in imagination, must necessarily produce but little effect

Scholars have long acknowledged Voltaire's influence on Keats; he read several of Voltaire's works. In a February 1818 letter to his brothers, Keats says he has been reading Voltaire and Gibbon, also a famous Freemason, and in a stream of consciousness letter to George and Georgianna in 1819, in which he piles one reference atop another, Keats again mentions Voltaire and Freemasons.[12] In addition, in one of his most significant philosophical and religious letters – the "Vale of Soul-making" letter – he writes that he has been reading Voltaire directly before he enters the crucial passages describing how he believes souls are to be created and describes Man's soul as being individualized and refined in strongly hermetic terms.[13] The same passages suggest his affinity with the views Barruel condemned and tied to both Voltaire's philosophies and the hermetic rituals of the Masons. In the letter, Keats opines that most religions created intermediaries in an attempt to make religion more understandable to the masses. In his attempt to explain to George what he conceives of as a "grander system of salvation than the chrystain religion," he writes:

> It is pretty generally suspected that the chr[i]stain scheme has been coppied from the ancient Persian and greek Philosophers. Why may they not have made this simple thing even more simple for common apprehension by introducing Mediators and Personages in the same manner as in the hethen mythology abstractions are personified – Seriously I think it probable that this System of Soul-making – may have been the Parent of all the more palpable and personal Schemes of Redemption, among the Zoroastrians the Christians and the Hindoos. For as one part of the human species must have their carved Jupiter; so another part must have the palpable and named Mediatior and saviour, their Christ their Oromanes and their Vishnu.[14]

While these concepts were by no means restricted to Freemasonry, the simplification Keats refers to does match the common and controversial claims put forth by many Masonic groups that argued that Freemasonry existed from the time of Adam as the "true" religion underlying the various versions put forth for the general public's understanding.

Masonry claimed to be based on a "Parent" religion in which man was able to engage the Deity directly through apprehension of Nature, and in the many exposures of Masonic rituals during the Romantic period, the rites of Masonry were described as designed to communicate to candidates "the whole science of the ancient truths and of the discoveries they had made by their profound meditations on the nature, the religion, the polity, and the rights of man."[15] As many exposures and lectures on Masonry made clear, initiates in the society prepared themselves first in the heart by examining their love for the Divine and for mankind and their desire to serve both, and Freemasonry's lessons were designed to reinforce that love without the

---

upon us'," and writes that these Masons would remove "the pains of hell from [their] moral code … We should be tempted to suppose that they knew no means of working their Salvation but by destroying the possibility of being damned" (Barruel 128–29). The Masonic sentiments are a match for those of Hunt and Shelley.

12  Keats, *Letters I* 237 and *Letters II* 68–69.
13  Keats, *Letters II* 102–103.
14  Keats, *Letters II* 102–103.
15  Barruel 139–40.

traditional barriers of religion, class or nationality. According to Gotthold Lessing, author of *Ernst and Falk*, a series of Masonic dialogues highly praised by Coleridge, Byron, and De Quincey, this was one of Masonry's most striking advantages.[16] Freemasons asserted that the universal nature of their philosophy had been recognized by philosophers of all civilized nations and had formed the basis for quite literally all the "Schemes of Redemption" to which Keats refers.[17]

In his accurate summary of the claims put forth to elucidate Freemasonry's ancient and universal status, based upon "divers works" by "learned" Masons, Barruel noted that:

> ... they will be found to contain merely this assertion ... "that in those ancient times when men first began to desert the primitive truths, to follow a religion and morality founded on superstition, some sages were to be met with who segregated themselves from the general mass of ignorance and corruption. These sages, perceiving that the grossness or the stupidity of the people rendered them incapable of profiting by their lessons, formed separate schools and disciples, to whom they transmitted the whole science of the ancient truths and of the discoveries they had made by their profound meditations on the nature, the religion, the polity, and the rights of man. ... The morality deduced from these principles was pure: it was grounded on the duties of charity, on the rights of Liberty, and on the means of living peaceably and happily. Lest these doctrines should lessen in value, should be falsified or be entirely lost, these sages commanded their disciples to keep them secret. ... These divers schools and the secrets of these mysteries have not been lost; the Philosophers of Greece transmitted them to those of Rome, and the Philosophers of all nations followed the same line ... The sages of divers nations by means of the signs which had been originally established, recognized each other, as the Free-masons do every where at this present day. The name only has been changed; and the secret has been handed down under the denomination of Free-masonry, as it was formerly under the sanction of the Magi, of the Priests of Memphis or of Eleusis, and of the Platonic or Eclectic Philosophers.[18]

In this fashion, Freemasonry's approach to religion during Keats's time resembled both Hunt's blend of natural religion, Deism, and emotion, a *Religion of the Heart*, and Voltaire's more scientific claims that the origins of specific faiths lay in Man's need to create them.[19]

Just as the French *philosophes* such as Voltaire became part of the mingled debate, others did as well. When Robert Ryan made the case for religion's relevance

---

16 Gotthold Lessing, *Ernst and Falk*, *Lessing's Masonic Dialogues*, trans. *The Builder* 1915–1929, ed. Robin L. Carr (1778; Bloomington, IL: The Masonic Book Club, 1991).

17 Barruel 139–40.

18 Barruel 139–40. Barruel does not say what Masonic work he is quoting, but this view is standard in texts such as William Hutchinson's *Spirit of Masonry*, Preston's *Illustrations of Masonry*, and Dermott's *Ahiman Rezon* amongst others.

19 Leigh Hunt, *The Religion of the Heart. A Manual of Faith and Duty* (London, 1853). Hunt composed "Christianism" and later *The Religion of the Heart* to help fulfill a "want" for a religion that could maintain reason but still "perpetuate the sense of the wonders and beauties of the sacred creation in which he believed." Michael Laplace-Sinatra, "'A Natural Piety': Leigh Hunt's The Religion of the Heart," *The Allen Review* 19 (1997) <http://www-oxford.op.org/allen/hunt.htm>.

in Keats's life in *Keats: The Religious Sense*, he did so by stressing how the public in general and Keats in particular were aware of the ways Edmund Burke and Thomas Paine linked politics and religion to their opposing views. Later, when he refined his arguments further in *The Romantic Reformation*, he asserted that "Keats began his poetic career as a devotee of mythology in the Humean and Gibbonesque mode" so prominent in the public sphere.[20] The public was also aware, however, that all of these men and others connected to them were associated with Freemasonry. Hume and Gibbon were Freemasons, and Burke was and is often listed as one, and the Lodge that claimed him as a member, Jerusalem Lodge, in a blatantly political move initiated John Wilkes into Freemasonry in 1769.[21] Given Burke's conservative stances, he probably came to regret offering a defense of Wilkes in his *Thoughts on the Present Discontents* written during the same period and published shortly thereafter. Wilkes quickly began to use Freemasonry for politicking and became notorious for it, even going so far as to join opposing Antient and Modern lodges, one of which espoused the type of hermetic, higher degree Freemasonry that Barruel and Robison warned so vigorously against.[22]

The connections between Wilkes and Freemasonry provide a good example of what appears to be interest on Keats's part as well as his deliberate use of hermetic allusions. In December of 1817, Keats followed with great interest the trial of William Hone taking place over a three-day period. Hone's prosecution centered around three works he had published early in the year: *The Late John Wilkes' Catechism*, *The Sinecurist's Creed*, and *The Political Litany*, and it is generally accepted that Keats wrote the sonnet "Before he went to live with owls and bats," also known as "Nebuchadnezzar's Dream," in celebration of Hone's acquittal on 20 December 1817. In his biography, *Keats*, Andrew Motion suggests that Keats, much like Hone, turned biblical references to political purposes, but that Keats chose the safer allegorical approach in his sonnet and continued his political commentary with oblique references in his review "Mr. Kean" that appeared in the *Champion* the day after Hone's acquittal.[23]

But the link between Keats's arguments in his sonnet and those in his review are stronger than Motion is aware. In his review, as Keats praises Kean's elocution and links it to poetic utterance, he exclaims, "The spiritual is felt when the very letters and prints of charactered language show like the hieroglyphics of beauty; – the mysterious signs of an immortal freemasonry!"[24] Kean was yet another well-known

20 Robert Ryan, *Keats: The Religious Sense* (Princeton: Princeton UP, 1976) 10; Robert Ryan, *The Romantic Reformation: English Politics in English Literature, 1789–1824* (Cambridge: Cambridge UP, 1997) 154.

21 Given the well known prerequisite that a man be "free" in order to become a Mason, the Masons' action clearly indicated their opinion of the charges of which Wilkes had been found guilty.

22 John Money, "The Masonic Moment; Or, Ritual, Replica, and Credit: John Wilkes, the Macaroni Parson, and the Making of the Middle-Class Mind," *The Journal of British Studies*, 32.4 (Oct. 1993): 358–95.

23 Andrew Motion, *Keats* (New York: Farrar, Straus and Giroux, 1998) 213–14.

24 John Keats, "Mr. Kean," *The Poetical Works & Other Writings of John Keats*, ed. H. Buxton Forman, rev. Maurice Buxton Forman, vol. 5 (New York: Phaeton Press, 1970) 229.

Freemason, and no doubt this factored in Keats's decision to make such specific use of the society's terminology, but considering Hone's trial at the time and Keats's sonnet, there is reason to believe the reference holds more significance. Hone's name also appears in relation to Freemasonry.

It was Hone who published the Hampden Club's Proceedings held at Freemason's Hall and Tavern only the year before in 1816, and Hone had been a member of the London Corresponding Society along with men tried for sedition in the 1790s who Coleridge deliberately bound to concepts of Freemasonry in a series of radical essays entitled "The Plot Discovered."[25] Keats was familiar with Coleridge's poetry, his more general writings and lectures, and his shift from liberal to increasingly conservative politics; given the heated debates surrounding Freemasonry and the sedition trials of the London Corresponding Society members, it is reasonable to argue he also would have been aware of Coleridge's published opinions on the issues.

In "The Plot Discovered," Coleridge demonstrated his knowledge of the claims made against Freemasonry prior to Barruel's and Robison's works. Beginning with the very title of the essay, he reversed the language of conspiracy to inveigh against the Hanoverian decree of 1793 that instituted repressive measures against reading libraries and societies, and closer to home, The Treason and Sedition Acts in Britain. The second concerned him more, especially because of the potential for abuse. He carefully built his argument against the Acts with references to "spells of despotism," "high-priests" and "a corrupt and abandoned ministry," all of which evoked the dark charges made against Freemasonry and its hermeticism, but Coleridge transferred such dangerous evocations to a government that would enforce a law enabling a man to be condemned on the most specious of evidence. As his indignation reached a high pitch, Coleridge declared:

> Know ye not, there is a numerous peace-establishment of King's tradesmen, of pensioners, of hired spies, of hungry informers, and of witnesses most learned in their profession, who have graduated in guilt and passed through all the degrees of serviceable iniquity from loss of memory to equivocation, and from equivocation to perjury? Of these mysterious Slave-masons know ye not who is their grand master?[26]

The references were unmistakable. The "mysterious" men who passed through grades and "degrees," however, were "Slave-masons" – the antithesis of the

25 *The Late John Wilkes' Catechism of a Ministerial Member; Taken from an Original Manuscript in Mr. Wilkes' Handwriting, never before printed, and adapted to the present Occasion. With Permission* (London: Printed for one of the Candidates for the Office of Printer to the King's Most Excellent Majesty, and Sold by William Hone 1817). *A Full Report of the Proceedings of the Meeting, Convened by the Hampden Club, which Took Place at the Freemason's Tavern, Great Queen-Street, Lincoln's Inn Fields, on Saturday, the 15th June, 1816, upon the Subject of Parliamentary Reform* (London: Published by Wm. Hone, Fleet-Street, 1816).

26 Samuel Taylor Coleridge, "The Plot Discovered," *The Collected Works of Samuel Taylor Coleridge: Lectures 1795 on Politics and Religion*, eds. Lewis Patton and Peter Mann (Princeton: Princeton UP, 1971) 291–92.

Freemasons – and they possessed a much more dangerous and corruptible "grand master." Coleridge made clear who that "grand master" was when he commanded readers to "read the trial of Gerald," and asked, "Have we not then the authority of Christ for asserting that men, who have been made Judges by a ministry and hope to be made Lord Chancellors, may and sometimes will be the creatures of that ministry?"[27] The infamous trials of men such as Thomas Muir in 1792 and Joseph Gerrald in 1794 had received extensive coverage. The outrage over the packed juries, the judges' blatant bias, and the instructions given to the jurors so there could be virtually no other verdict but guilty, guaranteed this. By using the language that he did and reversing the references, Coleridge linked reformers like the men of the London Corresponding Society to Freemasonry and to the truth, liberty, and light associated with Freemasonry in the liberal public discourse.

I would suggest Keats was doing much the same in celebration of Hone's acquittal. In addition, while the political overtones of Daniel's interpretation of Nebuchadnezzar are commonly understood, readers should also be aware that, like the Temple of Solomon that Nebuchadnezzar destroyed, the *Book of Daniel*, often played a prominent role in alchemical and Masonic allegories – including those related to the higher degrees where the import of prophetic dreams and Daniel's mystical, imaginative apprehension of their underlying truth served as allegorical representations of man's search for a better understanding of both himself and the Creator's will in order to better serve society.[28]

Framed as Keats's reference is, in a review which opens and closes with commentary on "unimaginative days ... of sickly safety and comfort," when the people are "*Habeas Corpus'd* ... out of all wonder," and in need of "cheer ... in the failure of [their] days," and examined with Masonic undertones in mind, Keats's reference to Freemasonry melds both the political and the poetic.[29] For Keats, the imagination played an essential role in man's physical and spiritual health, and both were bound to man's social and political state in his mind as well. Throughout his poetry and letters Keats consistently linked poetry's ability to stimulate the imagination with his hope to one day be "a friend to man" (*Ode on a Grecian Urn* 48). In a markedly hermetic sense, he hoped to "add a mite to that mass of beauty which is harvested from these [Nature's] grand materials, by the finest spirits, and put into ethereal existence for the relish of one's fellow," and in a similar vein but a political sense, he also hoped that his writings might "add a Mite of help to the Liberal side of the question."[30]

Like the Rosicrucians and the Freemasons who hoped by their work to "raise many and divers thoughts in men" to the benefit of all mankind and in particular "those which by reason of the course of the world ... are hindered through all manner of importunities of this our time" and are most in need of guidance to renew wisdom

27  Samuel Taylor Coleridge, "The Plot Discovered" 292.

28  John H. Van Gorden, *Biblical Characters in Freemasonry* (Lexington, Mass.: The Masonic Book Club, 1980) 46–47.

29  Keats, "Mr. Kean," 227 and 232 respectively.

30  Keats, letter to Tom Keats, 27 June 1818, *Letters I* 301; letter to Charles Dilke, 22 September 1818, *Letters II* 180.

and "all Arts … so that finally Man might thereby understand his own Nobleness and Worth" to effect "the love, help, comfort and strengthening of our Neighbors," Keats hoped to do the same.[31] Keats's review binds his views of poetry's role in society, and the compulsion he felt to offer poetry that might act as physic, to concepts associated with the secret societies.

Other similar connections between these issues and Keats's interests and writings also exist. Thomas Paine's associations with Freemasonry provide another example. In 1818, Richard Carlile published an unexpurgated version of an essay of Paine's first published in 1810 explicitly linking politics, religion, and Freemasonry.[32] Written sometime between 1803 and 1805, Paine's *The Origin of Freemasonry* appears to have been originally intended for inclusion in the third part of the *Age of Reason* and amply reveals Paine's familiarity with the brotherhood.[33] In the essay, he claimed that:

> Masonry (as I shall show from the customs, ceremonies, hieroglyphics, and chronology of Masonry) is derived from and is the remains of the religion of the ancient Druids; who, like the Magi of Persia and the Priests of Heliopolis in Egypt, were Priests of the Sun. They paid worship to this great luminary, as the great visible agent of a great invisible first cause whom they styled "Time without limits".[34]

Paine then used the conclusions he reached about Freemasonry to argue that it represented a purer and more reasonable form of worship than Christianity because it was "a more generalized Deistic religion" that preserved the older, universalized tenets in a form which all men could partake of and agree upon.[35]

Again, these concepts would have been of interest to Keats, and he would have been well aware of the inter-relationship between politics and religion. Keats's letters also indicate he may have been aware of Paine's essay. In a September 1819 letter to his brother George and sister-in-law Georgianna, Keats linked the present politics

---

31 The *Confessio Fraternitatis* and the *Fama Fraternitatis*, respectively. *Fama Fraternitatis*, trans. Thomas Vaughan (1652), transcriber, Kevin Day (Sept. 2002) <http://www.levity.com/alchemy/fama.html>. *Confessio Fraternitatis*, trans. Thomas Vaughan (1652), transcriber, Kevin Day (Sept. 2002) <http://www.levity.com/alchemy/confessi.html>.

32 The essay originally was published by Madame Bonneville, but she carefully omitted all anti-Christian references. Andrew Prescott, "'The Devil's Freemason': Richard Carlile and his Manual of Freemasonry," Lecture, the Sheffield Masonic Study Circle, 30 November 2000 <http://www.shef.ac.uk/~crf/papers/devil.htm>.

33 Thomas Paine, "The Origin of Freemasonry," *Writings of Thomas Paine*, ed. Moncure Daniels Conway, vol. 4 (New York: G. P. Putnam's Sons, 1896).

34 Paine 64. Paine's conclusion as to Freemasonry's origins was a common supposition. A quarter of a century earlier, William Preston discussed the subject in *Illustrations of Freemasonry* as did the following authors: William Hutchinson, *Spirit of Freemasonry*; Alex Lawrie, *History of Freemasonry*; George Oliver, *Antiquities of Freemasonry*. Similar speculations also appeared in the magazines. For example, in the February 1792 issue of *European Magazine*, a man speculated on connections between the words Mason and May, Druidic high ceremonies held in May, and the Druids as Masons.

35 Prescott.

of England to those of the past and the example as well as the problem posed by the French Revolution, where "the liberal writers of france and england sowed the seed of opposition to ... Tyranny – and it was swelling in the ground till it burst out in the french revolution."[36] The revolution's "unlucky termination," though, "put a stop to the rapid progress of free sentiments in England" and as a result, Keats believed those who would favor "despotism ... have made a handle of this event in every way to undermine our freedom. They have spread a horrid superstition against all innovation and improvement," and "the present struggle in England of the people is to destroy this superstition."[37]

Keats presented this struggle in moral terms that rose above politics and claimed "This is no contest between whig and tory – but between right and wrong," and he was convinced that a great change was coming as a result of this. He then proceeded to link these claims to those of religion, and specifically, the writings of Thomas Paine published by Carlile. He wrote:

> There are little signs wherby we may know how matters are going on – This makes the business about Carlisle the Bookseller of great moment in my mind. He has been selling deistical pamphlets, republished Tom Payne and many other works held in superstitious horror ... For this Conduct he I think has had above a dozen <Prosecutions> indictments issued against him ... After all they are afraid to prosecute: they are afraid of his defence: it would be published in all the papers all over the Empire: they shudder at this: the Trials would light a flame they could not extinguish. Do you not think this of great import?[38]

As Keats noted in a previous February 1819 letter to his brother, Carlile was originally arrested for his publications of 1818. One of those publications that would have been "held in superstitious horror" would have been Paine's essay in which he argued Freemasonry's original form of worship and "wise, elegant, philosophical religion, was the faith opposite to the faith of the gloomy Christian church."[39] Barruel's *Mémoires* and Robison's *Proofs of a Conspiracy* made clear the influence Freemasonry held and created just the "superstitious horror" of which Keats spoke by linking the "innovations" and philosophies underlying the French Revolution to Freemasonry and what they supposed to be its anti-Christian stance. And the public was aware of these issues well into the nineteenth century.

Just as Coleridge had made explicit reference to the Freemasons in "The Plot Discovered," he did so again in a long series of articles addressed to Mr Justice Fletcher published in *The Courier* from 1814 to 1815. In the *Courier* series of letters, Coleridge's views of Freemasonry were still positive despite his more conservative stance. He effusively praised "Lessing's exquisite Dialogues on Free-masonry, entitled Falk and Ernest," and condemned "that monstrous romance of the Illumino with which the fanatics, Barruel and Robison, astonished and terrified the good

---

36 Keats, *Letters II* 193.
37 Keats, *Letters II* 193.
38 Keats, *Letters II* 194.
39 Paine 66.

people of England, Ireland, and Vienna."[40] And as Coleridge's reference to Lessing indicates, Freemasonry was often connected to literary productions as well, and these too were interpreted as portions of the debates surrounding the society.

In 1789, Erasmus Darwin, another Freemason, anonymously published *The Loves of Plants*, the second part of *The Botanic Garden*, which soon appeared in its entirety in 1791. The popular poem was suffused with hermetic concepts such as an animating soul throughout Nature that created correspondences between the lowest life forms like plants and the highest form, man. Darwin made copious use of "the Rosicrucian doctrine of Gnomes, Sylphs, Nymphs, and Salamanders," "hieroglyphic figures," ancient allegories from the East, and allusions to the alchemical elements of earth, air, fire and water, all in the service of ideas branded by critics as either wild speculation and metaphysics or materialism and atheism.[41] As Keats's letters indicate, and as scholars such as Hermione De Almeida have stressed, Keats was familiar with Darwin's poetry and science and their political and religious ramifications.[42]

In 1798, when conspiracy fears were at their height, and Masonic groups were frequently under attack for occult, hermetic views, Canning printed his parody *The Loves of Triangles* in *The Anti-Jacobin*. The poem was deliberately designed to undercut the radical elements in Darwin's work, and Canning's choice of title and topic represented a calculated allusion to Freemasonry and its most celebrated science, Geometry. Considering the notoriety of *The Loves of Triangles*, it is highly unlikely Keats would have been unaware of it, and he certainly knew what may be considered Darwin's "answer" to it, the *Temple of Nature, or the Origin of Society, a Poem, with Philosophical Notes* published in 1803. This last again employed the language, imagery, and philosophies of hermeticism throughout while its very title defiantly referenced Darwin's determination to speak of philosophical matters as well as the Masonic "Temple of Nature," and the "Society" in which all men might meet and discover the Mysteries of Earth and Heaven.

The *Temple of Nature*'s verse and notes again prominently featured elements such as the Adonis myth, originating powers derived from a spirit essence, sages of the East, hieroglyphics, and the alchemical-philosophical theories of life as a series of interchanges between contraries. These frequent references to eternal change, the universal language or hieroglyphics of Nature used by the magi, and characters such as Adonis that signified life or animation in processes of decay and rebirth

---

40 Samuel Taylor Coleridge, "To Mr. Justice Fletcher, Letter II," *The Collected Works of Samuel Taylor Coleridge: Essays on His Times in The Morning Post and Courier*, vol. 2, ed. David V. Erdman (Princeton: Princeton UP, 1978) 382. "Letter II" was initially published in *The Courier* 29 September 1814. Coleridge annotated his own copy of Lessing's "Dialogues," considered translating them, and commented in a note he added to "To Mr. Justice Fletcher, Letter II," "I know nothing that is at once like them, and equal to them, but the Provincial Letters of Pascal" (382).

41 Erasmus Darwin, Apology, "The Economy of Vegetation," *The Botanic Garden* (London, 1791).

42 Hermione de Almeida, *Romantic Medicine and John Keats* (New York: Oxford UP, 1991).

were hallmarks of Rosicrucianism and Freemasonry.[43] The Adonis myth was used in the initiation rites of the Rosicrucian related higher degrees of Freemasonry, and the central myth in the lower degrees about the powerful Master Mason Hiram, a variation upon Adonis, figured forth the same allegorical experiences.

At the same time, the unrest of the period and fears of irreligion and conspiracy also found expression in countless gothic novels featuring members of the Rosicrucian and Illuminati secret societies that had been conflated with higher degree Freemasonry. Rosicrucian or Masonic machinery and variations on the philosophies of the societies appeared in many novels such as Walpole's *Castle of Otranto*, the Marquis de Grosse's *Horrid Mysteries*, Godwin's *St Leon*, Hogg's *Memoirs of Prince Abbey Haimatoff*, Shelley's *St Irvyne; or, the Rosicrucian*, several novels by Radcliffe and Scott, and even Peacock's gothic parody *Nightmare Abbey*.[44] The Rosicrucian elements formed the very basis for the plots and main characters of Godwin's and Shelley's novels, and without the Illuminati and Freemasons, *Horrid Mysteries* lost its plotline and *Nightmare Abbey* its punch line. We know Keats read many of these authors whose works drew heavily upon hermetic concepts and philosophies as well as specifically Rosicrucian novels such as Godwin's *St. Leon* which follows closely the myths of the secret brotherhood and delineates the fall of one of its members who attempted to use his wealth, wisdom and powers to the benefit of society only to find himself rejected, cast out and utterly disillusioned. The work clearly interested Keats, and in an 1819 letter to George and Georgianna, Keats commented on the novel as well as Hazlitt's analysis of it directly before copying out his poem "Bards of Passion and of Mirth" that contains various hermetic allusions.[45]

Mary Shelley exhibited a tendency similar to her father's when she too drew upon the philosophies surrounding Rosicrucianism to frame her own literary comment upon the possible repercussions of such concepts in society. She linked hermeticism to the debates surrounding materialist science and religion by making Victor Frankenstein an avid student of the alchemical philosophers Magnus and Paracelsus and by placing him at the University of Inglostadt where Adam Weishaupt founded his radical offshoot of Masonry, the Illuminati society. Although Keats does not mention *Frankenstein* in his letters, the passages drawing these connections were reprinted and commented upon in 1818 issues of the *Edinburgh Magazine* and the *Quarterly Review* that Keats read.

In another, more direct line of contact, Percy Shelley was also deeply interested in the alchemical philosophies that formed the basis for Rosicrucianism and found an outlet in the secret societies of the Romantic period. Shelley read and re-read works such as Godwin's *St. Leon* and Barruel's *Mémoires*. He told Hunt the same

---

43 See, for example, Erasmus Darwin's "Preface" and "Notes" to Canto I of *The Temple of Nature* in which he makes reference to all these elements.

44 The philosophical elements of Rosicrucianism and higher degree Freemasonry were understood in these novels. Scythrop Glowry, whose intent is to reform the world via a society of "mystical dispensers of liberty" or "illuminati," was a humorous version of Shelley that Shelley cheerfully acknowledged. Gary R. Dyer, "Peacock and the 'Philosophical Gas' of the Illuminati," *Secret Texts: The Literature of Secret Societies*, eds., Roberts Marie Mulvey and Hugh Ormsby-Lennon (New York: AMS Press, 1995) 188: 188–209.

45 Keats, *Letters II* 24–25.

societies and philosophies delineated by Godwin and Barruel appeared to him to be the perfect counter to "the enemies of liberty" at the *Quarterly Review*, and he proposed that they form a society of "enlightened unprejudiced members of the community."[46] To Peacock, with whom he often discussed hermetic concepts and Barruel's work, he wrote, "The quarterly is undoubtedly conducted with talent great talent & affords a dreadful preponderance against the cause of improvement. If a band of staunch reformers, resolute yet skilful infidels were united in so close & constant a league as that in which interest & fanatisism have joined the members of that literary coalition!"[47] The topic was also a favorite in conversations with his wife and friends, and Shelley proposed the formation of a similar society to Hogg and others too. Given his outspokenness, and his acknowledged incorporation of hermetic elements in his poetry, it is probable the topic also would have been discussed in the many gatherings of Hunt's circle that Keats attended.

It is also worth noting that Shelley's passions and interests culminated in the explicitly alchemical *Prometheus Unbound* that, in an August 1820 letter, Keats told Shelley he was "in expectation of … every day" and in "A Defense of Poetry."[48] In the same letter, Keats told Shelley that "a modern work it is said must have a purpose, which may be the God – *an artist* must serve Mammon – he must have 'self-concentration' selfishness perhaps," and advised Shelley to be "more of an artist, and 'load every rift' of your subject with ore."[49] Shortly afterwards Keats left the topic by writing "you must explain my metap[hysics] to yourself."[50] Shelley explained Keats's "metaphysics" by relating them to alchemical metaphor. A year later, he would argue in "Defense of Poetry" that "Poetry, and the principle of Self, of which money is the visible incarnation, are the God and the Mammon of the world," and that

> Poetry turns all things to loveliness: it exalts the beauty of that which is most beautiful, and it adds beauty to that which is most deformed: it marries exultation and horror; grief and pleasure, eternity and change; it subdues to union under its light yoke all irreconcilable things. It transmutes all that it touches, and every form moving within the radiance of its presence is changed by wondrous sympathy to an incarnation of the spirit which it breathes: its secret alchemy turns to potable gold the poisonous waters which flow from death through life; it strips the veil of familiarity from the world, and lays bare the naked and sleeping beauty which is the spirit of its forms.

In addition, with or without Rosicrucianism, the defiant co-opting of the hermetic terms and concepts that authors like Barruel and Robison had sensationalized was common amongst authors related to Keats's circle. Oftentimes, the authors co-opted the language to counter attacks using the same terminology. Anti-Jacobin publications

---

46  Percy Bysshe Shelley, *The Letters of Percy Bysshe Shelley*, ed. Frederick L. Jones, vol. 1 (Oxford: Clarendon Press, 1964) 54, and vol. 2, 81 respectively.

47  Shelley, *The Letters of Percy Bysshe Shelley*, ed. Frederick L. Jones, vol. 2 (Oxford: Clarendon Press, 1964) 81.

48  Keats, *Letters II* 323.

49  Keats, *Letters II* 323.

50  Keats, *Letters II* 323.

like the *Quarterly Review* may have sparked Shelley's fantasies about forming a society like those of the Masons and Illuminati to combat fanaticism precisely because the publications used the terminology of the societies against Shelley and his friends. In the October 1817 issue of *Blackwood's Magazine* containing the first essay of the series "On the Cockney School of Poetry," Z. described Hunt's politics as "Jacobin" and his religion as "a poor tame dilution of the blasphemies of the *Encylopaedie*."[51] The *Quarterly Review* of April 1818 made similar remarks about Hunt and likened Keats to a "disciple" and "neophyte" of Hunt, the "hierophant" of the "Cockney School."[52] The June 1818 reviewer in the *British Critic* called Keats "disciple" to his "Master" Hunt and claimed "Mr. Keats is not content with a half initiation into the school he has chosen."[53] And *Blackwood's* recycled the language in its August 1818 review calling Keats Hunt's "disciple" yet again. In the midst of the contemptuous reviews, the terminology bound the Cockney School to the secret societies whose social, political, and religious attitudes resembled their own and had posed a threat readers could easily understand.

William Hazlitt also used terminology associated with the secret societies in defiant public stances. In his essay "On the Conversation of Authors," Hazlitt recounted his experiences with the authors such as Keats in Hunt's circle who had been attacked by the conservative reviews. Hazlitt noted that, "the soul of conversation is sympathy," and "there is a Free-masonry in all things. You can only speak to be understood, but this you cannot be, except by those who are in the secret."[54] Shortly thereafter, he remarked "But when a set of adepts, of illuminati, get about a question, it is worth while to hear them talk," and he rejoiced to have been a part of the conversations and disputes. Given the ways in which men such as Hunt, Shelley, Keats, and he had been attacked or accused of irreligion and dangerous politics, Hazlitt's phrasing reveals a specific knowledge of just the interrelationships I have been discussing. The phrasing indicates knowledge on the part of his readers as well, and Keats's participation in gatherings with Hazlitt and his status as an avid reader of Hazlitt's works makes it safe to assume he would have understood.

While Byron was not a friend of Keats, he too used language associated with the secret societies to make his points and defend his writings against the reviewers. Byron employed similar techniques in works such as *Childe Harold* and *Don Juan*, as when in *Don Juan*, he wrote:

And therefore what I throw off is ideal –
Lower'd, leaven'd, like a history of freemasons;
Which bears the same relation to the real,

---

51  Z. (John Gibson Lockhart) "On the Cockney School of Poetry, No. I" *Blackwood's Edinburgh Magazine* (October 1817) 50.

52  For the full review, see Lewis M. Schwartz's, *Keats Reviewed by His Contemporaries: A Collection of Notices for the Years 1816–1821* (Metuchen, NJ: The Scarecrow Press, Inc., 1973) 129–33.

53  Schwartz 134, 137.

54  Hazlitt's "On the Conversation of Authors" was first published in the *London Magazine* in September, 1820. It may be found in *The Best of Hazlitt*, ed. P. P. Howe (London: Methuen, 1947).

As Captain Parry's voyage may do to Jason's.
The grand arcanum's not for men to see all;
My music has some mystic diapasons;
And there is much which could not be appreciated
In any manner by the uninitiated. (*Don Juan* Canto 14, Stanza 22)

The play on words here speaks to his views of his own writing and the public reception of it. Byron lightly adopted the alchemical language of Masonry to transmute the value of his works in opposition to critical reviews. He would take a more defiant stance in his *Vision of Judgment* answering Southey's charges of a "Satanic School" of authors including himself and Shelley. In Stanza LIV of Byron's *Vision of Judgment*, the spirits that Satan calls upon to prove his claim for George III's soul are likened to Freemasons, and soon thereafter John Wilkes, George Washington, and Benjamin Franklin, all Masons, are called to testify. Although the poem was not published until December 1822, and thus too late for Keats to have seen, it was published in John Hunt's *The Liberal*, and the connections again speak to a common knowledge amongst men of similar minds to Keats. In addition, Keats was familiar with *Manfred* and read it while he composed *Endymion*, and *Manfred* was widely acknowledged as a variation upon Goethe's *Faustus* – Goethe even wrote a review praising Byron's genius in adapting the tale. Goethe was also a Freemason deeply interested in hermeticism; he wove hermetic concepts and details throughout *Faustus* and many such as the Rosicrucian spirits appeared in *Manfred* as well.

While the above examples indicate the many points of contact between the social, political, and religious stances associated with the secret societies and those espoused by Keats, and while they delineate some of the ways the hermetic philosophies and terminology of the societies had been used in discourse directly related to Keats's concerns, it is also true that Keats could have encountered the philosophies and linguistics via other avenues as well. He could have drawn upon a number of sources we know he had access to or read that supplied elements of hermeticism without the direct political engagement and connotations I have noted. He possessed bound editions of *The Spectator*, and these contained articles that discussed common knowledge of Rosicrucianism and alchemy.[55] He also read Pope's *The Rape of the Lock*, with its Rosicrucian machinery and note for ladies to explain the Rosicrucian elements and spirits, and he likely knew Mozart's *The Magic Flute* with its hermeticism, Masonic allegory and elements of initiation. Keats delighted in Mozart's music, and in an 1816 verse epistle to Charles Cowden Clarke that is often cited by scholars as a virtual catalogue of Keats's early influences, he lists "divine Mozart" as an "inspiration / Of a peculiar sort, – a consummation" (110, 105–106).[56]

Apuleius's *The Golden Ass* provides yet another conjunction between hermeticism and the secret societies that Keats could have drawn upon. Keats familiarly referred

---

55  See the list of Keats's books compiled by Charles Brown in *The Keats Circle Letters and Papers 1816–1878*, ed. Hyder Edward Rollins, vol. II, 2nd edn (Cambridge, Mass.: Harvard UP, 1965) 259.

56  Keats, *Letters I* 112. Later, Keats writes to George of "a complete set" of Mozart during an evening at Novello's (*Letters II* 11).

his brother and sister-in-law to Apuleius's myth of Psyche in his April 1819 letter in which he includes his "Ode to Psyche."[57] Psyche's story formed the central book of Apuleius's *The Golden Ass* and acted as a microcosmic version of the initiation trials through which the main character of the book, Lucius, also passed. The final chapters of the work focused on Lucius's own transformation from ass back to man and his initiation into the mystery cults after he offered prayers to the Queen of Heaven and chose her as his Goddess. The book had been considered part of the *Hermetica* since the Renaissance, and during the Romantic period, *The Golden Ass* was widely understood as a basis for Rosicrucian and higher degree Masonic initiation rites, with good reason given the symbolic import of roses throughout the story and the multiple passages in which alchemical allegory was used to illustrate Lucius's gradual purification to make him suitable for service to both his goddess and mankind.[58] It was also known as a source for Mozart's *Magic Flute* – precisely because some Masonic rituals were derived from it.

Keats's reading included another text that, in turn, highlights still more points of contact. Brown lists two editions of Robert Burton's *Anatomy of Melancholy* in his inventory of Keats's books, and Keats made frequent allusions to the work in his letters. Overall, hermetic authors and their theories are referenced on at least 20 percent of the pages in Burton's work.[59] Furthermore, Burton devoted significant space in his *Anatomy of Melancholy* to several of Paracelsus's theories and drew upon both Agrippa's original alchemical conjectures in medicine and Paracelsus's refinements of the same in his discourses on the imagination, the humors, and psychology.[60] During the Romantic period, Paracelsus's theories were still studied and commented upon in medical schools where his works were acknowledged as precursors to chemistry and medical reforms. Like Keats, Paracelsus argued that medicine should be based not upon tradition, but upon treatments that had been "proved upon the pulses" of patients, and he claimed that what was conceived of by the imagination and spirit could only be put into action and brought home to a man through actual life experiences.[61]

---

57  Keats, *Letters II* 106.

58  In his address "To the Reader," William Adlington remarked that the allegorical tale would instruct readers so, "by the pleasantnesse thereof bee rather induced to the knowledge of their present estate, and thereby transforme themselves into the right and perfect shape of men." William Adlington, "To the Reader," *The Golden Asse* (1566), ed. Martin Guy (1996) <http://eserver.org/books/apuleius>.

59  Robert Burton, "Cure of Melancholy," *The Anatomy of Melancholy ... By Democritus Junior [pseud.]...* (Philadelphia: J. W. Moore; New York: J. Wiley, 1850). University of Michigan, "Making of America Books" <http://name.umdl.umich.edu/ACM8939.0001.001>. I have arrived at this figure through a search process the University of Michigan makes available in conjunction with its online version of the text, and using only the names of the major hermetic authors Agrippa, Magnus, Paracelsus, Hermes Trismegistus, and Apuleius, and the keyword Rosicrucian. Because I used only the most prominent names and did not do a complete search, it is likely more extensive analysis would yield an even higher percentage.

60  See for example, Burton's "Cure of Melancholy," part 2, sec. 4.

61  Robert Boyle, whose *Occasional Reflections*, Keats also owned, worked with many of Paracelsus's theories in his own lifelong experiments in alchemy.

Paracelsus's teachings were also considered an exemplar of hermeticism and remained familiar to many of the major authors of the Romantic period. De Quincey linked Paracelsus to the secret societies in his essays in *London Magazine* in which he noted the popularity of hermetic interpretations during the period. He displayed particular knowledge of Paracelsian concepts and theories throughout "Historico-Critical Inquiry," and "Secret Societies," but he is not alone in his knowledge. Godwin and Percy Shelley also associated Paracelsian philosophies with Rosicrucian hermetic Neo-Platonism in their writings. Mary Shelley displayed familiarity with Paracelsus's alchemical associations in her novel *Frankenstein*. Hazlitt encountered discourses on Paracelsus by Martin Luther in his translation of *Table Talk*; Hunt made reference to Paracelsus in his writings, and scholars have long noted Blake's, Darwin's, Wordsworth's and Coleridge's familiarity with him.

Given the broad-based knowledge, even if Keats somehow missed Paracelsus in his medical studies in general and his courses on the history of chemistry in particular, it is difficult to believe he would have been unaware of him. And, just as the philosophies upon which Paracelsus based his exoteric and esoteric alchemy and medical theorizing captured public attention and came to underpin the philosophies of the Rosicrucians, parallels in Keats's own theorizing indicate he too found them attractive. Several Paracelsian concepts central to Rosicrucianism match ideas Keats explored in his poetry and his letters.

Furthermore, considering Rosicrucianism's common association in the public mind to doctors and medicine, the high proportion of scientists and doctors who showed interest in Rosicrucianism throughout the seventeenth century, and those who joined Masonic lodges in the eighteenth and nineteenth centuries, these connections prove intriguing in terms of Keats's own tendency to turn the scientific to imaginative allegorical purpose. As many studies have shown, several founders of the Royal Society were deeply interested in Rosicrucianism and the hermetic, exoteric and esoteric philosophies of alchemy, and men such as Moray, Ashmole, Newton, and Boyle all spent significant time and effort engaged in the study of both.[62] More generally, at various times throughout the eighteenth century, up to a quarter of the Fellows of the Royal Society were Freemasons, and at Guy's Hospital, Masonic membership was consistently strong enough that in the 1840s a lodge was formed specifically for the doctors there.[63]

The philosophical explorations of the previous century formed the basis for many of the speculative philosophies influential during the Romantic period. Even the dialectical process of thesis, antithesis and synthesis put forth to elucidate man's progress or evolution in the world, the concept we now associate so readily with

---

62  B. J. T. Dobbs, *The Foundations of Newton's Alchemy or the Hunting of the Green Lyon* (Cambridge: Cambridge UP, 1975).

63  Michael Baigent, "Freemasonry, Hermetic Thought and the Royal Society of London" *Ars Quatuor Coronatum: Transactions of the Quatuor Coronati Lodge No. 2076* 109 (1996): 154–87. In "A Basic Historico-Chronological Model of the Western Hermetic Tradition," Trevor Stewart notes that "at any one time during the first half of the 18th century at least 25% of the Fellows of the Royal Society were Freemasons." 21 March 2003, *Societas Rosicruciana in Canada* <http://sric-canada.org/stewartintro.html>.

Hegelian philosophy, can be traced to the theological speculations contained in esoteric alchemy. The basic process mirrors that of alchemy and was expounded upon by Paracelsus, then adapted and used as a metaphor for the evolution of the personality by the Rosicrucians, and for the religious stages of enlightenment by mystics such as Swedenborg and Boehme, all of whose works influenced the philosophies and writings of Goethe, Novalis, Schelling, Hegel, and other Romantics.[64] The majority of these men also were involved in and associated with Freemasonry, and the transmission of the hermetic concepts long acknowledged as part and portion of *Naturphilosophie* ran not only through lines associated with literature but also medicine because of the remarkable number of doctors who joined Masonic societies. Considering scholars' acknowledgements of *Naturphilosophie*'s impact on British Romanticism, it is important we recognize that hermeticism formed the basis for much of the philosophical investigations.

In *Romantic Medicine and John Keats*, Hermione De Almeida presents readers with an assessment of the major debates of the Romantic period on subjects ranging from the nature of life, to theories of vitalism and mechanism, to electro-magnetism, evolution, and more. In each case, she documents the most influential writers and theorists of the period, including the proponents of *Naturphilosophie*, to whom she returns again and again. Analysis of the writings of men such as these, combined with discourses on the work of scientist philosophers such as Erasmus Darwin, forms the basis for much of her analysis of Keats's poetry. One point of connection between these men she argues as influential in Keats's understanding of medicine, however, is their sustained interest in hermetic philosophies. The majority of them were members of various Masonic societies, and several of them wrote works making explicit use of hermetic linguistics, and they certainly were aware of the origins of both the metaphors and allegories they chose to use and the concepts they chose to develop. When De Almeida writes that,

> ... readers of Keats usually assume that he derived his belief in the poet as physician from Wordsworth's concept, derived in turn from *Naturphilosophie*, that poetry medicines the mind. But concepts of service to humanity, usefulness, commitment to the alleviation of distress ... are all subjects that find place – perhaps first for Keats – in the ethical teachings and practice of Romantic medicine ...

she notes another possible avenue from which Keats may have garnered his ideas, but it is important to realize that this is not a separate pathway from that of *Naturphilosophie*.[65] The aspects are part of one continuum in thought and practice dating back to Ficino's and Paracelsus's concept of the priest-physician who provides physic to both spirit and body via the imagination.

Finally, Keats's long established interest in Neo-Platonism also would have provided him with access to hermetic concepts and language. Thomas Taylor provided readers with introductions and translations to the works of Plato, Proclus, Plotinus, Porphyry, and Iamblichus, as well as many of the texts of the Egyptian, Chaldean,

---

64  Glenn Alexander Magee makes the case for broad influence throughout *Hegel and the Hermetic Tradition* (Ithaca: Cornell UP, 2001).

65  De Almeida 38.

and Eleusinian Mystery Societies, and these works had played a significant role in hermetic studies for centuries. Horace Walpole had good reason to link Taylor to the mystic Swedenborg, and when the *Edinburgh Review* wrote that, "the ravings of Jacob Behmen are not a more abominable interpretation of the New Testament than the commentaries of Proclus and Company are of the writings of Plato," the assessment was not without precedent.[66] By the Romantic period topics such as hermeticism, Neo-Platonism, and the philosophies of Pythagoras all had become closely related in the public mind, and even scholarship of the period did not make the sorts of differentiations we would expect today. Authors with whom Keats was very familiar, men such as Lempriere, made little distinction between Pythagorean, Platonic, and Neo-Platonic metaphysics. All three were commonly recognized as central to hermetic and specifically alchemical speculations that secret societies of the Romantic period relied upon for "the enlightenment, elevation, [and] perfection of humanity by developing the moral powers of nature, and their happy consummation in the eventual peace, happiness and illumination of our species."[67]

Keats himself makes unmistakable use of hermetic, Rosicrucian, and Masonic lore throughout his verse. In the 1818 fragment "Where's the Poet? Show him! show him" and the later "Bards of Passion and of Mirth," Keats transfers to the poet the fabled abilities of Rosicrucian or Masonic adepts and highlights various characteristics associated with the societies' rituals. *Endymion*, both in structural and conceptual design, follows the traditional, allegorical Rosicrucian stages of advancement through the elements as representative of gained wisdom and spiritual growth, and Keats also follows exactly the Rosicrucian doctrines of spirits or sylphs as representative of the four elements in his 1819 work *Song of the Four Fairies*. Likewise, Rosicrucian and Masonic elements arguably form a significant subtext to both *Hyperion* poems with their emphasis on mystic visions, revelatory rites, and the dying into life of both the poet and the god Apollo. And *Lamia* contains Hermes, the lovely and volatile serpent Lamia, and the philosopher Apollonius, all long associated with Rosicrucian lore and Mysteries.

As a result of these many connections, there is ample evidence to justify an examination of Keats's poetry and letters in light of the hermeticism contained in the secret societies. Keats habitually incorporated in his writings terms and ideas from his reading in wide-ranging fields. He often examined materials, mixed them in unusual ways, and created new meanings and new implications in an effort to formulate imaginative truths he believed could provide physic during those "unimaginative days" "of sickly safety and comfort."[68] Like the societies of the period, the process

---

66 Kathleen Raine, "Thomas Taylor in England," *Thomas Taylor the Platonist: Selected Writings*, eds. Kathleen Raine and George Mills Harper (Princeton: Princeton University Press, 1969) 29.

67 Rev. A. F. A. Woodford, "Freemasonry and Hermeticism," *Ars Quatuor Coronatorum: Being the Transactions of the Lodge Quatuor Coronati, No. 2076*, 1 (1886): 28. Woodford connects the philosophies to "all occult and mysterious, primeval and religious lore ... that found an outcome in alchemy, astrology, the mysterious learning, [and] the aporreta of the East which is repeated in Hebraic Cabala, and was preserved originally in the [Greek] Mysteries" (28).

68 Keats, "Mr. Kean" 227.

he embraced included imagination and science, and material and spiritual awareness, as well as an implicit recognition that though he was "straining at particles of light in the midst of a great darkness," he might arrive at knowledge of some value.[69]

If Keats was a realist, it is important to acknowledge he was a realist who also never was able "to perceive how any thing can be known for truth by consequitive reasoning," and who placed a high value on knowledge and truth gained not only through absolute proof but also speculation.[70] If we accept his opinion that "a Question is the best beacon towards a little Speculation," then Keats's question "Can it be that even the greatest Philosopher ever arrived at his goal without putting aside numerous objections?" indicates he was willing to explore "the Penetralium of mystery," even if it meant gaining only "half knowledge."[71] If facts and reason, consecutive logic, might "clip an angel's wings," then he was willing to dispense with them, and there is reason to believe he also was willing to explore the philosophies and concepts underpinning Rosicrucianism and Freemasonry that permeated the period.

His writings suggest that he used the hermetic concepts underlying Rosicrucianism and Freemasonry to examine his evolving philosophical ideas. The allusions in his letters and poetry appear to be his attempts to merge his philosophies on life and poetry, much the same way elements were combined in the alchemist's flask to create a more meaningful whole. The imagery used refers to and elaborates on the endeavor itself as well as his successes and failures. Rosicrucianism and Freemasonry during the Romantic period were cultural phenomena that served as a nexus for scientific, political, philosophical, and religious debate. To suppose that Keats was unaware of them and to discount his use of hermetic concepts and linguistics in his writing is akin to returning to views of his disengagement with his times that scholars have worked so hard to disprove. But, to allow their presence and import grants us another way to interpret his writings and his thoughts.

---

69  Keats, Letter to George Keats, *Letters II* 80.

70  Keats, Letter to Bailey, 22 November 1817, *Letters I* 185.

71  Keats, Letter to Bailey, 22 November 1817, *Letters I* 185; Letter to Bailey 30 October 1817, *Letters I* 175; Letter to George and Tom Keats, 27 December 1817, *Letters I* 193.

Chapter Three

# Hieroglyphics: Hermetic Recovery in Keats's Poetry

Popular theories about Rosicrucianism and Freemasonry provided readers with a direct conduit to the hermeticism of previous centuries that became mingled during the Romantic period with broader concepts of social reformation, politics and religion, and Keats, like so many others of the period, appears to have been aware of this. His writings provide evidence that he was aware of various hermetic concepts and that he related them to both his philosophical speculations and his goals as a poet. Similarly, variations on an intriguing sonnet by John Taylor and Richard Woodhouse indicate that Keats's friends associated characteristics of the Rosicrucian and Masonic brotherhoods with Keats as well.

In her 1925 biography *John Keats*, Amy Lowell introduced scholars to the sonnet "The Poet" from the Pierpont Morgan Woodhouse Collection of Keatsiana. For years, scholars thought that Keats had written "The Poet," in part because Lowell found the unattributed sonnet in a section Richard Woodhouse had labeled as "Poem, &c. by, or relating to, John Keats," and had noted "All that are not by Keats, have the names of the authors added." [1] Then, E. L. Brooks discovered that *London Magazine* had published a variation of "The Poet" signed "S." in October 1821, and Mabel Steele found evidence indicating that James Hessey believed John Taylor wrote the sonnet published in *London Magazine*.[2] Steele suggested that Taylor gave the sonnet to Woodhouse to place with his other Keatsiana, and Woodhouse modified the poem to his own taste while copying it into his book but forgot to provide an author's name.

Although it is impossible to know for certain who wrote the version in Woodhouse's collection, it is certain that Woodhouse identified the poem with Keats and that the sonnet contains highly specific allusions that highlight the skills associated with the Rosicrucian adepts – both of the mythical Renaissance society and the Masonic organizations of the Romantic period. In effect, the poet of the sonnet is a Rosicrucian:

> The Poet
> At morn, at noon, at Eve, and Middle Night
>   He passes forth into the charmed air,

---

1    Woodhouse quoted by Amy Lowell, *John Keats*, vol. 1 (Boston: Houghton Mifflin Co., 1925) 60–61.

2    E. L. Brooks "'The Poet' an Error in the Keats Canon?," *Modern Language Notes* 67.7 (Nov. 1952): 450–54. Mabel A. E. Steele "The Authorship of 'The Poet' and Other Sonnets: Selections from a 19th Century Manuscript Anthology," *Keats–Shelley Journal* 5 (Winter 1956): 69–80.

With Talisman to call up spirits rare
From plant, cave, rock, and fountain. – To his sight
The husk of natural objects opens quite
    To the core: and every secret essence there
    Reveals the elements of good and fair;
Making him see, where Learning hath no light.
Sometimes, above the gross and palpable things
    Of this diurnal sphere, his spirit flies
    On awful wing; and with its destined skies
Holds premature and mystic communings:
    Till such unearthly intercourses shed
    A visible halo round his living [mortal] head.[3]

The poet goes about his tasks at specific divisions of the day that mirror those described in various Rosicrucian and Masonic texts in which "morn," "noon," "Eve" and "Middle Night" are designated as symbolic points in rituals, and adepts are charged to divide their different "works" by such times.[4] His abilities also correspond exactly to those of the Rosicrucians and higher degree Masons who were fabled to converse with "spirits rare" drawn from the elements of the world and to possess the skill of reading "natural objects," and seeing within them "every secret essence." In his condemnations of the Rosicrucian lodges and the Cabalistic or Occult Freemasons, Barruel specifically noted the supposed abilities of adepts to physically or imaginatively enter into communion with the spirits of the elements as well as their purported access to the revelatory knowledge of Nature which could not be gained solely by traditional means of study.[5]

According to the Rosicrucian manifestos the *Fama* and *Confessio*, these abilities and "mystic communings" formed part of the "Philosophy of Nature" or occult knowledge central to the Rosicrucian goal of helping mankind. Even the phrase, "Making him see, where Learning hath no light," echoes both Rosicrucian and higher degree Masonic precepts stating that while conventional learning, the arts

---

3    "The Poet," written in Woodhouse's hand, *John Keats: Poems, Transcripts, Letters, &c. Facsimiles of Richard Woodhouse's Scrapbook Materials in the Pierpont Morgan Library*, ed. Jack Stillinger, vol. 4 (New York: Garland Publishing, Inc. 1985) 305. In the running header, Stillinger attributes the poem to Taylor, but the sestet of this version differs so strongly from the sonnet Hessey attributed to Taylor that it is possible this version is not by Taylor.

4    See for example the divisions of day and night in the 1760 ritual exposure *Three Distinct Knocks* contained in A. C. F. Jackson's *English Masonic Exposures 1760–1769* (London: Lewis Masonic, 1986) 73.

5    The Abbé Barruel, *The AntiChristian and Antisocial Conspiracy. An Extract from the French of the Abbé Barruel, to which Is Prefixed Jachin and Boaz, or an Authentic Key to the Door of Free-Masonry Ancient and Modern* (Lancaster: Joseph Ehrenfried, 1812) 120–23. Writers sympathetic to Masonry, including Lessing, knew such claims were metaphorical. In the "Fourth Conversation" of *Ernst and Falk*, Ernst speaks with disgust of those who want to learn the secrets of gold making, conjuring spirits, and the like, but Falk, who has deeper knowledge of Freemasonry, gently mocks him for taking such aims literally and attempts to guide him to a better estimation of their philosophical worth. Gotthold Ephraim Lessing, *Lessing's Masonic Dialogues*, ed. Robin L. Carr, trans. *The Builder* 1915–1929 (1778; Bloomington, IL: The Masonic Book Club, 1991).

and sciences, were vital to man's progress, the ultimate secrets of nature and thus the ultimate access to inner wisdom could not be taught or learned by conventional means but only by mystical, imaginative apprehension and revelation in the heart. The sonnet that Woodhouse recorded and associated with Keats portrays the poet – who he is and what he does – using explicitly Rosicrucian and Masonic attributes.

In addition, although Woodhouse may have made alterations to the sonnet now attributed to Taylor, the version that appeared in *London Magazine* also presents the poet as possessing traits long associated with the secret societies. While the octet of the published version remains much the same, the sestet emphasizes the broad sympathies of the poet in a fashion that strongly evokes a major characteristic of Freemasonry – the society's ability to find common ground and create ties among men of differing religious, social, and national distinctions who might otherwise "have remain'd at a perpetual distance."[6] The sestet declares:

> The Poet's sympathies are not confined
> To kindred, country, climate, class or kind,
> And yet they glow intense. – Oh! were he wise,
> Duly to commune with his destined skies
> Then, as of old, might inspiration shed
> A visible glory round his hallow'd head.[7]

The lines might just as well refer to the Freemasons who, in their widely published *Constitutions*, proudly asserted that their brotherly love knew no common boundaries because Masons met as equals "on the Level" regardless of class, and were of "all *Nations*, *Tongues*, *Kindreds*, and *Languages*."[8] Indeed, many writers such as Lessing and De Quincey considered this to be Freemasonry's distinguishing feature and greatest potential.[9]

Regardless of whether scholars acknowledge the sonnet as by Keats or as about Keats, as Brooks and others such as Earl Wasserman have stressed, "The Poet" corresponds closely with much of Keats's own poetry.[10] Keats himself alluded to similar ideas and displayed a markedly similar Rosicrucian/Masonic perspective in the 1818 fragment beginning "Where's the Poet? Show him! show him!" The fragment is usually read as an extension of both the concept of sympathy expressed in

---

6    James Anderson, *The Constitutions of the Free-Masons Containing the History, Charges, Regulations, &c. of that Most Ancient and Right Worshipful Fraternity* (London 1723; Philadelphia: Benjamin Franklin, 1734). *An Online Electronic Edition*, ed. Paul Royster, University of Nebraska Lincoln Libraries, 14 February 2006 <http://digitalcommons.unl.edu/libraryscience/25> 48.

7    "The Poet," *London Magazine* (October 1821) as quoted by Brooks 451.

8    Anderson 53.

9    In *Ernst and Falk*, Lessing refers repeatedly to the ways in which Freemasonry can enable men to extend their sympathies beyond, as the sonnet says, "kindred, country, climate, class, or kind," and uses all these same terms, although not all in one phrase.

10  Earl Wasserman later conceded that the *London Magazine* sonnet was most likely not by Keats, but he provides a particularly useful summary of parallels in Keats's writings in his response to Brooks's article: Earl Wasserman, "Keats's Sonnet 'The Poet'," *Modern Language Notes* 67.7 (Nov. 1952): 454–56.

*Endymion* and Keats's conception of the "camelion Poet" described in his 27 October 1818 letter to Woodhouse, but the fragment is also a specific response to critical attacks.[11] Woodhouse had expressed concern that Keats might cease to write poetry, in part because of the vitriolic reviews of *Endymion*, in which Keats was mocked as one "not content with a half initiation into the school he has chosen," and as a "disciple" and "neophyte" of his "Master" Hunt.[12] Keats's response to Woodhouse encompassed not only lessons learned from the process of writing *Endymion* but also his evolving sense of a poet's abilities and duties as well as a defiant appropriation of the language of the secret societies that was used against him.

The poet of 1818 who declares himself a "camelion" partakes of the knowledge that the character Endymion gains through his initiation trials. He knows what Endymion learns – that affinity both with man and the natural world are necessary before one can understand and create "Greater things." This philosophy centering upon strengthening the imagination and the sympathies in order to see into the life of things and thereby provide men with greater understanding and spiritual solace played a central role in Rosicrucian and Masonic teachings, and here, as elsewhere, Keats is drawing upon the same.[13] Keats presents the poet as entering into direct communion with the natural world that includes mankind as well as other living creatures:

> Where's the Poet? show him! show him,
> Muses nine! that I may know him!
> 'Tis the man who with a man
>     Is an equal, be he King,
> Or poorest of the beggar-clan,
>     Or any other wondrous thing
> A man may be 'twixt ape and Plato;
>     'Tis the man who with a bird,
> Wren or Eagle, finds his way to
>     All its instincts; he hath heard
> The Lion's roaring, and can tell
>     What his horny throat expresseth,
> And to him the Tiger's yell

---

11  John Keats, *The Letters of John Keats, 1814–1821*, ed. Hyder Rollins, vol. 1 (Cambridge, Mass.: Harvard UP, 1958) 386–88. Hereafter, this work will be referred to as *Letters I*.

12  The *British Critic* (June 1818), the *Quarterly Review* (April 1818), and *Blackwood's Edinburgh Magazine* (August 1818). For the full reviews, see Lewis M. Schwartz's, *Keats Reviewed by His Contemporaries: A Collection of Notices for the Years 1816–1821* (Metuchen, NJ: The Scarecrow Press, Inc., 1973) 129–37.

13  The role of the imagination in exciting the sympathies and leading to a gradual inculcation of wisdom was vital to Rosicrucian and Masonic philosophies derived from Paracelsus's writings in which the roles of philosopher-alchemist, artist, and physician were conflated and described as that of the "cabalistic 'rector'." Paracelsus, *Opera Omnia*, tom. II, 472. A. *De Virtute Imaginativa*, tract II, trans. C. H. Josten, Desiree Hirst, *Hidden Riches: Traditional Symbolism from the Renaissance to Blake* (New York: Barnes & Noble, Inc., 1964) 67.

Comes articulate and presseth
On his ear like mother-tongue

The poet is equal with kings and beggars, and this was the essence of both Rosicrucianism and Freemasonry's catchwords of equality and brotherhood. The societies' insistence "that not only princes, men of rank, rich men, and learned men, but also mean and inconsiderable persons, are admitted to their communion, provided they have pure and disinterested purposes, and are able and willing to exert themselves for the ends of the institution" was viewed by De Quincey and others as a significant means by which the societies encouraged "the ties of social obligation," and throughout the Romantic period, Freemasonry's liberal and revolutionary aspects were linked to this claim to equality.[14]

Moreover, the higher degrees of Freemasonry, including the Rosicrucian related degrees, made use of the animals described in Keats's poem in their rituals and iconography.[15] The lion and the eagle were associated with higher knowledge and skills and commonly found in alchemical and Rosicrucian texts which described in allegorical terms the process by which man gained successive degrees of wisdom and sympathetic understanding of others and the world around him. And, in an interesting twist with political implications, Barruel and De Quincey noted that the lion and ape were symbols adopted by the "Jacobite" "Scotch" degrees.[16] Similarly, the figures of the man, the eagle, and the lion appeared on the "Principal Banners" of the Royal Arch degrees, and frequently in decorative Masonic items as well as texts.[17] Keats's poem even depicts the wisdom and understanding that the Rosicrucian and higher degree Masonic adepts were fabled to possess whereby they could enter into communion with birds and animals and converse with them in their own tongues.

Rosicrucian concepts also appear in the poem "Bards of Passion and of Mirth." Keats mentions the poem in a letter to George right before he recounts Hazlitt's character analysis of the Rosicrucian *St Leon* and copies the poem into the letter directly afterwards.[18] The bards enjoy a "double-lived" immortality because their souls remain on earth in the form of their poetry while also existing in heaven (4). And like the Rosicrucians, the poets' souls

... of heaven commune
With the spheres of Sun & Moon;

---

14  Thomas De Quincey, "Historico-Critical Inquiry into the Origins of the Rosicrucians and the Free-Masons," *De Quincey's Collected Writings: Tales and Prose Phantasies*, ed. David Masson, vol. 13 (Edinburgh: Adam & Charles Black, 1897) 404–405 and 389, respectively.

15  Various eighteenth-century compendiums such as the *Geheime Figuren der Rosenkreuzer...* (Altona 1785, 1788) described Rosicrucian symbology.

16  De Quincey 438.

17  Roy A. Wells, *Some Royal Arch Terms Examined* (London: Lewis Masonic, 1978) 64–67.

18  John Keats, letter to George and Georgianna, 16 December 1818–4 January 1819, *The Letters of John Keats, 1814–1821*, ed. Hyder Rollins, vol. 2 (Cambridge, Mass.: Harvard UP, 1958) 24–25. Hereafter, this work will be referred to as *Letters II*.

With the noise of fountains wondrous,
And the parle of voices thunderous;
With the Whisper of heavens trees,
And one anothers, in soft ease
Seated on elysian Lawns ... (5–11)

They enter into the life of the world and "grand materials" around them consisting both of nature in general and the four elements, moving from the fire of sun and moon, to the waters of fountains, to the sounds of voices and whispers born in air, to the trees and lawns and flowers, even unto the nightingale who sings

... Melodious truth divine
Philosophic numbers fine;
Tales and golden histories
Of Heaven and its Mysteries. (19–22)

Keats's images allude to several key elements in Rosicrucian lore. The "Melodious truth," tied as it is to song, appears to refer to the music of the spheres hinted at in the previous lines, and this music, last heard by the philosopher Pythagoras whose teachings were absorbed into Rosicrucian philosophy, leads to "Philosophic numbers fine." The sacredness of numbers also was understood as part of the divine Mysteries and the Cabala the Rosicrucians professed knowledge of, and the numbers also played a role in various initiation rites, so it is not surprising to see Keats immediately referring to "golden histories / Of Heaven and its Mysteries." And, while these ideas were widespread, their appearance in Keats's verse directly following his references to a Rosicrucian related work suggest a process of association typical of Keats and strongly imply that his bards possess the powers of the Rosicrucians.

Their similarity also extends unto the benefits they offer mankind. Although the natural wonders that Keats describes and the nightingale who sings of golden histories and mysteries are located in Elysian realms where nature has been refined to a sublime state, they are still linked to the natural world and to the "souls" the poets have left behind. The "souls" still on Earth are the poems they have written and they serve a vital function – they literally guide those "mortals of the little week" who "must sojourn with their cares" (30).[19] They "teach" "the way," to find the poets' purer souls in heaven by speaking both

Of their sorrows and delights
Of their Passions and their spites;
Of their glory and their shame –
What doth strengthen and what maim. (26, 31–34).

Through the insights they provide in which these contrary aspects of life are mingled and fused, they teach the way and process by which men may gain "Wisdom," and that wisdom is the same as that found in the Rosicrucian and Masonic texts and rites (36).

---

19  The line "must soujourn with their cares" is found in the letter version of the poem in *Letters II* 24–25.

While the references in these poems are certainly more fanciful than the scientific, chemical aspects of Keats's allusions that Stuart Sperry, Donald Goellnicht, and others have asserted describe Keats's poetic process via terms related to distillation, refinement and purification, both sides are vital to any interpretation of his writings. Keats's Rosicrucian descriptions of the poet, the man who actually creates poetry by a process of distilling and refining his impressions of and knowledge from the world around him, should be acknowledged and examined further.

Keats's use of the imagery and linguistics commonly related to the Rosicrucians and Freemasons extends well beyond fables or even chemical or alchemical metaphors. When he describes his philosophies in his letters or alludes to them in his poetry, and when he addresses the issues of the imagination's and poetry's roles in life, Keats also makes use of an entire range of hermetic symbols scholars have traditionally associated with classical mythology and especially Apollo in his writing. In a situation similar to that with Keats's alchemical and chemical terminology, the emblems and associations traditionally linked to Apollo in Keats studies, while retaining their Apollonian meanings, accrue additional metaphysical import when their hermetic meanings are applied.

In his work *The Starlit Dome*, G. Wilson Knight offers readers an interpretation of Keats's poetry based upon a method of "decipherment, like the decipherment of pictographs."[20] He argues that close analysis of recurring images and figures such as Apollo and of the associations such elements create in the mind can lead to more fruitful interpretations of Keats's poetry. The method is a familiar one and has been used many times with good effect to study Keats's poetry and in particular the mythological symbols he appropriates.[21] The key, of course, is an explanation of the symbolic language Keats uses, a way for readers to decipher the images and the linguistics used to convey them by connecting them to given meanings. Such an approach, however, requires that those who attempt the decipherment be fully aware of the range of associations a symbol possessed during the poet's time. In a sense, we become archeologists examining cultural artifacts, and while we may guess at meanings as scholars of Keats's time guessed at the characters carved on the Rosetta Stone, without full context, we find ourselves in the same position as the speaker in *Hyperion* describing

> ... hieroglyphics old,
> Which sages and keen-eyed astrologers
> Then living on the earth, with labouring thought
> Won from the gaze of many centuries:
> Now lost, save what we find on remnants huge

---

20  W. F. Jackson Knight, introduction, *The Starlit Dome, Studies in the Poetry of Vision* by G. Wilson Knight (1943; New York: Barnes & Noble, 1960) xii.

21  To cite only two examples: 25 years after the publication of *The Starlit Dome*, Walter H. Evert followed the same approach in his *Aesthetic and Myth in the Poetry of Keats* (Princeton: Princeton UP, 1965), and a quarter of a century later in *Romantic Medicine and John Keats* (New York: Oxford UP, 1991), Hermione De Almeida incorporated her interpretations of the myths upon which Keats seemed to place the most value in her analysis of his writings.

Of stone, or marble swart; their import gone,
Their wisdom long since fled. (I.277–83)

Recovering the Rosicrucian and Masonic associations popularly attached to mythology during the Romantic period offers a means to more fully decipher Keats's own hieroglyphics by adding connotations that were equally prevalent during Keats's time. The Romantic period was one in which authors regularly syncretized mythologies in an attempt to create a unifying vision. Thus, the associations made in relation to myths and even specific gods were often extended to include similar ones from other cultures as well as associations that had accrued in Western culture over the years. This is certainly the case with many of the myths and symbols Keats regularly used, in part because they had long since been appropriated by the Rosicrucians and later the Freemasons.

Recognizing such associations alters more traditional interpretations of Keats's writings, particularly his longer poems. Usually interpreted as reformulations of myths, *Endymion*, *Hyperion*, *Lamia*, and *Fall of Hyperion* are essentially allegorical poems, and when examined with aspects of Rosicrucianism and Freemasonry in mind, these works gain new significance.[22] Allegory was the chosen mode of expression for the rituals, texts, and mythmaking surrounding the secret societies, and these would have provided Keats with not only symbolism and vocabulary well-suited for expression of the philosophical concepts he was examining but also structural frameworks for his poems. Even scholars who acknowledge the allegorical nature of *Endymion* tend to characterize Keats as lacking a plan or understanding of the significance of many ideas put forth within the poem until he had almost completed his work. This encourages some to discount the more metaphysical aspects of the poem. Parallels in *Endymion* to Rosicrucian and Masonic literature, however, both in structure and symbolism, counter this tendency.

*Endymion* reads like a Rosicrucian or Masonic work allegorizing a quest for wisdom and greater perfection in man realized through a process that develops the sympathies via the imagination. Similarly, Keats's *Hyperion*s contain the elements of initiation into a Temple of Knowledge, where Wisdom, Strength and Beauty, the three "pillars" supporting the Masonic Temple, play key roles, and the impending deification is of Apollo who long served as representative of the mystical "Light" for which Rosicrucian and Masonic candidates strove. Moreover, Keats's very choice of the allegorical mode suggests serious intent on his part to use poetry to fully engage in a process of philosophical inquiry about the human experience in which all meet and all may do "some good for the world ... in a thousand ways all equally dutiful to the command of Great Nature."[23]

Keats's avowed goals, and his belief that "a Man's life of any worth is a continual allegory – and very few eyes can see the Mystery of his life – a life like the scriptures, figurative – which such people can no more make out than they can the hebrew Bible," bear striking resemblance to Rosicrucian and Masonic assertions that the

---

22  See Evert's discussions of allegory in both the Introduction and the chapter titled "Endymion" in *Aesthetic and Myth in the Poetry of Keats*.

23  Keats, letter to John Taylor, 24 April 1818, *Letters I* 271.

true Mysteries of their craft were to be discovered not in literal interpretation of their exposed rituals or texts but rather within the men themselves, the lives they lived, and the experiences they garnered in their initiations.[24] Keats's goals to grow in wisdom and spirituality also match those of the societies. Although *Endymion* is rarely read as consistent with Keats's later philosophies and views, when it is considered in light of such allegories and the goals and philosophical elements of Rosicrucianism and Freemasonry, it reveals distinct parallels in thought and perspective to Keats's later work.

As is the case with most symbols, when several are viewed in conjunction they accrue greater significance as their meanings multiply, but even narrowing the focus to encompass only a few Rosicrucian and Masonic symbols in Keats's poetry can alter our analysis in subtle but significant ways. Scholars traditionally have worked with an analogical process they ascribed to Keats, suggesting that once a range of meaning was decided upon and linked to specific kinds of images, linguistics, or figures, it could be applied with a fair amount of consistency regardless of whether precisely the same elements occurred in every instance in Keats's writings.[25] This methodology is particularly apt when Rosicrucianism's and Freemasonry's lines of association are considered – both in Keats's writings and the Romantic period's cultural matrix in general. If we accept such an approach, several of the most common symbols associated with Rosicrucianism and Freemasonry during Keats's time function as placeholders for larger philosophical concepts in his poetry, and just as some scholars have used various, consistently appearing Apollonian attributes in Keats's poetry as guides to wider interpretations of his writings, the same practice proves effective when his use of hermetic symbols and terms is considered.

Once one becomes aware of the way in which the symbolism of the secret societies permeated Romantic culture, it is possible to trace symbols in Keats's poetry back to hermetic ideas and recover the import those symbols and ideas once contained. Keats's hieroglyphics in the passage from *Hyperion* cited above, for example, and in his 1817 review of Kean where he exclaims "The spiritual is felt when the very letters and prints of charactered language show like the hieroglyphics of beauty; – the mysterious signs of an immortal freemasonry!," are references to the hermetic symbols and ideas derived from Paracelsian and Rosicrucian texts and transferred to Freemasonry.[26] In both cases, Keats links "the hieroglyphics of beauty," with the role poetry plays in providing man a means to bring himself back into harmony with Nature and thereby regain health.

Hieroglyphics, astrologers, and sages possessed of wisdom from the East all played roles in the Rosicrucian and Masonic mythologies. The texts of both societies asserted their right to designate their emblems as hieroglyphics and connected them

---

24 Keats, letter to George and Georgianna Keats, 19 February 1819, *Letters II* 67.

25 Evert uses this method as do many other Keats scholars. In her study of Keats's understanding of Romantic science and medicine, Hermione De Almeida works by analogy in her interpretations of the role myth plays in Keats's poetry and Robert Ryan does so as well in his researches of Keats's views of religion.

26 Keats, "Mr. Kean," *The Poetical Works & Other Writings of John Keats*, ed. H. Buxton Forman, rev. Maurice Buxton Forman, vol. 5 (New York: Phaeton Press, 1970) 229.

to the ancient history of the Egyptians as well as Hermes Trismegistus and the sages of the East. The Rosicrucians claimed to possess a secret "Magical Language and writing," composed of hieroglyphics – "those great letters and characters which the Lord god hath written and imprinted in heaven and earth's edifice."[27] Similarly, all degrees of Freemasonry were said to possess "hieroglyphical emblems" and portions of each rite of initiation were given to explaining these as illustrations of Masonry's "principles and mystic secrets."[28]

Such explanations commonly appeared in the many Masonic exposures as well as authorized Masonic texts such as William Preston's *Illustrations of Masonry* and various Masonic guides and monitors where readers were told that the hieroglyphics concealed mysteries of Masonry from those who might do the brotherhood harm and presented a means to gradually inculcate knowledge in the initiates that, if exposed in full, would be too great to grasp. Many writers both Rosicrucian and Masonic strengthened such hermetic connotations of hieroglyphics with brief "histories" in which they presented Hermes Trismegistus as the inventor of hieroglyphics and the Cabala and linked both to astrology, "the mother of astronomy ... the study of Nature, and the knowledge of the secret virtues of the heavens ... the sun, moon, and stars ... placed in the firmament to be *signs*."[29]

These writers also explicitly presented the knowledge figured forth by such "signs" as having a metaphysical and humanistic import. The Rosicrucians claimed for themselves the titles of magus and sage and counted astrology as a key art in which they might discover "the clear and manifested Light and Truth" of the "Librum Naturae," but also espoused the belief that "man's nature" as "the compleatest image of the whole universe, containing in itself the whole heavenly harmony," provided "the Seals, and Characters of all the Stars, and Celestiall influences, and those as the more efficacious, which are less differing from the Celestiall nature."[30] Implicit in such claims was the belief that man possessed a spark of God's celestial light and divinity because man was "light and life, like God the Father of whom Man was born," and "if therefore you learn to know yourself ... you will return to life."[31]

In addition, hieroglyphics were commonly understood to include all of Nature and to constitute "a symbolic alphabet: the code of a lost wisdom which it was man's task to decipher," and adepts were taught that "by exploring nature, reassembling

27  *The Confessio Fraternitatis*, trans. Thomas Vaughan (1652), transcriber, Kevin Day (Sept. 2002) <http://www.levity.com/alchemy/confessi.html>.

28  William Preston, *Illustrations of Masonry* (1772; Louisville: American Masonic Publishing Association, 1858) 97.

29  Preston 97–98.

30  The first two quotations are from the *Fama*, but many of these ideas also are reiterated in the *Confessio* where the "magical characters" of the Rosicrucian language are linked to knowledge gained from their studies of the heavens and all of nature. The final quotation is from Agrippa's *Three Books of Occult Philosophy*, Book I, Chapter 33 that also was fabled to have been found in Rosenkreutz's tomb. *The Fama Fraternitatis* (1614), ed. Adam McLean <http://www.levity.com/alchemy/fama.html>.

31  *The Poimandres of the Corpus Hermeticum*, trans. Francis Yates, *Giordano Bruno and the Hermetic Tradition* (Chicago: University of Chicago Press, 1964) 25.

'the scatter'd parts of the immortal body', man was elucidating *himself.*"[32] The Rosicrucian adepts encountered this task in the allegorical processes of alchemy where art transformed the materials of nature into the sublime through a process of decomposition, purification, and re-integration, and the Master Masons of the higher degrees faced the same challenge in allegorical rituals where they were charged to read the signs in order to discover the master builder Hiram, who they were told they represented, and reassemble and re-inter his disintegrated body.

Masonic *Monitors* of the early nineteenth century further elaborated on these concepts via copious notes explaining that their hieroglyphics functioned as "emblems or signs of divine, sacred, or supernatural things by which they are distinguished from common symbols, which are signs of sensible or natural things."[33] The same texts stressed such emblems were also intended to "inform the understanding, correct the passions ... guide the will" and "discover the majestic form of divinity" by which man might derive true principles of philosophy founded upon strength, wisdom and beauty and overarched with love.[34] Thus, for the Rosicrucians and the Freemasons, hieroglyphics served as a means to teach candidates "Wisdom, which might partly renew and reduce all Arts ... to perfection; so that finally Man might thereby understand his own Nobleness and Worth, and why he is called Microcosmus, and how far his knowledge extendeth in Nature."[35] The adepts or initiates were required to study both Nature and themselves to discover the lost secrets (in hermetic terms also the Cabala or lost word) that would lead them to a better understanding of themselves – self-knowledge that in turn enabled them to better serve both Man and their God. Nature contained the symbolic alphabet – the hieroglyphics – they must learn to read, just as Glaucus and Endymion in *Endymion* must learn to read the mystical symbolic alphabet of nature in Glaucus's cloak and mysterious book so they can free themselves and revivify the lost lovers.

As suggested by my reference to *Endymion*, I believe that Keats had in mind much more than "common symbols" when he referenced the emblems or *signs* of Nature in his writing. In May of 1817, roughly a fortnight after he embarked on *Endymion*, Keats wrote to Haydon "I must think that difficulties nerve the Spirit of a Man – they make our Prime Objects a Refuge as well as a Passion," and he declared that he looked "upon the Sun the Moon the Stars, the Earth and its contents as materials to form greater things – that is to say ethereal things –."[36] Although he quickly added "but here I am talking like a Madman greater things that our Creator

---

32  Bernard Blackstone, *The Consecrated Urn, an Interpretation of Keats in Terms of Growth and*
Form (London: Longmans, Green and Co., 1959) 34–35.

33  Thomas Smith Webb's *The Freemason's Monitor or Illustrations of Masonry* (Salem: Cushing & Appleton, 1818) 114. I have quoted from a Monitor easily available to scholars in the United States, but British Monitors of the early nineteenth century are virtually identical in their expositions of Masonic hieroglyphics. I have consulted over a dozen Monitors from both the US and England, ranging in date from 1801 to 1818. In cases where the wording differs, the changes are minor.

34  Webb 149.

35  *Fama Fraternitatis.*

36  Keats, *Letters I*, 141 and 143.

himself made!!" the similarity of his own conception to that of the Rosicrucians and Freemasons cannot be discounted.

Keats's comments not only indicate a clear sense of objects in their material sense but also an understanding that such objects function as the means by which to go beyond materialism. His references to the heavens and Earth appear in the midst of a serious examination of his own strengths and failings and the "Sin" of self-delusion, and his allusions indicate that the same process by which materials are etherealized includes an increasing self-knowledge. Keats's "Prime Object" was poetry and, more than that, poetry that served not only as personal refuge and passion, but also as an exploratory process for his own education and as a physic for mankind in general. He reiterated this same concept in June 1818 when during his Northern tour he wrote to Tom:

> I shall learn poetry here and shall henceforth write more than ever, for the abstract endeavor of being able to add a mite to that mass of beauty which is harvested from these grand materials, by the finest spirits, and put into ethereal existence for the relish of one's fellows.[37]

The "ethereal things" Keats would create from such "grand materials" are in effect a universal panacea such as the Rosicrucians labored for even as they stipulated that "true Philosophers" were well aware that the material manifestation of it was "but a parergon" of the abstract true elixir.[38] The flow of ideas and the language in Keats's letters echo those of the Rosicrucians and Freemasons whose "doctrines," as one scholar has argued, "imbued as they were with an experimental, experiential, creative and immensely personal vision – found expression in a peculiar symbolic or hieroglyphic language, an idiom alchemical in nature but ever more religious-philosophic than physical-chemical in intent."[39] Keats's "grand materials" function both as poetic Prima Materia and *signs* or hieroglyphics that can provide wisdom, self-knowledge, inspiration and refuge to those with the ability to see.

Given such associations as these, the larger context in which Keats's poetic passage from *Hyperion* occurs becomes even more symbolic of Rosicrucian and Masonic ideals. Keats's "hieroglyphics old" represent the "sweet-shaped lightnings" of Hyperion's chariot, the silver winged "planet orb of fire, whereon he rode / Each day from east to west the heavens through, / Spun round in sable curtaining of clouds," but "Not therefore veiled quite, blindfold, and hid" (*Hyperion*, II.276; 269–72). Both the chariot of the sun and the sun god himself form a matrix of meaning in Rosicrucian and Masonic lore, and there is good reason, beyond the references to hieroglyphics, sages, and wisdom, to interpret Hyperion's chariot in hermetic terms. Unlike the biblical chariots of fire or even those commonly depicted in classical mythology, Hyperion's is an "orb of fire" with "argent wings," and this is precisely the emblem by which the Rosicrucians and higher degree Masons figured forth the wisdom and spiritual illumination available to man from a combination of study,

---

37　Keats, letter to Tom, 27 June 1818, *Letters I* 301.

38　*Fama Fraternitatis*.

39　Lance S. Owens, "Joseph Smith and Kabbalah: The Occult Connection," *Dialogue: A Journal of Mormon Thought* 27. 3 (1994): 117–94.

insight into Nature, and direct apprehension of truth and beauty via the imagination and senses.

This light signified the means by which the soul journeyed through mortal life to immortal liberation. Thus, the winged orb or chariot was representative not only of the sun god's progress through the sky from East to West but also of a philosophy in which man's "labouring thought" enabled him to win from concealment an understanding and manifestation of what the Rosicrucians called the "Wisdom of God" or the "Brightness of Eternal Light."[40] Masons, moreover, equated the same "Light" with truth, "the divine attribute, and the foundation of every virtue" man must discover in his heart and cultivate for the benefit of his own soul's elevation and that of others.[41]

Finally, Apollo appeared prominently in both Rosicrucian and Masonic allegories and philosophies where the sun was equated with the familiar connotations given the god, including life and, in a conflation of all the meanings discussed, the metaphysical equivalent of the alchemical processes by which matter passed through stages of death, rebirth, and regeneration. In alchemical-philosophical terms, man attained a higher state akin to deification or divinity by acquiring the wisdom necessary to "die into life" as Apollo does in the *Hyperion* fragment (III.130).[42] When we consider that Hyperion's chariot will become Apollo's, and Apollo as the god of prophecy, physic, poetry, and the wisdom contained therein will be the inspiration of poets and communicate his gifts to those who dedicate themselves to the task of helping humanity, the many hermetic associations enrich Keats's lovely image. They invest it with prophetic foresight and the hope that what Apollo will soon possess will not remain veiled to the poet – he too will partake of the glory and "symbols divine, / Manifestations of that beauteous life / Diffus'd unseen throughout eternal space" (*Hyperion*, I.316–18).

In addition, Keats's language also lights the way to a wide range of Rosicrucian and Masonic meanings associated with not only Apollo but also Hermes or Mercury. Virtually all critics who make use of myth as a means for analysis of Keats's poetry and philosophies grant Apollo a prominent role if not the pre-eminent one in their studies, and many use Apollo as a touchstone for Keats's other mythological allusions. When Evert analyzed the recurring images and linguistics in Keats's poetry, he ascribed to Keats a metaphysics in which both nature and man are "subject to the influence of a single beneficent power, or law, which manifests itself in and through them."[43] He described that power as a "law of universal harmony, by which all existing things are held in a balanced interrelationship with each other, and initially discrete elements are fused, through an assimilative growth process, into

---

40 *Fama Fraternitatis*. The symbol is also Egyptian, however its appropriation in Rosicrucian texts and hieroglyphics as well as the symbology of Masonic degrees and rites, including its presence in staging of Mozart's *Magic Flute*, gave it a popular currency explicitly connecting it to the wisdom hard won from study to which Keats refers.

41 Webb 67.

42 Herbert Silberer, "The Royal Art," *Hidden Symbolism of Alchemy and the Occult Arts*, prev. *Problems of Mysticism and Its Symbolism*, trans. Smith Ely Jelliffe (New York: Dover Publications, Inc., 1971) 373–416.

43 Evert 30.

new, organically integrated entities."[44] He concluded that Apollo was not only the exemplar of this power but also Keats's symbolic center from which virtually all his most significant allusions originated.[45] These same assertions, however, also apply to Freemasonry and its assumed precursor Rosicrucianism which not only advocated the same conception of harmony and integration Evert describes via their alchemical metaphors and symbolism but also used both Apollo and Hermes-Mercury to elucidate their philosophies.

The references to the sun and light and Apollo and Hermes in various Rosicrucian degrees and higher Masonic degrees such as the Knights of the Sun were presented to the public as representative of a form of natural religion with a "celestial temple," encompassing a harmonious relationship between man and nature, "which the ETERNAL had himself erected upon earth to sublime virtue."[46] Masonic writers often described their temple as universal, and when tracing Freemasonry's origins, claimed that those who understood the "true religion" knew that all the world "was filled with his presence, and he was not hidden from the most distant quarters of creation" and "wheresoever under the sun they worshipped, they regarded themselves as being in the dwelling-place of the Divinity," in part because the sun was "the great symbol of the Deity."[47] They also informed readers that Freemasonry's mysteries and principles were closely related to the Pythagorean system of philosophy that they claimed could be found both in the mythology surrounding Apollo and Hermes-Mercury as well as the teachings of Hermes Trismegistus.[48]

Similarly, researchers into Freemasonry often took note of the many references to the sun as one of the "Lights" appearing in Masonic rituals and its frequent presence on Masonic aprons, medals, tracing boards, and plates where conjunctions of the sun and moon were often depicted as well as the blazing chariot and a "flaming star."[49] Some such as Thomas Paine devoted considerable time to studying the connections between ancient mythologies and Freemasonry's use of the sun symbol and concluded that regardless of Masonry's religious affiliations, its theological origins could be traced back to ancient sun worship and the principles that entailed.[50] Paine argued that Freemasonry was based on an ancient, universal religion whose principles had since been lost to the greater world, and Masonic texts, even those claiming that Freemasonry was not a religion, supported this notion by asserting that

---

44  Evert 31.

45  Evert 38.

46  Barruel 100–101. Barruel of course presented such "modern philosophism" as malicious.

47  William Hutchinson *The Spirit of Freemasonry* (1775; New York: Bell Publishing Co., 1982) 112–13.

48  Hutchinson 116–18.

49  For example, see the transcripts of the rituals of first, second and third degree Masons in *Three Distinct Knocks* in Jackson's *English Masonic Exposures 1760–1769*.

50  Thomas Paine, "The Origin of Freemasonry," *Writings of Thomas Paine*, ed. Moncure Daniels Conway, vol. 4 (New York: G. P. Putnam's Sons, 1896) 64.

**Adran Saesneg ac Ysgrifennu Creadigol**

**Athrofa Llenyddiaeth, Ieithoedd a'r
Celfyddydau Creadigol**

Adeilad Hugh Owen, Penglais, Aberystwyth
Ceredigion, Cymru, DU SY23 3DY

Ffôn: (01970) 622534
Ffacs: (01970) 622530
E-bost: saesneg@aber.ac.uk
Gwefan: www.aber.ac.uk/saesneg

Gyda Chyfarchion

**Department of English and Creative Writing**

**Institute of Literature, Languages and
Creative Arts**

Hugh Owen Building, Penglais, Aberystwyth
Ceredigion, Wales, UK SY23 3DY

Tel: (01970) 622534
Fax: (01970) 622530
E-mail: english@aber.ac.uk
Website: www.aber.ac.uk/english

With Compliments

PRIFYSGOL
ABERYSTWYTH
UNIVERSITY

the philosophies upon which it was based could be traced back to the beginnings of man.[51]

The same works delineating the mystical aspects of Freemasonry's symbols also stressed the society's practical humanism and identified the mythological figures of Apollo and Hermes as emblematic of the Masonic aspirations to gain knowledge and serve mankind. Thus, the mythologies and concepts surrounding Apollo and Hermes were widely understood to function as keys to the philosophies of the secret societies, and the varied interpretations given these mirror the many theories scholars put forth to explain Keats's own allusions.[52] During the Romantic period, Apollo's many attributes and roles had become so mixed and melded with other myths that they often had become indistinguishable. In the case of Rosicrucian and Masonic mythologies, Apollo and Hermes-Mercury, and the symbols associated with them, essentially served as interchangeable emblems of hermetic philosophies that carried positive connotations.

-----

51  When the *Constitutions* was first published in 1723, it included a "history" of Freemasonry that claimed the society's origins lay in the times before the Flood and that traced the brotherhood's existence throughout history, linking it to Noah's sons, Hermes, the Tower of Babel, Abraham, the sages of Egypt, Solomon's Temple, and so forth. To this mythical history were soon added many others and claims of Masonry's primeval status appeared in the majority of authorized Masonic texts.

52  There are, however, some differences between modern interpretations of these myths and the inclusive nature ascribed to them during the Romantic period. Some scholars have isolated various elements and separated concepts which were once considered interrelated. For example, when Hermione De Almeida examined Apollo's role in Keats's writings, she saw within Apollo not a universal harmony but an inherent division. "The dark underside of the myth of Apollo," with its associations of pestilence and what she identified as "a tradition of false medicine, of magic or sorcery," led her to separate rather than fuse the elements of the myths and images surrounding the god (39; 20–21). In effect, she took characteristics of Apollo and split them – those to which she attributed a positive reading she related to Apollo, and "a tradition of true or sacred medicine" and "altruistic healing," but those she viewed as negative, "false or profane medicine" and "self-interested and often deadly magic" she identified as belonging to Hermes-Mercury (18). While De Almeida clearly acknowledged "Apollo's 'dual nature'," and "the manifold associations of Apollo's power," the tendency of her analysis was to work against it (17). To make her case, she used Tooke's myth in which Apollo invents both the lyre and music and Hermes is portrayed as a thief who steals the lyre to force Apollo to give him the caduceus (20–21). But both Spence and Lempriere, favorites of Keats, gave the credit for the invention to Hermes-Mercury. The same story is related by Horace and Ovid, and its details suggest Keats was familiar with Hermes's pre-eminent skills. According to the alternative storyline, Hermes invented the lyre from a tortoise shell and the entrails of a kine he stole from Apollo. When Apollo confronted Hermes with the theft, Hermes so charmed him with his music that Apollo was appeased and agreed to trade the cattle for the lyre. Later, Hermes invented the pipe to amuse himself as he watched over the cattle, and Apollo again became entranced with the music and desired the pipe. Hermes traded the pipe for the caduceus in return. This exchange casts Hermes in a very different light than many Keats scholars are accustomed to, but the more positive characterizations of Hermes in which his skills are blended with Apollo's do match closely the texts of the period.

In order to trace the ways in which Apollo and Hermes became related, it is necessary to recall the emphasis placed upon wisdom from the East in Rosicrucian and Masonic mythologies. As Keats's references to hieroglyphics suggest, Egypt and its mysteries were among the most prominent associations with the East during his time, not only because of the many publications of Neo-Platonic works asserting that the Greek philosophers derived their knowledge from the sages of Egypt but also the interest in Egyptian antiquities sparked by the Napoleonic campaigns. It was a natural tendency of the Romantic period to seek correspondences between the Egyptian gods and those of the Greeks and Romans, and the god Thoth was one whose connections had long since been established in Neo-Platonic and hermetic texts.

In Egyptian mythology, Thoth served many functions. He was the god of the moon as well as the representative of the sun god Ra, a messenger to the judges of the underworld, the patron of all learning and philosophy, and the inventor of languages and writing. In addition, in the myths surrounding Osiris, he appeared in a role similar to that of a physician; he protected the pregnant Isis, aided in the delivery of her son, and healed Horus when he was wounded. The Greeks considered the multi-purpose god to be synonymous with Hermes and often referred to both as Thoth "the thrice great" or Hermes "the thrice great," and by the end of the third century AD both gods had become conflated with a divinely inspired mortal who took the name Hermes Trismegistus. Hermes Trismegistus became the designated author of choice for the works of the *Hermetica* and countless treatises in the related fields of alchemy and medicine as well as various occult sciences stressing the gifts of prophecy, theology and the attendant implications of divine wisdom and philosophy.[53]

There are many parallels between Thoth, the Greek god Hermes, often referred to in Romantic literature by his Roman counterpart Mercury, and the figure Hermes Trismegistus. Both Thoth and Hermes-Mercury acted as messengers to various gods; both were closely related to their respective sun gods; both played significant roles in the process of conducting souls to their judged places in the underworld; and both were explicitly recognized as masters of language and eloquence. Furthermore, both also played roles in the healing arts. Although Joseph Spence, who was a Freemason, was reluctant to discuss what he called the "mystical part of [Hermes-Mercury's] character" in *Polymetis*, he noted that Horace included "a very extraordinary account of Mercury's descending to Ades [*sic*], and his causing a cessation of the sufferings there."[54] And in a story that bears important relation to Keats's use of classical myth, Hermes was fabled to have delivered Asclepius from his mother Coronis's womb as her body lay burning on its funeral bier. Asclepius was Apollo's son later deified, the famous physician who restored Glaucus to life, and the father of Hygeia and Panacea.[55]

---

53   E. J. Holmyard, *Alchemy* (New York: Dover Publications, Inc., 1990) 97–100.

54   Joseph Spence, *Polymetis* (London: 1747; New York: Garland Publishing, Inc., 1976) 106.

55   The story of Hermes and Asclepius is in Thomas Taylor's translation of Pausanias's *Description of Greece* entitled *Pausanias: The Description of Greece* (London: 1794). The possible links here multiply, especially in the context of *Endymion* with Peona and her well-

These many characteristics of the gods reveal how Hermes-Mercury became mingled with Apollo in Rosicrucian and Masonic mythology and symbology. Lempriere's *Classical Dictionary* and Tooke's *Pantheon* both describe Apollo as the god of the fine arts, including medicine, rhetoric, poetry and music, as well as the god of prophecy and revelatory wisdom, yet virtually all these functions were also ascribed to Thoth and by analogy Hermes-Mercury. In addition, the interchangeable figure of Hermes Trismegistus was granted pre-eminent authority over all these fields and was claimed as author of the most famous texts relating to these fields for centuries. When we consider that authors such as Ovid, Horace and later Spence, also claimed for Hermes-Mercury, not Apollo, the invention of the lyre and the gift of music, it becomes even more difficult to separate these gods, and in Keats's case, I suspect he, like the Rosicrucians and the Masons, often did not.

Indeed, a careful study of Keats's allusions to Hermes reveals that although the critical tendency has been to associate Apollo with the natural world and particularly the elements of gold and silver, the processes of transformation, and the various forms of gradual illumination in Keats's verse and letters, there is ample reason to relate Hermes to these as well.[56] Doing so not only alters the interpretations of Keats's poems, but also reveals a definitive connection between the philosophical concepts discussed in Keats's letters and those expressed more figuratively in his poetry.

In a general sense, the true gold associated with Hermes and Apollo in the processes of the philosopher-alchemists is linked to the "gold image" Walter Evert has called "a sort of universal catalyst" that appears throughout Keats's poetry and combines both his philosophies of poetry and life.[57] If Hermes-Mercury acts as a volatizing principle, he is also Apollonian in his transformative powers. Recognizing the hermetic conflation of symbolism in Hermes and Apollo enables us to expand our interpretations of Keats's writing and include not only a traditional organic or natural process but also a correspondent and explicit alchemical or chemical process that communicates the same concepts and includes Keats's ever-present awareness that the means by which a poet arrives at his goals and his imaginative truths is often as vital as the results of his poetry. These, in turn, allow us to also examine Keats's poetry and letters from Rosicrucian and Masonic perspectives, and when we do, the hermetic associations affirm and magnify previous interpretations of Keats's imagery even while allowing for a greater flexibility in critical approach.

Keats frequently bestows upon Hermes-Mercury the same attributes of Apollo that scholars have used to decipher the meanings in his poetry. In *I stood tip-toe* visions that lead to poetry are closely linked to an open, "light-hearted" sensation the poet describes as "as light, and free / As though the fanning wings of Mercury / Had played upon my heels" (23–26). References to Mercury also include those in Book I of *Endymion* where Pan, the son of Hermes-Mercury, shares with him the role of

---

noted connection to Panacea, and Endymion's and Glaucus's restoring of life to the lovers by means of magic to name only two.

56  Evert discusses the symbolic associations of Apollo in Keats's letters and poetry throughout his chapter "Imitatio Apollinis" 23–87.

57  Evert 50.

presiding over herds and shepherds. Directly following the sacrifice to Pan and the narrator's description of Apollo's "golden splendour," as "A heavenly beacon," that leads to "high contemplating," the shepherds "by divine converse" turn to Elysium and "each one his own anticipated bliss" (I.349; 353–54; 371; 373). One wishes that he will find his child, who will "through those regions be / His messenger, his little Mercury," and while the image fits Hermes-Mercury's functions perfectly, it also is linked to images and concepts we commonly associate with Apollo in Keats's poetry (I.383–84). The setting and light reminiscent of Apollo have led them to a "divine converse" that includes the imaginative vision of the shepherd's "little Mercury" who "with the balmiest leaves his temple bind[s]," (I.382) in an act reminiscent of not only soothing, medicinal balms but also the crowning of poets, as well as Keats's assertion in his 22 November 1817 letter to Bailey that he views the truth of the imagination as akin to "Adam's dream – he awoke and found it truth."[58]

While some might argue the shepherd's wish does not constitute a vision, Keats does provide evidence in his letters that it should be interpreted so. In his November letter, Keats's own musings on the afterlife create a striking parallel when he speculates that "we shall enjoy ourselves here after by having what we called happiness on Earth repeated in a finer tone and so repeated … Adam's dream will do here and seems to be a conviction that Imagination and its empyreal reflection is the same as human Life and its spiritual repetition."[59] Keats argues such things are "Truth" and stipulates we must make use of the imagination to discover them. The positive aspect of imaginative projection in dreams lifts such imaginings into the realm of divine vision, and the prophetic and healthful nature of such visions is here linked to both Hermes-Mercury and Apollo.

When, near the end of Book II, Hermes appears again, the same allusions to visions implied in Book I and stated in *I stood tip-toe* are compounded with the music of the lyre and the pipe. After a night of love, Endymion awakes alone, but the extreme rage of "Love's madness" he felt previously "had pass'd away" and instead, "The lyre of his soul Eolian tun'd / Forgot all violence, and but commun'd with melancholy thought" (II.866–68). Only a few lines later, the imagery of the lyre leads to that of "Hermes' pipe" and "ravishments more keen" (II.876–77). The musical allusions are initially linked to a tempering of Endymion's emotions, and though the visions he first sees are such that they "might have dismay'd / Alecto's serpents," they diffuse themselves into contemplation of his life and those "ravishments" that spur him to necessary action as he rushes into "the earth's deep maw" and "all its buried magic" (II.876; 899–900). The imagery here is one of solace and required physic common both to Apollo and Hermes who once soothed the disquieted souls of Hades, and at other times, spurred mortals to action. In essence, it is beneficial.

The same connotations hold true for the direct reference to Hermes. Although some scholars such as De Almeida have read the effect of Hermes' pipe negatively, it is important to recall that visions and music that might "dismay" Alecto's serpents can be read positively. Alecto was one of the implacable furies with serpents for hair; to dismay her serpents implies a counter to the excessive rage they represent.

---

58  Keats, *Letters I* 184–85.
59  Keats, *Letters I* 184–85.

Furthermore, the phrase "ravishments more keen / Than Hermes' pipe, when anxious he did lean / Over eclipsing eyes," calls to mind much the same effect. The allusion is to a story Keats will reference again in his 1819 sonnet *As Hermes once took to his feathers light* about Dante's lovers Paolo and Francesca. According to the myth, Zeus transformed his lover Io into a heifer that his wife then claimed. Rightly suspicious, Hera set Argus with his thousand eyes to watch over the heifer, but Zeus sent Hermes to try to rescue the maiden. Disguised as a shepherd, Hermes played music and told tales to lull the monster to sleep. In both cases, Hermes's actions are helpful rather than harmful, and significantly, the passages of Keats's verse in which the allusions appear are ones to which Keats attached positive emotions. In the case of *Endymion*, the character Endymion wants the ravishments more keen, and in the case of the sonnet about Paolo and Francesca, Keats describes the dream that led to it as pleasurable and soothing. Hermes's music, by lyre or pipe, relieves the violent emotions and as such it becomes linked to the harmony and physic attributed to Apollo.

The sonnet *As Hermes once took to his feathers light* reinforces the likelihood that Keats held such associations between Hermes and Apollo in his mind. He writes:

> As Hermes once took to his feathers light,
> > When lulled Argus, baffled, swoon'd and slept,
> So on a Delphic reed, my idle spright
> > So play'd, so charm'd, so conquer'd, so bereft
> The dragon-world of all its hundred eyes;
> > And setting it asleep, so fled away – (1–6)

Hermes's music is conflated with that of the poet's "spright" who plays upon a "Delphic reed" sacred to Apollo, and the charmed music leads to a vision of solace where the poet kisses a beautiful girl and "lovers need not tell / Their sorrows" (11–12). Keats viewed the vision in a markedly positive light. When he copied the sonnet into a letter to George and Georgianna in April of 1819 he introduced the poem by writing:

> I had passed many days in rather a low state of mind and in the midst of them I dreamt of being in that region of Hell. The dream was one of the most delightful enjoyments I ever had in my life – ... in the midst of all this cold and darkness I was warm – even flowery tree tops sprung up and we rested on them sometimes with the lightness of a cloud till the wind blew us away again – ... o that I could dream it every night.[60]

He suggests the dream rejuvenated him, and the echoes of lightness both in sense and in heart that he associates with Hermes-Mercury in *I stood tip-toe* are reinforced in this letter where "flowery tree tops" spring up in the same manner as the natural world of delight that appears to lead the speaker to poetry in the earlier work.

Just as Hermes's music tends to offer physic we normally associate with Apollo in Keats's poetry, his wand or caduceus is often figured in the same way. In Book IV

---

60 Keats, *Letters II* 91. De Almeida characterizes "Hermes's false medicine" and "dangerous fancies" as receiving "special mention" in this sonnet and describes Argus as "hapless," but Keats's letter makes it clear he viewed the dream in a far different light (39).

of *Endymion*, the Indian maid ascribes to Hermes's caduceus the ability to transform and thereby restore life. She does so by referring to Hyacinthus – the youth Apollo loved and mortally injured by accident but could not save. She cries out:

> "O for Hermes' wand,
> To touch this flower into human shape!
> That woodland Hyacinthus could escape
> From his green prison, and here kneeling down
> Call me his queen, his second life's fair crown!
> Ah me, how I could love! (IV.66–71)

The powers of transformation and regeneration into a "second life" bestowed by Hermes's wand are the reverse process of Apollo's actions when he discovered he could not heal Hyacinthus's wound, but both sides are ones which yield life and both are linked to love.

Throughout Book IV of *Endymion*, Keats consistently portrays the Indian maid's views as positive. He clarifies this position outside the poem as well when he writes to Bailey that

> I am certain of nothing but of the holiness of the Heart's affections and the truth of Imagination – What the Imagination seizes as Beauty must be truth – whether it existed before or not – for I have the same Idea of all our Passions as of Love they are all in their sublime, creative of essential Beauty –

and then refers him to the maid's song "O Sorrow" as "a representation from the fancy of the probable mode of operating in these Matters."[61] This, too, is the same letter where Keats ties these concepts of love and Imagination to "Adam's dream" which becomes "Truth," and indicates that the afterlife will be the happiness of this life transmuted by Imagination and love into a "finer tone." Just as "Adam's dream" leads to "Truth," the Indian maid's dreams of love do as well, and it is the Indian maid's plight that Keats has in mind, since her song occurs almost immediately after Endymion hears her invoke Hermes and falls in love with her. Given the ways Keats binds these associations together, it seems both Hermes's and Apollo's powers are in play, and such a reading is only reinforced by Hermes's next appearance as Mercury.

When the Indian maid completes her "Sorrow Song" and Endymion openly declares his love for her, a cry of "fearful tone" echoes through the forest, and the new lovers cling to each other, "waiting for some destruction," but it is "foot-feather'd," "sublime" Mercury who appears and not the traditional arrows of a jealous goddess (IV.323; 330–31). Instead of vengeance, as before when his music provided Endymion the passion and will to continue his quest deep into the earth with all its magic, Mercury gives the lovers the necessary means to continue their journey – this time into the air. Light and "sublime," he comes from heaven and swiftly returns there after the magic of his caduceus creates steeds for Endymion and

---

61 Keats, *Letters I* 184–85. The 22 November 1817 letter has long been recognized by scholars as integral to Keats's philosophies. Here, as elsewhere, Keats indicates that "dreams" are not as distinct from "visions" in his philosophies as scholars tend to portray them.

the maiden to mount to heaven, and yet again Keats combines the effect of Hermes-Mercury's magic with Apollonian imagery. The steeds fly through the air "high as eagles," and "like two drops of dew / Exhal'd to Phoebus' lips" they leave the earth "unseen, alone ... but that the free, / The buoyant life of song can floating be / Above their heads" (IV.348–53). And, in a clear allusion to the function scholars typically ascribe to Apollo as one who provides vision and poetic inspiration, the song that floats above them becomes the poet as well, who asks his muse "am I inspired?," then answers his own question affirmatively by stating "I must spread my pinions wide" and "I have beneath my glance / Those towering horses ..." (IV.354; 358–59).

Keats's poem *Mother of Hermes! And still youthful Maia* further indicates that he associated poetic inspiration with both Hermes and Apollo. Maia is first and foremost "Mother of Hermes" and the poet petitions to sing to her, to hymn her, to woo her or seek her smiles because "they once were sought ... by bards who died content ... leaving great verse unto a little clan" (1; 6–8). Moreover, he specifically requests of her that she grant him the "old vigour" possessed by the bards (9). Such relationships between Hermes and Apollo exist throughout Keats's poetry and compound until we reach *Lamia* where the identification of Hermes with Apollo is so pervasive virtually every descriptive term given Hermes also matches Apollo.

In *Lamia*, Keats describes Hermes as leaving his "golden throne," and arriving at Crete in "a celestial heat" of passion "that from a whiteness, as the lily clear, / Blush'd into roses 'mid his golden hair" (I.8; 22; 24–25). Then, again, Lamia tells the god she saw him "sitting, on a throne of gold," and though she says he does not hear Apollo's soothing music, she relates him to the god nonetheless, by saying:

> I dreamt I saw thee, robed in purple flakes,
> Break amorous through the clouds, as morning breaks,
> And, swiftly as a bright Phoebean dart,
> Strike for the Cretan isle; and here thou art! (I.70; 76–79)

Keats equates Hermes with Apollo's sun imagery, and Lamia's dream itself is prophetic. The passage combines Apollo's physical characteristics and his functions and transfers all of them to Hermes. Later, Hermes is described as a "bright planet," at whose brilliance the nymph initially fades, "like a moon in wane," but recovers when she feels his warmth, and in deliberate contrast to the flower "That faints into itself at evening hour," she "like new flowers at morning song of bees / Bloom'd, and gave up her honey to the lees" (I.87; 136–43).[62] Finally, throughout the opening stanzas, Keats repeatedly describes both the god and his actions with adjectives such as light, warm and burning.

As a result of the many conflations throughout Keats's poetic career, Apollo and Hermes-Mercury, while retaining their classical attributes, also take on Rosicrucian and Masonic ones that alter in significant ways the conclusions scholars reach

---

62 Critics often describe the nymph's discovery as a betrayal, as part of a decidedly negative bargain made between Hermes and Lamia in which the nymph loses out, but to do so is to focus solely on her sudden fear and ignore entirely her presence *as the bargain was struck* "near-smiling on the green" and her warm and amorous response to Hermes once he has allayed her fears.

when they use these gods as a means to interpret Keats's poetry. Many scholars have traditionally viewed Apollo as positive and Hermes as suspect. Hermione de Almeida, for example, has attributed "false practice" to Hermes-Mercury and attached negative connotations to him in poems such as *Endymion* and *Lamia*. She has described Hermes-Mercury as representative of "trickery and haste" and harmful transformative powers attributed "not to patiently acquired medicine but to the god of quick fixes."[63] But, there are many instances in which Keats applies to Hermes positive, Apollonian characteristics, and in medicine derived from Renaissance hermetic philosophies some transformations were regarded as beneficial and absolutely vital. As we have seen, Keats himself consistently refers to the process of poetry as one in which the "materials" of the natural world, including life, are transmuted to form "Greater things," and from early on he makes positive reference to many transmutations.

In his light verse *To George Felton Matthew*, no matter how dubious his taste, Keats grants to Matthew greater poetic powers than his own and claims the muse "will [his] every dwelling grace," and fill with sunlight because Apollo has blessed Matthew with a series of transformations from flower, to fish, to swan, and last to human form ("To George Felton Matthew," 1.74–89). The Indian maiden's wish for Hermes's beneficial transformational powers also has been noted. And while some Keatsian transmutations are not beneficial – he portrays Circe's actions in *Endymion* in a decidedly negative light – there is no need to associate Hermes with Circe as scholars sometimes do. In fact, there is ample reason to present the two as foes considering that in traditional mythology it is Hermes who provides Odysseus with the means to resist Circe's charms and advises him how best to make her do his will. And if the hermetic connotations associated with Hermes are considered, the case De Almeida makes for Keats's awareness of the dangers of "trickery," "haste" and "quick fixes" actually becomes clearer and stronger because Circe, distinct from Hermes, is representative not of hermetic philosophies but of the sorcery and false magic they warned against.

When the hermetic philosophies incorporating both Apollo and Hermes are fully taken into account, their emphasis upon the effort, patience and perseverance required to arrive at the hermetic goals makes it clear that "quick fixes" were to be denigrated. Even while acknowledging the possibilities of "false practice," and warning against them, hermetic texts consistently presented views of both gods as necessary to processes associated with physical and spiritual well being. The same Rosicrucian texts and alchemical allegories that described Apollo and Hermes in terms of the desired light and wisdom, and literally designated Mercury as the catalyst by which transformations took place and the hoped for Elixir was obtained, continually warned readers to be on guard against false physic that offered easy success.[64]

---

63  De Almeida 18; 20–21.

64  The *Fama*, the *Confessio*, and *The Chymical Wedding* all contain lengthy warnings that were often reiterated in the prefaces affixed to translations such as Thomas Vaughan's; later Masonic writers made much the same arguments; and writers such as Goethe represented them as well in their fictions.

Making a distinction between an enchantress such as Circe who represents a magic based on negative phantasy and Hermes who more frequently was associated with hermetic philosophies in which transformation is a process completed only by mixing pain, sorrow and toil with hard won love and knowledge better allows for the complexity inherent in Keats's poetry. This is especially true in poems such as *Lamia* where scholars often begin their analysis, positive or negative, by discussing Hermes's and Lamia's interactions. As De Almeida notes in her chapter entitled "The Ambiguity of Snakes," snakes were associated with Thoth, Hermes-Mercury, and Apollo.[65] All of these gods held symbolic significance in hermetic philosophies in general, and alchemical ones in particular, and snakes did as well. When in 1820, Hazlitt remarked that "The principle of the imagination resembles the emblem of the serpent, by which the ancients typified wisdom and the universe, with undulating fold, for ever varying and for ever flowing into itself, – circular, and without beginning or end," he was reiterating the very rationale behind the snake's symbolism in alchemical philosophies.[66]

In addition, Lamia's actual transmutation from snake to woman clearly resembles a chemical process, but that chemical chain reaction is initiated by Hermes and proceeds in a traditional *alchemical* fashion. To somewhat modify Sperry's well known summation of the episode, Lamia is consumed by what resembles nothing so much as the beginning stages of an alchemical transformation:

> ... her elfin blood in madness ran,
> Her mouth foam'd, and the grass, therewith besprent,
> Wither'd at dew so sweet and virulent;
> Her eyes in torture fix'd, and anguish drear,
> Hot, glaz'd, and wide, with lid-lashes all sear,
> Flash'd phosphor and sharp sparks, without one cooling tear.
> The colours all inflam'd throughout her train,
> She writh'd about, convuls'd with scarlet pain:
> A deep volcanian yellow took the place
> Of all her milder-mooned body's grace;
> And, as the lava ravishes the mead,
> Spoilt all her silver mail, and golden brede;
> Made gloom of all her frecklings, streaks and bars,
> Eclips'd her crescents, and lick'd up her stars:
> So that, in moments few, she was undrest
> Of all her sapphires, greens, and amethyst,
> And rubious-argent: of all these bereft,
> Nothing but pain and ugliness were left.
> Still shown her crown; that vanish'd, also she
> Melted and disappear'd as suddenly;

---

65 De Almeida 182–96.

66 As quoted by De Almeida 194. See too *The Complete Works of William Hazlitt*, ed. P. P. Howe. 21 vols. (London: J. M. Dent, 1930–34) 18:371. De Almeida also notes that in Erasmus Darwin's *The Botanic Garden*, Darwin informed readers that the Egyptian Medusa was representative of divine wisdom. Given Darwin's well known membership in Freemasonry, such a connection would have reinforced the hermetic associations of snakes in readers' minds (193).

And in the air, her new voice luting soft,
Cried, "Lycius! Gentle Lycius!" (I.147–68)

As Sperry explains, "a sort of chemical analysis or separation of elements takes place," and Lamia is destroyed only "to ascend from the throes of her ordeal transformed," and "like a vaporous distillation, she flies off, changed to a radiant but almost incorporeal lady."[67] Her experience corresponds exactly with the general alchemical processes in which matter was broken down and separated by means of corrosives and fire, oftentimes ignited by "sulphur," which represented "the Expansive force in Nature" and caused "dissolution" and "evaporation" as it consumed the matter it worked upon, leaving behind a charred or calcinated material that could be again dissolved by recombination with the vapors.[68]

Similarly, whether it is Lamia's "elfin blood" or the foam from her mouth, or both, that is a "dew so sweet and virulent," Keats's choice of words calls to mind a very specific alchemical term long associated with Rosicrucian lore in which the Latin "Ros" for "dew" was used to signify a universal solvent that acted in the manner Keats describes. Likewise, Lamia's searing and sparking as she combusts, and her sudden alterations when her "peacock" colors flash and are consumed, rather than overdone or gaudy as some critics believe, mimic those occurring in alchemical experiments as the process of purification via separation and recombination continued. Alchemists often referred to a burst of fugitive colors symbolizing the progression of a transformation as a "peacock's tail," and even Lamia's crown of stars, last to disappear as she is etherealized, accords well with the ignition of gases in the alchemist's flask.

Furthermore, it is significant that Apollonius of Tyana, the philosopher typically noted as the basis for Keats's character Apollonius, whose gaze ultimately makes Lamia dissolve and vanish, was claimed to be a disciple of Pythagorean philosophies, an author of alchemical texts, and one of the supposed discoverers of the *Emerald Table* attributed variously to Hermes or Hermes Trismegistus.[69] Scholars cite a passage in Burton's *Anatomy of Melancholy* taken from Philostratus's *The Life of Apollonius of Tyana* as Keats's source for the Lamia story, but Keats also may have been aware of connotations associated with Apollonius other than his vanquishing of the Lamia. The passage from Burton certainly is a primary source, but there is no reason to believe the single short passage was Keats's only exposure to information about Apollonius. Burton refers to the philosopher in his preface and throughout *Anatomy of Melancholy*, and the story of the philosopher was well known, in part because of the arguments surrounding his "miracles." Because Apollonius's life story resembled Christ's, those who argued Christ was a man rather than God incarnate often referenced Apollonius in their arguments. As Keats did not believe

---

67  Stuart Sperry, *Keats the Poet* (Princeton: Princeton UP, 1973) 302.

68  For a description of these processes readers may consult Gareth Roberts, *The Mirror of Alchemy: Alchemical Ideas and Images in Manuscripts and Books from Antiquity to the Seventeenth Century* (Toronto: University of Toronto Press, 1994) 57, and C. A. Burland, *The Art of the Alchemists* (London: Weidenfeld & Nicolson, 1967) 72.

69  Holmyard 99.

in the divinity of Christ, he could have known of Apollonius from sources other than Burton.

Throughout Philostratus's *Life of Apollonius*, the author took great pains to distinguish between false magic and that derived from divine wisdom and the study of Nature, and he linked Apollonius's abilities to the knowledge he gained both from Pythagoras and in travels to the East where he ostensibly met and studied with the Magi and sages. Apollonius's exploits made this distinction a particularly important one because he was fabled to have possessed miraculous healing powers, the knowledge of the Elixir, prophetic insight, and the ability to converse in all languages, including those of the animals and birds. Alchemists had long considered Apollonius of Tyana an alchemical adept and teacher of the secrets of Hermes, and he was said to possess precisely the same knowledge and abilities attributed to the Rosicrucians and espouse much the same metaphysics that writers such as William Hutchinson claimed as the basis for Freemasonry's most ancient ideals.[70]

At the same time, however, Apollonius's skills also formed a point of contention. While some authors such as Butler remarked in *Hudibras* that the Rosicrucians claimed affiliation with Apollonius and suggested that their entire fable of Christian Rosenkreutz was based upon the philosopher, others like Thomas Vaughan in his widely circulated preface to his English translation of the Rosicrucian manifestos presented Apollonius as a pretender to the secrets of nature and largely ignorant of not only Pythagoras's philosophies but also the true Mysteries of the East from which the Rosicrucians derived their arts.[71] Vaughan asserted that Apollonius possessed only the most superficial knowledge of the arts attributed to him and instead presented evidence that the Rosicrucians' wisdom came not second-hand from a second-rate philosopher, but rather from the original sages and magi in the East.

After spending considerable time noting and "proving" Apollonius's "gross Ignorance" and lack of "Philosophy," Vaughan concluded, "now if any man will say, that the Brachmans did impart their Mysteries to him, it is apparent enough they did not," and "for my own part, if I durst think him a Philosopher, I should seat him with the Stoics; for he was a great Master of Moral Seventies, and this is all the Character I can give him."[72] The characterization Vaughan employs will strike many readers of Keats's *Lamia* as a particularly apt description of the philosopher who is "austere" with "eye severe" and possessing a "sophist's spleen," and whom Lycius calls at various points "the ghost of folly haunting my sweet dreams," and one who uses "unlawful magic, and enticing lies" (II.157–58, 172; I.377; II.285–86).

The many connections between Hermes, Lamia, Apollonius and alchemy indicate that Lamia's transformation should be read as an alchemical process, and moreover,

---

70 F. C. Coneybeare, preface, *Philostratus's The Life of Apollonius of Tyana*, trans. F. C. Coneybeare (Cambridge, Mass.: Loeb Classical Library, Harvard UP, 1912; 1969).

71 Part II, Canto 3, lines 609–64 of *Hudibras* feature an extended dispute between Hudibras and the charlatan magician Sidrophello about the Rosicrucians and alchemical authors such as Agrippa, Paracelsus, and Boehme as well as Trismegistus, Pythagoras, Zoroaster and Apollonius.

72 Thomas Vaughan, preface, *The Fame and Confession of the Fraternity of R: C: commonly, of the Rosie Cross...* (London: J. M. for Giles Calvert, 1652) <http://www.levity.com/alchemy/vaughanp.html>.

one in which hermetic philosophies figure prominently. Hermes-Mercury acts not as negative or false magic but rather as the catalyst he represented in hermetic lore. As a result, Lamia symbolically represents an element in a process rather than the immoral force posited by scholars who attribute some of her negative aspects, in part, to her interactions with Hermes. When considered in this manner, it becomes clear that, contrary to the suggestions of many critics, the opening episode between Lamia and Hermes does serve a purpose necessary to the rest of the story. Nor is Lamia "shifty," "unknowable" or "destructive" simply because her metamorphosis "defies moral evaluation" as Barry Gradman argues in his work *Metamorphosis in Keats*, where he contends "the somewhat ludicrous travail of her change makes it seem suspect and malign."[73] Instead, she resembles a material that shifts based upon the imagination and desire the philosopher-alchemists posited as key to their work.

Originally trapped in the form of the snake, she becomes fluid thanks to Hermes-Mercury's transformative touch, and she is representative of what Diane Brotemarkle refers to in *Imagination and Myths in John Keats's Poetry* as that which the Imagination works upon through mediators in the form of Hermes and then Lycius.[74] I would add too that she becomes subject to Imagination's counter that, in this poem, Keats figures forth as "*cold* Philosophy" that denies all "charms" and "mysteries," strips the rainbow of its mystical or "awful" aspects, and "clip[s] and Angel's wings" (II.229–35). In this sense, she is much more representative of what men such as Lycius and Apollonius project upon her, and this matches both alchemical allegories and the esoteric alchemical philosophies that warned adepts success and failure depended more upon the mental and spiritual states they projected upon the materials being worked than the materials themselves.

Keats reminds the reader throughout, there is little hope this "experiment" will have a happy ending. There is "woe" and "ruin" in store, but Lamia is not the active cause, and one could argue her demise is caused by extremes in which Lycius demands all and then Apollonius denies all, and both run counter to the hermetic philosophies stressing integration, harmony, and balance. The concept of Lycius and Apollonius as representative of extremes is a common one in analysis. Brotemarkle represents Lycius as the artistic sensibility and Apollonius as "the utilitarian spirit calling the mysterious beauty to account for her identity" and requiring her to "justify her existence" as part and portion of imagination and art.[75] Hermione de Almeida also presents the two men as extremes in her chapter "The Ambiguity of Snakes," but for her they represent extremes in capacities of self-deceit and trickery or sophistry of others.[76] And Clarence D. Thorpe offers the widely accepted argument that in *Lamia* Keats expresses the dangers of "two falsities" in which Lycius's conception

---

73 Barry Gradman, *Metamorphosis in Keats* (New York: New York UP, 1980) 105–106. Gradman draws upon Sperry's assessment in *Keats the Poet* that Keats describes her transformation "rather ludicrously," but Sperry concedes a greater complexity when it comes to her "moral stance" (302).

74 Diane Brotemarkle, *Imagination and Myths in John Keats's Poetry* (San Francisco: Mellen Research UP, 1993) 94–95.

75 Brotemarkle 99. The argument is made throughout her chapter "Lamia: From Honey to Poison?" 81–106.

76 De Almeida 182–96.

of Lamia "represent[s] an existence of phantasy – pure dream," but "Apollonius, on the other hand, stands for cold and factual reasoned knowledge."[77]

Significantly, though, all three stances allow for the poem as an allegorical representation of the challenges inherent in hermetic philosophy, particularly because Keats deliberately evokes sympathy for Lamia. Throughout most of the poem, Lamia does not so much act as react to those around her. She becomes what Lycius desires and demands, thereby relinquishing her immortality and placing herself in harm's way. Then, in Apollonius's case, she is quite literally dissolved – both "material" and life are lost – because he mentally denies the mystery and mysticism inherent in her beauty, and thereby removes the spiritual component necessary to maintain the alchemical process.

When reading the poem with hermetic philosophies in mind, one can appreciate the outcome that has dissatisfied so many readers and scholars. Lamia is simultaneously the focus of both Apollonius's and Lycius's "work," but the true focus of the poem is the contrasting roles of imagination and reason, and the integration of these as well as the need to find and accept a balance between joy and sorrow, the material and spiritual, reality and dreams. As Paracelsus, the Rosicrucians, and later the Freemasons all taught in their various texts and doctrines, the wisdom to which man aspired in hopes of better understanding his own nature and his place in the world, so that he might ultimately achieve transcendence, was grounded in a fruitful experience of all of life's realities. Delight and pleasure could not be "unperplex'd" (I.327) from sorrow, the "noisy world almost forsworn," or youths "from every ill / Of life ... preserv'd" as the characters wish them to be, but neither could all mystery be reduced to a "dull catalogue of common things" (II.33; 296–97; 233). Because the characters cannot move past their desires to do just these things, however, the work, as symbolized by Lamia, is doomed to destruction.

The ambiguity so many readers find in *Lamia* is the continual condition of philosophical alchemy, in which the desire for perfection is always present, but so is the knowledge that to achieve the perfected state one must fuse contraries, and a successful outcome was always in doubt.[78] Indeed, adepts were often warned that failure in this task was almost always guaranteed because the very desire that compelled men to attempt the "Great Work" could also lead them astray. The impulse to separate out joy, deny reality, and immerse oneself in the false gold of a phantasy was acknowledged as the greatest danger, and in a metaphysical sense, even the ultimate achievement of transcendence was understood as something perhaps only fully attainable after death.

---

77 Clarence D. Thorpe, preface, *John Keats: Complete Poems and Selected Letters* (New York: Odyssey Press, 1935) xliii–xliv.

78 David Perkins refers to this impulse as "the quest for permanence" and writes that "One aspect, for example, is typified by romantic transcendentalism or romantic Platonism, except that here they are discussed in terms of emotional response." The emotional response he refers to was a vital component of Freemasonry's blend of transcendentalism and Neo-Platonism. David Perkins, *The Quest for Permanence: The Symbolism of Wordsworth, Shelley and Keats* (Cambridge, Mass.: Harvard UP, 1965) 3.

As in Keats's "Vale of Soul-making," the best that could be aspired to in this physical life was to gain wisdom of both mind and heart, to "feel and suffer in a thousand diverse ways," and so create individualized souls with identities which still might be "sparks of the divinity," "sparks of his own essence" that after death could return to union with the divinity but nonetheless possess "a bliss peculiar to each one's individual existence."[79] Implicit in Keats's statements throughout his Soul-making letter is his belief that the imagination plays a vital role in achieving this goal, and because it is imagination that acts upon and transmutes Lamia in a traditional hermetic fashion, here again, recognizing the correlations to hermetic philosophies shifts interpretations of the poem. Rosicrucian and Masonic philosophies maintained that while the possibility of ever achieving the ultimate goal remained in doubt, doubt did not preclude the effort, or the hope, and the attempts themselves could help man to individualize his soul just as Keats suggests. The value, then, remained, albeit as one granted after death.

When *Lamia* is considered with this in mind, the poem becomes an allegory reflecting both the desire for such a state and an attempt to achieve it, but a flawed one similar to others that Keats suggests in his letters and poetry simply cannot succeed because the participants do not pursue an integration of all life's experiences in which "the heart must feel and suffers in a thousand diverse ways!" It does not, however, negate the attempt. The poet may hope for a state of happiness, and his poetry may help him and others move closer to that state, provided readers understand that he recognizes the allure of self-deception as ever present in the process and knows even if man may somehow avoid the dangers, the salvation offered by the imagination may occur only after mortal life has passed.

Thus, *Lamia*, long considered by critics as a repudiation of ideas espoused by Keats in his earlier letters and his poetry such as *Endymion*, represents instead a more sophisticated acknowledgement of the difficulties that underlie the task Keats has set himself as poet who will provide physic to man in both humanistic and spiritual contexts. Keats's ideals and chosen process remain consistent, even as he illustrates the ways in which men can lose their way, and these concepts were central to several of Keats's most crucial philosophical speculations in his letters and poetry long before he composed *Lamia*.

---

79 Keats, letter to George and Georgianna, 21 April 1819, *Letters II* 102–103. As Alexander Piatigorsky notes, these concepts were embodied in both the Rosicrucian and Masonic rituals and legends. Alexander Piatigorsky, *Who's Afraid of Freemasons? The Phenomenon of Freemasonry* (London: The Harvill Press, 1997) 294–310.

# Chapter Four

# Hermeticism in the *Endymion* Letters

Keats's letters of 1817 to Benjamin Bailey have often played key roles in the analysis of his thought and poetry, in part because they serve as a starting point for elucidation of his philosophies. So much of what he discusses at length in his letters to Bailey reappears in letters to others and in his poetry that any examination of Keats's writings must take these into account.

Scholars tend to divide their analysis of the letters to Bailey upon lines separating the spiritual from the material. Some interpret Keats's language in Neo-Platonic or theological terms and attribute it to his exposure to Platonic texts via Bailey and their conversations about religion. Others argue that the same language is derived from Keats's chemical studies and suggest that because of Bailey's academic nature, Keats felt comfortable using scientific terms with him.[1] But, while scholars such as Stuart Sperry and Donald Goellnicht rightly point to chemical terms, and note that Keats was not the first to describe the poetic process using such terms, they inevitably provide examples of previous authors who were exposed to explicitly hermetic texts.[2] Wordsworth and Coleridge are both frequently cited, and both were very familiar with Boehme, whose ideas were derived from Paracelsian philosophy, associated with Rosicrucianism, and figured forth via alchemical allegory and linguistics. Erasmus Darwin's and Goethe's works are also often cited, and again, both men studied alchemy and both men were Freemasons. The alchemical origins of both chemistry and the terminology Keats uses, and the popular associations of that terminology with the societies and their philosophies, makes it far more likely that Keats's language represents a stance between the two interpretive poles scholars have argued and in the scientific and metaphysical blend Paracelsus created and the secret societies adopted and popularized.

Given the Neo-Platonic currents and metaphysical aspects of the Paracelsian and Rosicrucian alchemical philosophies which also formed the basis for much of Freemasonry's symbolism, and Keats's exposure to Paracelsus in his studies as well as the strictly material aspects of chemistry and medicine Paracelsus pioneered, Keats probably intended his comments to Bailey to be interpreted in spiritual and material ways. While staying with Bailey, Keats discussed philosophy, theology, and Neo-Platonism as well as his theories surrounding poetry, and Bailey's familiarity with both the metaphysical and scientific realms would have made him a wonderful audience. Paracelsian, Rosicrucian, and Masonic ideas and texts with explicit

---

1    Donald C. Goellnicht, *The Poet-Physician: Keats and Medical Science* (Pittsburgh: University of Pittsburgh Press, 1984) 53. Stuart Sperry, "The Chemistry of the Poetic Process," *Keats the Poet* (Princeton: Princeton UP, 1973) 30–71.

2    Goellnicht 54.

examples of alchemical metaphors illustrating the benefits the imagination and the imaginative process could provide to man's spirit seem to be likely sources for Keats's vocabulary.

For example, in a late October 1817 letter to Bailey, Keats appears to be examining many hermetic ideas espoused by Paracelsus, the Rosicrucians, and various Masonic groups and synthesizing them with his own perspectives. Although each reference or concept appears insignificant in isolation, when we follow the flow of Keats's thoughts and the context in which he expresses them, the overall effect is striking. When he wrote to Bailey, Keats was immersed in Book IV of *Endymion* and attempting to finish despite various concerns and distractions, including a growing desire to be done with the poem and a nagging sense that he had been neglecting Bailey. Throughout the letter, he counters his sense of guilt and his inclinations with allusions that recall his belief that poetry in general, and ostensibly his own, may yet do some good in the world. In the process, he draws together various concepts such as the Paracelsian contention that man's health and spirits are intimately connected and the corresponding belief that imagination plays a central role in mediating between the two.

In his letter, Keats first provides Bailey with a portion of the opening to Book IV of *Endymion* that acts as a framing device for the speculations with which he follows it. He writes:

Muse of my Native Land. Loftiest Muse!
O First born of the Mountains, by the hues
Of Heaven on the spiritual air begot –
Long didst thou sit alone in northern grot ...
... Long didst thou sit amid our regions wild
Wrapt in a deep, prophetic Solitude.
There came a hebrew voice of solemn Mood
Yet wast thou patient: then sang forth the Nine
Apollo's garland; yet didst thou divine
Such homebred Glory, that they cry'd in vain ...
... A higher Summons – still didst thou betake
Thee to thy darling hopes. O thou has won
A full accomplishment – the thing is done
Which undone these our latter days had risen
On barren Souls. O Muse thou knowest what prison
Of flesh and bone curbs and confines and frets
Our Spirit Wings: despondency besets
Our pillows and the fresh tomorrow morn
Seems to give forth its light in very scorn
Of our dull uninspired snail paced lives.
Long have I said "how happy he who shrives
To thee" – but then I thought on Poets gone
And could not pray – nor can I now – so on
I move to the end in Humbleness of Heart. [3]

---

3    John Keats, *The Letters of John Keats, 1814–1821*, ed. Hyder Rollins, vol. 1 (Cambridge, Mass.: Harvard UP, 1958) 172–73. Hereafter, this work will be referred to as *Letters I*.

England's Muse is given full praise for her perseverance despite the long time in which she waited for fruition of her hopes, "wrapt in a deep, prophetic Solitude," resisting the calls of "a hebrew voice of solemn Mood," and "the Nine Apollo's Garland," and her description as well as her actions reflect hermetic philosophies. Her "prophetic solitude" and the "hebrew voice" she hears speak to the long held associations of hermeticism with prophecy and the Hebrew Cabala. Keats eventually changed the second phrase to "an eastern voice," for the printed version of the poem, and the later variation emphasizes a positive and powerful knowledge like that embodied by Apollo's nine and Ausonia and reinforces the hermetic allusion because of the Romantic period's broader assumption that the wisdom of the *Hermetica* and the spiritual guidance it contained originated in the East.[4]

In addition, there is yet another reason to view Keats's English Muse in hermetic terms. She is "by the hues of Heaven on the spiritual air begot," thereby resembling one of the Paracelsian intermediary spirits born of the ether and popularly known in various Rosicrucian texts. In accordance with the Rosicrucian doctrine of spirits, she provides an inspiration that counters the "despondency" of "dull uninspired snail paced lives" that "frets our Spirit Wings." And, in alchemical terms, her origins and residence in something more than the common atmosphere suggest her function as well. As Walter Pagel explains in his work *Paracelsus: An Introduction to Philosophical Medicine in the Era of the Renaissance*, alchemical philosophy included a "spiritual air" that "concentrates into itself all the celestial influxes and … like a divine mirror … reflects all things made by nature and art and all languages and speech. Penetrating into the pores of the skin, it forces all that it carries into man – to whom it appears in the form of dreams and prophecies."[5]

This same "air" became more commonly known as "ether," and during the Romantic period, theories surrounding ether received widespread attention in a variety of fields and also became linked to the secret societies.[6] In the same passages of *Proofs of a Conspiracy* in which Robison denounced Paine and Priestly, he also lamented that Newton had ever popularized the theory of ether and castigated "the unmeaning jargon of Dr. Hartley," who dared to suggest that "supreme intelligence" might be "a more extensive, and (perhaps they will call it) refined undulation, pervading or mixing with all others."[7] Newton's concept of ether was based in part

---

4    Masonic author W. L. Wilmshurst explains the symbolic significance of the East as "East is our eternal source of Light and Life," and "every candidate finds himself in a state of Darkness, in the West," but "after many tribulations and adversities incident to human life, he may at length ascend purified and chastened by experience, to larger life in the Eternal East." The East represents spirituality and wisdom gained via life in the West or "the world of reason" (29–30). W. L. Wilmshurst, *The Meaning of Masonry. A Philosophical Exposition of the Character of the Craft* (London: Lund, Humphries & Co.; Whitefish, MT: Kessinger Publishing, 2007).

5    Walter Pagel, *Paracelsus: An Introduction to Philosophical Medicine in the Era of the Renaissance* (Basel: Karger, 1958) 299.

6    Sperry provides an overview of theories surrounding ether and sensation in "A Poetry of Sensation," *Keats the Poet* 3–29.

7    John Robison, *Proofs of a Conspiracy Against All the Religions and Governments of Europe Carried on in the Secret Meetings of Freemasons, Illuminati and Reading Societies*

on the philosophies and processes of alchemy, and we now know that the majority of his life's work was spent engaged in alchemical studies and a religious, philosophical pursuit for mystic truth, and that this fact was better known during the eighteenth century – particularly by the men of the Royal Society whose historical founders expressed similar interests.[8] And, as Hermione de Almeida notes throughout *Romantic Medicine and John Keats*, medicine was one of the fields of study in which the concept of ether was discussed, and it was used in debates on principles of vitalism that hearkened back to many of the same Renaissance world views scholars such as Abrams have designated as grounded in hermeticism.

The spiritual air of alchemical philosophy became an object of study in relation to concepts of sensation, instinct and imagination, and while many critics stress Keats's scientific knowledge of ether, his poetry suggests he also was aware of the hermetic connotations, and references to the air in his poetry preceding *Endymion* support this view. In *Sleep and Poetry*, sleep's "soothing," "healthful" functions give way quite naturally to poetry that comes upon men

> ... sometimes like a gentle whispering
> Of all secrets of some wond'rous thing
> That breathes about us in the vacant air;
> So that we look around with prying stare,
> Perhaps to see shapes of light, aerial limning,
> And catch soft floatings from a faint-heard hymning;
> ... Sometimes it gives a glory to the voice,
> And from the heart up-springs, rejoice! Rejoice!
> Sounds which will reach the Framer of all things,
> And die away in ardent mutterings. (2; 7; 229–40)

Poetry, like Keats's Muse born of spiritual air, is depicted as a breeze that grants men visions, lifts their hearts, and inspires their voices with an "awful, sweet and holy" response to the Divinity (*Sleep and Poetry* 25). It breathes "rich benedictions" and acts as "a friend / To soothe the cares, and lift the thoughts of man" (*Sleep and Poetry*, 222; 246–47).

Similarly, it is to "Poesy," that Keats offers "ardent prayer" and asks that poetry might:

> Yield from thy sanctuary some clear air,
> Smoothed for intoxication ...
> ... that I may die a death
> Of luxury, and my young spirit follow
> The morning sun-beams to the great Apollo
> Like a fresh sacrifice; or if I can bear
> The o'erwhelming sweets, 'twill bring me to the fair
> Visions of all places ... (*Sleep and Poetry*, 53–63).

---

(New York; London, 1798; Whitefish, MT: Kessinger Publishing, 2007) 276–78.

8    B.J.T. Dobbs, *The Foundations of Netwon's Alchemy or the Hunting of the Green Lyon* (Cambridge: Cambridge UP, 1975) and *The Janus Face of Genius: The Role of Alchemy in Newton's Thought* (Cambridge: Cambridge UP, 1991). Boyle and Leibniz shared his fascination and devoted significant effort to the same studies, as did Ashmole and others.

Poesy's "clear air" intoxicates like an elixir, and though its supplicant may die, his death is one which exalts his spirit and draws him to heaven, and in an indication of future intent, if he is strong enough, the speaker, like Endymion, and the narrator of his tale and later of *The Fall of Hyperion*, will gain visions and insight beyond the traditional scope of mortal man. If he can survive, it will enable him to

> Write on my tablets all that was permitted,
> All that was for our human senses fitted.
> Then the events of this wide world I'd seize
> Like a strong giant, and my spirit teaze
> Till at its shoulders it should proudly see
> Wings to find out an immortality. (*Sleep and Poetry*, 79–84)

The immortality he seeks is bound to the poetry he will create that is inspired by this potent spiritual air. These lines presage those Keats directs to his English Muse and both rely upon a conception of air similar to that espoused by Paracelsus and the Rosicrucians. Indeed, Keats's English Muse literally acts as its summation, linking nature and art to both the heavens and man and providing an inspiration and physic so vital to the imagination and spirit that she resists the highest "Summons" of her counterparts.

His Muse has won "A full accomplishment – the thing is done / Which undone these our latter days had risen / On barren Souls," and her knowledge of "what prison / Of flesh and bone curbs and confines and frets / Our Spirit Wings" enables her to offer succor. So much so that Keats asserts "'Long have I said 'how happy he who shrive{s} / To thee'," although when he thinks of what he might be compared to "Poets gone," he cannot pray to her and so must "move to the end in Humbleness of Heart." Nonetheless, in these lines, he provides both her task, that of the great poets, and though he feels humbled, his own as well. He praises her and would pray to her were he not so aware of how far his own accomplishment lies in view of hers and poets passed, yet his humility does not negate his hope. Like her, he too has been "alone," "confined at Hampstead" by his will to finish his poem despite his knowledge of "How much toil! How many days!" and "what desperate turmoil!" he will endure before achieving "the vast idea ... the end and aim of Poesy" as "a friend to sooth the cares, and lift the thoughts of man" (*Sleep and Poetry*, 307–308; 291–93; 245–47).[9]

Keats has taken the ideas of the ethereal quintessence and the spirits and transferred them to the Muse, and his conception of the Muse and the poetry she inspires is the counterpart to Paracelsus's philosophy that "Imagination is Creative Power," "Medicine uses imagination fixed," and "He who is born in imagination discovers the latent forces of Nature," by which, if he is resolute, he "can accomplish all things," both medically and spiritually.[10] In addition, because Keats's Muse acts not only as representative of imagination but also poetry and the function it serves, the poets she inspires also become intermediaries just as Paracelsus envisioned

---

9   Keats, *Letters I* 172.

10  Paracelsus, "Interpretatio alia Totius Astronomiae," *The Life and Soul of Paracelsus*, trans. and ed. John Hargrave (London: Victor Gollancz, Ltd., 1951) 102.

alchemist-physicians fulfilling the same role by preparing the medicines for man's body and spirit that the common man could not prepare himself. The entire system of correspondences and the process of analogy Keats suggests echoes that of the Rosicrucians who knew well that man was beset by care, "fear, hunger, poverty, sickness and age," that left the heart and spirit in despondency but believed that the harmony of the divine, Nature, and man could be renewed through the gifts of imagination, revelation and knowledge both of the self and the world.[11]

The medicine – whether it is the hermetic physic or poetry – ministers to both the body and the spirit, and Keats makes this same connection in his thought processes as his letter to Bailey continues. Aside from the way in which the poetic passage calls to mind the arguments of *Sleep and Poetry* with its suggestion of poetry as counter to the "despondency that besets our Pillows," references to health – his own, Tom's, Bailey's and others' – run throughout the letter. They also form a significant portion of Keats's postscript which itself refers back to a passage in the middle of the letter, adding another hermetic nuance. Keats remarks in his postscript that "A Question is the best beacon towards a little Speculation," because Bailey has asked after his "health and spirits," and comments "Health and Spirits can only belong unalloyed to the selfish Man – the Man who thinks much of his fellows can never be in Spirits." Immediately afterwards, he follows this with a second postscript in which he asks Bailey's forgiveness for having written too brief a letter.

His "neglect" of Bailey has been bothering him, and Bailey's kindness has stung him to remorse. His own tendency to isolate himself from his friends and immerse himself in work but then be troubled by his conscience leads him, in the body of the letter,

> to suppose that there are no Men thoroughly wicked – so as never to be self-spiritualized into a kind of sublime Misery ... he is the only Man "who has kept watch on man's Mortality" who has philanthropy enough to overcome the disposition [to] an indolent enjoyment of intellect – who is brave enough to volunteer for uncomfortable hours.[12]

An "x" appears directly after this comment, and Hyder Rollins notes that it links this passage not to the first postscript, but rather, the second in which Keats again apologizes for not writing sooner or more. However, both postscripts are pertinent to the passage. The "Misery" Keats mentions in the body of the letter is caused by the same sort of self-awareness that he links to low spirits and poor health, and both passages contain echoes of alchemy in the phrases "self-spiritualized into a kind of sublime" and "unalloyed" health and spirits.

Throughout his career, Keats links poetry to his conviction that the welfare of the body and soul are related. His thoughts both in the letter and the postscript, following as they do the verse from *Endymion*, support and parallel claims he makes later in *The Fall of Hyperion*. The visionary poet learns from the Muse-like "High Prophetess" Moneta that "None can usurp this height ... But those to whom the miseries of the world are misery, and will not let them rest," and he explicitly posits

---

11  *Confessio Fraternitatis*, trans. Thomas Vaughan (1652), transcriber, Kevin Day (Sept. 2002), <http://www.levity.com/alchemy/confessi.html>.

12  Keats, *Letters I* 173.

himself as "favored for unworthiness" and "medicin'd" by the "propitious parley" her visions offer directly before he states "sure a poet is a sage; a humanist, physician to all men" (I.147–48; 183; 189–90). In this sense, Keats's description of the poet as sage, humanist and physician matches that of Rosicrucians – it is their description as well.

With such connotations in mind, Keats's choice to characterize his thoughts as "Speculation" and his use of the terms "unalloyed," "self-spiritualized" and "sublime" directly relate them to the primacy of the imagination in alchemical philosophy. They echo Paracelsus's opinion that the imagination is the "spirit which speculates" and enables man to investigate his own nature and the arts and sciences so he can do both "the work of the cabbalistic 'rector'," and administer to the "corporeal" body.[13] Like Keats, the alchemist-philosophers acknowledged that the state of the world was such that "Health and Spirits can only belong unalloyed to the selfish Man," and considered their Philosopher's Stone a metaphor for the reformation of the world and man so that health and spirits might be improved in all men. This concept is reiterated throughout both the *Fama* and the *Confessio* and in which they differentiate their true alchemy from that of "false Alchemists" whose "lying tinctures" do nothing to lessen the world's "innumerable miseries."[14]

Furthermore, implicit in this is the oft-stressed realization by the Rosicrucian alchemists and Keats that their respective tasks would be enormously difficult. In works such as the *Fama, Confessio* and *Chymical Wedding*, as well as countless other texts, adepts were continually warned that the path to success was strewn with obstacles, and success was dependent on their industry as well as wisdom and insight granted by a divine power. Oftentimes, as in the *Chymical Wedding*, the adept was portrayed as poignantly aware of his own unworthiness and even lack of knowledge but determined to continue in his task and rely upon his faith and hope. In addition, the same concepts were figured forth in various ceremonies surrounding higher degree Freemasonry, and because the ceremonies employed hermetic symbolism and had been widely publicized, Keats might well have been aware of them.

For example, in the initiation rituals for the Royal Arch degrees of Masonry, a candidate found himself literally and metaphorically "in a state of darkness," blindfolded and bound in ropes to symbolize his ignorance, and enjoined by "Sojourners" to embark upon a "mystical quest" through a "difficult and dangerous pass" entailing physical obstacles such as the "rugged road" and veils symbolizing the four elements.[15] He was, however, consoled and urged on by the promise that though he would be led in unknown paths, in the inner sanctum of the temple, the darkness would be made light and the wisdom of the secret mysteries would be revealed to him, and from these, he would gain his freedom. Like the speaker in

---

13 Paracelsus, *Opera Omnia*, tom. II, 472. A. *De Virtute Imaginativa*, tract II, trans. C. H. Josten, as quoted by Desiree Hirst, *Hidden Riches: Traditional Symbolism from the Renaissance to Blake* (New York: Barnes & Noble, Inc., 1964) 66–67.

14 *Confessio Fraternitatis.*

15 Alexander Piatigorsky, *Who's Afraid of Freemasons? The Phenomenon of Freemasonry* (London: The Harvill Press, 1997) 132–37. The quotes are taken directly from the ritual Piatigorsky provides.

*Sleep and Poetry*, those who were "athirst to gain a noble end, thirsty every hour" were charged to fight "Despondence" though not yet

> ...wealthy in the dower
> Of spanning wisdom; though [they] did not know
> The shiftings of the mighty winds that blow
> Hither and thither all the changing thoughts
> Of man: though no great ministering reason sorts
> Out the dark mysteries of human souls
> To clear conceiving ...

precisely because the "vast idea" and hope were held out before them from which they might "glean" their "liberty" (281–92).

While this last passage from *Sleep and Poetry* predates Keats's October letter, the concepts within it match the flow of thoughts in his letter where references to his diligence and hard work inevitably refer to poetry and his conception of the poet as one who must withstand "uncomfortable hours" to be a friend to man, thereby providing yet another link between his comments to Bailey and the hermetic philosophies I have been discussing. Keats's verse praising the English Muse's perseverance also is bounded before and after by lines in which he worries about how little attention he has paid his friends and then almost immediately reiterates his determination to "keep as tight a reign as possible" until he has completed *Endymion*. His belief that only a man "who has philanthropy enough to overcome the disposition to an indolent enjoyment of intellect" can "[keep] watch on man's Mortality" leads him directly to a critique of Wordsworth's "Gypsies," and though he thinks it unfair to attack Wordsworth on the subject, his major point is that the poem seems "to have been written in one of the most comfortable Moods of his life" and thus is not so much a "Speculation" or "search after Truth" as "a kind of sketchy intellectual Landscape." And finally, his postscript on the possibility of unalloyed health and spirits places the reader right back into the midst of these lines.

If this were the only letter in which connections exist between hermetic philosophies and Keats's own, such arguments as I have made could be dismissed, but other letters of a similar nature soon follow. In November, Keats writes to Bailey and makes significant reference to sensations in such a way that hermetic philosophies are again called to mind. In his November 3 letter, Keats writes of "the great Consolations of Religion and undepraved Sensations. of the Beautiful, the poetical in all things."[16] Robert Ryan argues, correctly I believe, that "Keats seems to mean that a clear perception of the beauty to be found everywhere in the universe – a beauty that is regular and orderly and therefore the work of a Creator ... is enough to convince anyone whose sensations are not depraved ... that a benevolent deity presides over our destiny."[17] He bases his conclusion upon a contention that Keats is using "sensation" in a way Bailey would have understood based upon his studies of the Scottish moral sense philosopher Francis Hutcheson. Ryan, however, is not the first to attempt to decipher Keats's November letters to Bailey based upon

---

16  Keats, *Letters I* 179.
17  Robert Ryan, *Keats: The Religious Sense* (Princeton: Princeton UP, 1976) 127.

an understanding of the concept of sensation, and a brief review of some of the arguments put forth can better illustrate both how Keats may be employing views influenced by hermeticism and how these views encompass a broader range of meaning than many may suspect.

When Stuart Sperry addressed the issues surrounding Keats's conception of sensation in the opening chapter of his work *Keats the Poet*, he acknowledged both the importance of the term in any study of Keats's letters and poetry and the lack of agreement among scholars when it comes to just what Keats meant by the term.[18] As Sperry noted, some such as Sir Sidney Colvin have argued that "what [Keats] means are intuitions of the mind and spirit ... independent of all consecutive stages and formal processes of thinking," and Clarence Thorpe defined Keats's use of the term as "feelings or intuitions, the pure activity of the imagination."[19] On the opposite end of the spectrum were opinions such as those offered by Walter Jackson Bate who believed Keats followed "Hazlitt's constant use of the word 'sensations' in the traditional empirical sense – as virtually equivalent to concrete experience."[20] Somewhat more in the middle, Sperry offered his own assessment, that "Keats's use of the word, while denoting specific physical impressions, moves beyond the realm of sense experience," and "encompasses much more – feeling, sensibility, and the world of interior consciousness."[21] Ultimately, Sperry concluded that while Keats appeared to conceive of sensation as "a *process*, an assimilation of outer stimulus and inner response," he "never use[d] 'sensation' to refer to anything that might be described as immediate apprehension of a higher reality," and "there is no need for, nor does Keats's metaphor advance, any transcendental hypothesis to account for it."[22]

There is reason, however, to combine the differing views of all these scholars, and Sperry's acknowledgement of sensation as a "process" offers the means by which to do so. Keats has been using hermetic allusions and, as will become clear, he does so throughout his November letters to Bailey, and hermeticism did contain within it elements of transcendental mysticism. The secret societies of Keats's time employed a hermetic blend derived from Paracelsian and Rosicrucian theories linking sensations, the imagination, and the spirit, and these theories explicitly posited sensation as just the process Sperry describes. At the most basic level, sensation was understood as Hazlitt and Bate described it, but it progressed by degrees to encompass much more including the emotional and intellectual aspects Sperry recognizes in Keats's use of the term, and stimulating the sensations was understood as a vital way for man to approach an "apprehension of a higher reality." When Sperry remarks that Keats's understanding of sensation and its use in his poetry reflect the intellectual milieu of

---

18  Sperry 3.

19  Sir Sidney Colvin, *John Keats: His Life and Poetry, His Friends, Critics, and After-Fame* (London: C. Scribner Sons, 1917) 155. Clarence Dewitt Thorpe, *The Mind of John Keats* (New York: Oxford UP, 1926) 64. Sperry provides both of these quotes. I am indebted to his analysis throughout his chapter "A Poetry of Sensation" and draw heavily upon his gathering of the evidence (3–29).

20  Walter Jackson Bate, *John Keats* (Cambridge, Mass: Harvard UP, 1963) 240.

21  Sperry 5–6.

22  Sperry 6–7.

the Romantic period, he is correct. Many of the theories of the philosophers who attempted to bridge the gap between nature and mind, and even of those who asserted sensation resided primarily in the mind distinct from matter, possessed elements of hermeticism. Hartley's philosophy taken from Newton and based on "the notion of a very subtle and elastic fluid or 'Aether' diffused throughout space and occupying even 'the Pores of gross Bodies,'" made explicit use of a concept derived from the Paracelsian theories of spiritual air we have already seen in Keats's writing.[23]

Similarly, other philosophers who proposed a progression through the senses in conjunction with a refinement of the imaginative powers as a vital part of the physical and mental improvement of men were also Freemasons, and some were linked in the public mind with the higher "Occult" or "Scotch" degrees conflated with alchemical and Rosicrucian theories. Hume, D'Alembert, and Stewart were famous members of Masonic degrees. Theories such as Stewart's that "nothing but a species of *instinct*, more sure in its operation than reason itself, could so forcibly transport us across the gulf by which mind seems to be separated from the material world," paralleled arguments made in Masonic texts, lectures and rituals in which men were encouraged to follow a program of sense development that began in the material, but ultimately strove for an instinctual and imaginative apprehension of beauty, wisdom and self-knowledge in an attempt to bring the self into harmony with nature and the will of the Creator. Masonic rituals included a process by which candidates moved through symbolic points of the compass representative of their journey through life. The Northern point on the ritual compass represented man's senses not yet turned to refined purpose, but as men progressed through their journey, they learned to use their senses to help them gain wisdom and reach an "illuminated human intelligence and understanding, which results from the material brain-mind being thoroughly permeated and enlightened by the Spiritual Principle."[24]

As a result of such associations, there is no need to overlook any of Keats's many uses of the term sensations; they all played a role in the progression. Likewise, there is no reason to insist that Keats's metaphors and analogies have no link to transcendental philosophies. In fact, philosophies with transcendental implications such as those that Hutcheson espoused parallel those expressed in various Masonic books of the period like William Preston's *Illustrations of Masonry* and William Hutchinson's *Spirit of Freemasonry* in which "our ability to perceive regularity, order, and harmony in the universe ... an 'internal sense,' distinct from the five external senses" was designated as part and portion of the "sensations" and encouraged.[25] Following the same philosophies of the Rosicrucians, the Freemasons also argued that study of the arts and sciences, the beauties of nature, and the affection of the heart – all elements which engaged the traditional five senses – could lead to an amplification of this internal strength. Indeed, William Preston made an argument similar to Hutcheson's in his lectures discussing the beauties of Geometry that served as a preface to his own Hutchesonian portrayal of "The Senses." According to Preston, "the contemplation of this science in a moral and comprehensive view

23 Sperry 20.
24 Wilmshurst 93; 103.
25 Ryan 125.

fills the mind with rapture," and all the Liberal Arts as well as Nature espouse a "symmetry, beauty, and order" that yield "pleasing and delightful themes, and naturally lead to the source whence the whole is derived."[26]

The arguments regarding sense and perception made in Rosicrucian and Masonic texts in general also can be extended to include underlying hermetic philosophies that made an even more explicit link between the "Sensations" and the spiritual. And, given the way in which Keats elaborates upon his belief in "a Life of Sensations" in his 22 November 1817 letter to Bailey and intermingles the concepts of Sensation and Imagination, all the while making use of markedly alchemical terminology, that letter too should be examined with hermetic – specifically Paracelsian and by extension Rosicrucian and Masonic – philosophies in mind. Just as Keats's 3 November letter has been the focus of much scholarly debate, his 22 November letter has as well, and perhaps even more so because this is the letter in which Keats discusses his conjectures about the nature of the afterlife. The letter, much like his later Vale of Soul-making letter, represents one of his rare and detailed expositions about religious questions and his philosophy of life that scholars rely upon for guidance when they study these issues in his letters and then apply their analyses to his poetry. Because of the letter's importance, the appearance within it of several Paracelsian philosophies demands an extended discussion of these concepts in order to fully understand how their presence may alter our interpretations of Keats's speculations, and the best way to understand their effect is to give them in full.

The alchemical philosophies put forth by Paracelsus stressed that all of creation, including man, was comprised of two bodies – the visible and the invisible, the material and the spiritual, the corporal and the eternal. In his work *Archidoxis*, Paracelsus explained that "every man is made up of two portions, that is to say, of a material and of a spiritual body. Matter gives the body, the blood, the flesh; but the spirit gives hearing, sight, feeling, touch and taste."[27] Sensation, even at its most basic, was understood as a portion of the spirit. The senses were viewed as the means by which the imagination was stimulated, and because their inlets were in the physical body of man, they formed a necessary conduit between the material and the spiritual. This same concept, so integral to Paracelsian theories also found expression in the catechisms of Masonic rituals of Keats's time where initiates were taught the physical senses functioned as entrances to the spiritual mysteries of Masonry by enabling man to fully engage his imagination in a study of the "Seven Liberal Sciences" and those "teachings of the heart" that led him to the "Light."[28]

---

26 William Preston, *Illustrations of Masonry* (1772; Louisville: American Masonic Publishing Association, 1858) 43. See also Ibid. at Part IV, "Remarks on the Second Lecture," for further discussion of the senses.

27 Paracelsus, *Paracelsus: Essential Readings*, trans. and ed. Nicholas Goodrick-Clarke (Wellingborough: Crucible, Thorsons Publishing Group, 1990) 67.

28 See, for example, *Three Distinct Knocks* in A. C. F. Jackson's *English Masonic Exposures 1760–1769* (London: Lewis Masonic, 1986) 78–79. The Master of the Lodge quizzes initiates as to why "Five make a Lodge?"; "Because every Man is endued with Five Senses." As the questioning continues the candidate explains that the senses and the Seven Liberal Sciences are instrumental in a full understanding of "the Word" and "the Light" to

Ultimately, what the imagination derived from the senses and created based upon them took precedence over materiality. As the "Creative Power," imagination existed "in the perfect spirit."[29] Thus, Paracelsus and the Rosicrucians were able to maintain that "Because Man does not imagine perfectly at all times, arts and sciences are uncertain," but nonetheless "in fact, they are certain and [when] obtained by means of imagination, can give true results. Imagination takes precedence over all."[30] Moreover, as the means by which man could discern the signs of the true, invisible world and ultimately take part in the spiritual life, the imagination created a reality unattainable by simple, "corporeal understanding." As a one Masonic catechism expressed the concept when candidates were quizzed about the truths they experienced through their senses during the ritual, it was "Nothing that reason can grasp."[31]

In *De Virtute Imaginitiva* Paracelsus emphasized the imagination's role in perception and described the imaginative process as a mingling of mind and materials, and he declared the operations of the imagination as indispensable to alchemical-philosophical physic. The imaginative mind not only drew in materials through the corporeal senses and transmuted them, but also went forth and penetrated into the life of the world around it. According to Paracelsus, "the power and nature of Imagination … cannot imagine anything, unless the things to be imagined are attracted to it by its imaginative power," and

> By this [imaginative] spirit are born into the world clever and industrious people … This one or that invents such through his fancy and thinks things out with a more intent speculation than one who is vacuous, though assiduous. Thus it comes about that a man after laying aside his corporeal understanding … and after putting on a spiritual one, nevertheless remains corporeal in his cunning and subtlety in his art. Of that mettle are excellent craftsmen and others who are born from this spirit, for it is this spirit which speculates, it is he who possesses the attractive power which is linked to the impressions. He that can penetrate there and can make his imagination sufficiently intensive, he already knows the work of the cabalistic 'rector' and no difficulty of any kind will stand in his way.[32]

These are the same concepts in play in Keats's November 22 letter to Bailey. As we follow Keats's thoughts through the letter, he moves from a brief mention of "Men of Power" or "Men of Genius" who "are great as certain ethereal Chemicals operating on the Mass of neutral intellect – by they have not any individuality, any determined Character," to an extended discussion of "the authenticity of the Imagination" which he values above "consequitive reasoning," to references to the Sensations and the Imagination as creative of "a Shadow of reality to come," that parallels Paracelsus's

---

which all Masons wish to be brought. At the ritual's start, the candidate expresses his desire to be "To be brought to the Light" and his preparations for this "In my [his] Heart" (70; 66).

29  Paracelsus, "Interpretatio alia Totius Astronomiae," 102.

30  Paracelsus, "Interpretatio alia Totius Astronomiae," 102.

31  Herbert Silberer, *Hidden Symbolism of Alchemy and the Occult Arts*, prev. *Problems of Mysticism and Its Symbolism*, trans. Smith Ely Jelliffe (New York: Dover Publications, Inc., 1971) 383–84.

32  Paracelsus, *Opera Omnia*, tom. II, 472. A. *De Virtute Imaginativa*, tract II, 66–67.

belief that the imagination reveals "traces" or "signatures" of the "real," invisible world.[33]

As Sperry and Goellnicht have noted in their discussions of this letter, Keats's "'Men of Genius' have no 'individuality,' no 'determined Character,'" and instead "act as catalysts in the creative process of transmuting material 'things' into art," but in this function these men also fulfill a metaphorical role as the Philosopher's Stone of alchemy which also exists above "individuality." By a series of correspondences, those who strive for the poetic goals become alchemists whose work in turn acts upon the world. Their imaginative efforts transmute materials into art that then stimulates the senses and operates via the imagination upon men in the world at large, providing the spiritual aid and solace that was a goal of the Rosicrucian and Masonic societies.

This is not an entirely new notion for Keats, and is in fact often linked in his mind with many of the same topics as those appearing in this November letter. Roughly a fortnight after Keats first embarked upon *Endymion*, in May 1817, he wrote to Haydon discussing "difficulties" that "nerve the Spirit of a Man – they make our Prime Objects a Refuge as well as a Passion," while also asserting that as an artist, Haydon would understand "the turmoil and anxiety, the sacrifice of all what is called comfort" to the greater goal. Then, he linked these thoughts to consolations to be derived from "the looking upon the Sun the Moon the Stars, the Earth and its contents as materials to form greater things – that is to say ethereal things –."[34] Goellnicht believes Keats has the same chemical process in mind here, but he does not discuss the most definitive link between the two letters – alchemy.[35] Like the philosopher-alchemists, Keats views Nature, and more specifically the traditional symbolic elements of the sun, moon, stars, and Earth, as the *Materia Prima* from which the ethereal quintessence may be derived.[36] "Men of Genius," then, are the artistic "craftsmen" Paracelsus praises who are able to take these materials and create from them both art and the ethereal physic derived from it, and they do so through the medium of imagination.

While Keats spends little time discussing these "Men of Genius," and cuts short his thoughts because he "long[s] to be talking about the Imagination," there is further evidence the two topics are connected. He asserts his thoughts on both are "truth" – a strong claim for Keats – and when he again returns to the subject of these men in a letter to Woodhouse discussing "the poetical Character," they bear strong resemblance to those Paracelsus describes as born with the imaginative spirit. According to Keats, the "poetical Character ... is not itself – it has no self – it is every

33 Keats, *Letters I* 184–85.

34 Keats, *Letters I* 141–43.

35 Donald C. Goellnicht, "Keats's Chemical Composition," *Critical Essays on John Keats*, ed. Hermione de Almeida (Boston: G. K. Hall & Co., 1990) 150.

36 Maureen Roberts supports this view in "Beautiful Circuiting: The Alchemical Imagination in English Romanticism," *The Diamond Path: Individuation as Soul-making in the Works of John Keats* (1997) <http://www.cgjungpage.org/articles/robertm4.html>. Roberts argues that Keats uses alchemical metaphors, but she does not provide cultural sources for his knowledge. Instead, she follows Jung's proposal that alchemical metaphors are psychological archetypes and uses them as a basis for a Jungian reading of Keats.

thing and nothing," and "A Poet is the most unpoetical of any thing in existence; because he has no Identity – he is continually in for – and filling some other Body –."[37] In other words, the "poetical Character," like the imagination, enables the poet to penetrate intensively into the life of people and objects that surround him, and just as Paracelsus declares "it is this spirit which speculates," Keats notes that the "relish" the "poetical Character" takes in all things "end[s] in speculation."[38]

Likewise, Paracelsus defines this power as both a going forth and a drawing in, an "attraction," and Keats does as well. As Keats explains to Woodhouse, "When I am in a room with People if I ever am free from speculating on creations of my own brain, then not myself goes home to myself: but the identity of every one in the room begins to press upon me that, I am in a very little time anhilated."[39] As Woodhouse's letter written about the same time to John Taylor makes clear, this description formed part of a fuller discussion amongst the men on this topic, and Woodhouse's summation of Keats's ideas elucidates the connections further. He writes:

> The highest order of Poet ... will have as high an imag[ination] that he will be able to throw his own soul into ... any object he sees or imagines, so as to see feel <&> be sensible of, & express, all that the object itself wo[uld] see feel <&> be sensible of or express – & he will speak out of that object – so that his own self will with the Exception of the Mechanical part be "annihilated." ... And it is a fact that he [Keats] does ... by the power of his Imag[ination] create ideal personages substances & Powers – that he lives for a time in their souls or Essences or ideas –[40]

Woodhouse makes a distinction here when he notes "with the Exception of the Mechanical," and that too matches Paracelsus's distinctions between the corporeal or material and the spiritual, although both remain linked. When a poet such as Keats lays "aside his corporeal understanding" and puts "on a spiritual one," he "remains corporeal in his cunning and subtlety in his art" even while he sees into the "Essences or ideas" his imagination creates.

Keats's definition of "Men of Genius ... Men of Power" and his experience as a poet correspond so closely to Paracelsus's men of imagination that it seems only natural he would describe such men as "great as certain ethereal Chemicals operating on the Mass of neutral intellect." The alchemical metaphor, with its emphasis on the ethereal, draws from the same tradition as the underlying ideas. And, because the imagination is the salient feature of these men and the poet, when Keats's thoughts turn fully to "the authenticity of the Imagination" the transition too is entirely natural.

---

37  Keats, letter to Woodhouse, 27 October 1818, *Letters I* 386–87. The letter reveals that more than a year later, Keats's ideas on the subject have not changed appreciably. Rollins writes that Woodhouse copied "continually in for" in this passage, but "George Beaumont, *TLS*, 27 February, 1 May 1930, pp. 166, 370, emends it to 'informing'" (387). The change, however, only highlights the way in which this aspect of the imagination functions as an interchange of powers that both went out and drew in.

38  Keats, *Letters I* 387.

39  Keats, *Letters I* 387.

40  Woodhouse, *Letters I* 389. Rollins dates the letter as "About 27 October 1818."

Scholars have long considered this passage on the imagination as central to Keats's philosophies regarding not only poetry but also life in general and even the possibility of an afterlife. Given its importance, and the ways in which Keats appears to be moving through hermetic thoughts and his examples by a process of association, it is best understood when read in full. In response to some doubt on Bailey's part, Keats writes:

> O I wish I was as certain of the end of all your troubles as that of your momentary start about the authenticity of the Imagination. I am certain of nothing but of the holiness of the Heart's affections and the truth of Imagination – What the Imagination seizes as Beauty must be truth – whether it existed before or not – for I have the same Idea of all our Passions as of Love they are all in their sublime, creative of essential Beauty – In a Word, you may know my favorite Speculation by my first Book and the little song I sent in my last – which is a representation from the fancy of the probable mode of operating in these Matters – The Imagination may be compared to Adam's dream – he awoke and found it truth. I am the more zealous in this affair, because I have never yet been able to perceive how any thing can be known for truth by consequitive reasoning – and yet it must be – Can it be that even the greatest Philosopher ever arrived at his goal without putting aside numerous objections – However it may be, O for a Life of Sensations rather than of Thoughts! It is "a Vision in the form of Youth" a Shadow of reality to come – and this consideration has further convinced me for it has come as auxiliary to another favorite Speculation of mine, that we shall enjoy ourselves here after by having what we called happiness on Earth repeated in a finer tone and so repeated – And yet such a fate can only befall those who delight in sensations rather than hunger as you do after Truth – Adam's dream will do here and seems to be a conviction that Imagination and its empyreal reflection is the same as human Life and its spiritual repetition. But as I was saying – the simple imaginative Mind may have its rewards in the repetition of its own silent Working coming continually on the spirit with a fine suddenness – to compare great things with small – have you never by being surprised with an old melody – in a delicious place – by a delicious voice, felt over again your very speculations and surmises at the time it first operated on your soul – do you not remember forming to yourself the singer's face more beautiful than it was possible and yet with the elevation of the Moment you did not think it so – even then you were mounted on the Wings of Imagination so high – that the Prototype must be here after – that delicious face you will see – What a time! I am continually running away from the subject – sure this cannot be exactly the case with a complex Mind – one that is imaginative and at the same time careful of its fruits – who would exist partly on sensation partly on thought – to whom it is necessary that years should bring the philosophic Mind – such an one I consider your's and therefore it is necessary to your eternal Happiness that you not only <have> drink this old Wine of Heaven which I shall call the redigestion of our most ethereal Musings on earth; but also increase in knowledge and know all things.[41]

Here again, Keats's Imagination functions in the same manner as its Paracelsian counterpart and his thoughts are a synthesis of various alchemical-philosophical concepts. Keats begins by asserting both "the authenticity," "the truth of Imagination," and that "What the Imagination seizes as Beauty must be truth – whether it existed before or not." We know from his November 3 letter that this seizing is an act of

---

41  Keats, *Letters I* 184–86.

perception of "the undepraved Sensation of the Beautiful, the poetical in all things." We know from both his and Woodhouse's comments that the poetical here, like "all our Passions ... in their sublime," refers to the essence of things into which the poet is able to enter. As I have noted, this matches Paracelsus's description of those artists born with the imaginative spirit, and Keats's contention here also echoes Paracelsus's opinion that "the power and nature of Imagination ... cannot imagine anything, unless the things to be imagined are attracted to it by its imaginative power." The imagination is Paracelsus's "Creative Power" that draws upon sensation, and when in "perfect spirit," or to use Keats's descriptive and alchemical terms, when "in their sublime," the passions interacting with the imagination yield an "essential" beauty. Furthermore, Keats believes that this is true *"whether it existed before or not,"* regardless of whether it is a *product* of the imagination and not independent of it, and here again he follows the same thought process as Paracelsus who argues that things "obtained by means of imagination can give true results."[42]

In yet another parallel, Keats claims he is "the more zealous in this affair, because I have never yet been able to perceive how any thing can be known for truth by consequitive reasoning." Even while conceding, "it must be," Keats, like Paracelsus, does not place an absolute certainty in man's conception of the "arts and sciences" or "consequitive reasoning." Indeed, he immediately undercuts the phrase "it must be" by questioning whether "the greatest Philosopher ever arrived at his goal without putting aside numerous objections" – and before the internal debate can distract him further, he returns to his emphasis upon imagination, effectively granting it the greater certainty when he declares "O for a Life of Sensations rather than of Thoughts!" Sensations take precedence as "'a Vision in the form of Youth' a Shadow of reality to come," and Keats's reasoning calls to mind the Paracelsian arguments that the Sensations stimulate the imagination and "he who possesses the attractive power which is linked to the impressions," "he knows the work of the cabbalistic 'rector'," and can discover the traces and signatures of the invisible world's "reality" within this one.

Moreover, Keats's perception of Sensations contains within it both the traditional senses as well as the suggestion that they affect the spirit; when he compares "great things with small" he offers the example of a melody placed within a context engaging all the senses that "operated on the soul" at that moment. Paracelsus's traces and signatures also seem to be Keats's "Shadow of reality to come," and their similarity is reinforced by Keats's "auxiliary" "Speculation" that "happiness on Earth" will be "repeated in a finer tone" in the afterlife. Like Paracelsus, Keats argues that this world is an imperfect version of the invisible world, it is a "Shadow" of "reality," and what we perceive here exists in the purer or "finer tone" there.

To explain further Keats offers, "Adam's dream ... a conviction that Imagination and its empyreal reflection is the same as human Life and its spiritual repetition," and all the terms he uses not only reinforce the Paracelsian conception but also carry more general hermetic associations. Arthur Edward Waite, a scholar of hermeticism in Rosicrucian and Masonic societies, has characterized philosophical alchemy's goal as "the attainment of all desire in the order which is called absolute, because

---

42  Italics mine.

after its attainment all that we understand by the soul's dream has passed into the soul's reality. It is the dream of Divine Union, and eternity cannot exhaust the stages of its fulfillment," and this, as a guiding principle, certainly fits portions of Keats's own description.[43]

In addition, although "Adam's dream" is traditionally cited as a reference to Milton's *Paradise Lost*, Adam also figured prominently in Rosicrucian texts and Masonic histories. He was considered the original possessor of cabalistic knowledge and the gift of prophecy, the original man imbued with "Wisdom ... the Breath of the Power of God, and a pure Influence ... an undefiled Mirror of the Majesty of God, and an Image of his Goodness," that "foreknoweth Signs and Wonders."[44] Keats also describes Adam's dream in terms of a "mirror," one that reflects perfectly Paracelsus's special air that functions as "a divine mirror" and penetrates man, thereby yielding "dreams and prophecies," much in the same way Keats's English Muse, born of "spiritual air" inspires the Imagination. Keats's series of correspondences between Adam's dream, the Imagination and its "empyreal reflection," and "human Life and its spiritual repetition," turn upon hermetic concepts. The pivot point, the word "empyreal," with its alchemical associations not only with the heavens and celestial air but also pure fire and light, and the highest degree of refinement attainable, makes this clear.[45]

Even when Keats rebukes himself, as he finds himself "continually running away from the subject" and attempts to come to some final statement, he reveals that his mind has not entirely dropped the threads that run throughout his argument. His reference to the "complex Mind – one that is imaginative and at the same time careful of its fruits – who would exist partly on sensation partly on thought," will become "the philosophic Mind" of a "Man of Genius" and still follows the

---

43 Arthur Edward Waite, "The Pictorial Symbols of Alchemy," *Occult Review* 8.5 (Nov. 1908) <http://www.adepti.com/docs/ps2.pdf>.

44 *Fama Fraternitatis*, trans. Thomas Vaughan (1652), transcriber, Kevin Day (Sept. 2002), <http://www.levity.com/alchemy/fama.html>.

45 While I have chosen to use Paracelsus's original theorizing for the sake of clarity, Keats could have come across these ideas in any number of alchemical texts or works related to the secret societies as well as Burton's *Anatomy of Melancholy*. For example, the alchemical author and assumed Rosicrucian Michael Sendivogius wrote in his treatise *New Chemical Light*:

the Sages have been taught of God that this natural world is only an image and material copy of a heavenly and spiritual pattern: that the very existence of this world is based upon the reality of its celestial archetype; and that God has created it in imitation of the spiritual and invisible universe, in order that men might be the better enabled to comprehend His heavenly teaching, and the wonders of His absolute and ineffable power and wisdom. Thus the Sage sees heaven reflected in Nature as in a mirror and he pursues this Art, not for the sake of gold or silver, but for the love of the knowledge which it reveals.

This popular work ran to over thirty editions in English and new editions were still being issued at the end of the eighteenth century. Michael Sendivogius, "Part Two, Concerning Sulphur, Concerning Elementary Fire," *New Chemical Light*, transc. Jerry Bujas, <http://www.levity.com/alchemy/newchem3.html>.

Paracelsian and Rosicrucian precepts that such a man think "things out with a more intent speculation than one who is vacuous, though assiduous," and his final words on the subject to Bailey gather together all the hermetic elements in an exceptionally Paracelsian prescription.

He tells Bailey "it is necessary to your eternal Happiness that you not only <have> drink this old Wine of Heaven which I shall call the redigestion of our most ethereal Musings on earth; but also increase in knowledge and know all things." Sperry and Goellnicht have argued that when Keats uses the term "digest" he is employing chemical meanings involving a gentle heat and a moisture that dissolve materials in order to purify and then recombine them.[46] In this case, while such chemical meanings certainly may be in play, there is more to Keats words. However Keats may view the process of poetry, the prescription for happiness is directed to Bailey, not himself. Furthermore, the end product, the "Wine of Heaven," is created from "ethereal Musings" – substances *already* purified and in airy form, and Keats has prescribed this Wine to Bailey to "drink." The reference is more literal than many suspect, and it may seem odd, but when understood in Paracelsian terms, it makes perfect sense. According to Paracelsus's alchemical theories of concordance, the ethereal quintessence formed the basis for medicines that were then administered to the patient whose stomach became, in turn, the alchemist that "joined together" and "brought into mutual agreement" both the spirit and body and nature and man.[47]

Like Paracelsus, Keats recommends to Bailey a wine or elixir created from the fruits of the Imagination that works on the body and spirit in conjunction with a course of mental development that reflects the charges given to Rosicrucian adepts that they continually strive for knowledge. The metaphor of digestion he chooses is taken directly from Paracelsus and his "Chemistical" philosophies and his choice of a "Wine of Heaven" necessary to the "philosophic Mind," echoes a common alchemical reference to "philosophic wine" employed by Paracelsus as well as others to signify the same element and process.[48]

Taken as a whole, added associations such as these show that, contrary to Robert Ryan's contentions in *Keats: The Religious Sense*, Keats did find both "encouragement to the spirit and nourishment to the imagination."[49] So much so, in fact, that he offers

---

46  Goellnicht, *The Poet-Physician: Keats and Medical Science* 59. Sperry 45.

47  E. J. Holmyard, *Alchemy* (New York: Dover Publications, Inc., 1990) provides a translated excerpt of *Paragranum* that illustrates these concepts: "The medicine must be brought into an airy form ... the *quantum esse* ... [and] this Arcanum is a chaos [gas]" that is created so that "the stomach ... is the alchemist" and "this is the way to heal and restore health" (172–73).

48  "Chemistical followers" is the designation given to "Rosicrucians" by Robert Burton, but the Freemasons also emphasize this striving after knowledge. The phrase "increase in knowledge" appears both in the "Book of Daniel" in the Bible – a text used by higher degree Masons – and in the charges to Masonic initiates of the second degree of Masonry. For discourses on philosophic wine readers may consult any number of alchemical texts such as chapters XII and XIV in *Paracelsus his Aurora, & Treasure of the Philosophers... Faithfully Englished. And Published by J.H. Oxon,* transc. Dusan Mileusnic (London, 1659) <http://www.levity.com/alchemy/paracel3.html>.

49  Ryan 208.

his own views as encouragement and nourishment to others. They also indicate that while Keats certainly believed Beauty and poetry could provide solace in this life, they served an equally vital role in the spiritual growth necessary for life to be "repeated in a finer tone" in the next.[50] The hermetic references emphasize Keats's willingness to believe in an immortal soul. Without knowledge of the philosophies behind phrases such as "repeated in a finer tone," many critics, like Ronald Sharp, find such references "peculiar" and assume Keats believed our only rewards were to be found in this life, but once understood, the associations reconcile the spiritual interpretations of Keats's philosophies by men such as Ryan and Sharp.[51] They also acknowledge that although, as Goellnicht says, "Keats's poetry remains rooted in the empirical world," the branches his speculations create touch upon the ethereal.[52]

When scholars such as Goellnicht contend that "the abstract 'truth'" rarely concerns Keats because the abstract seems too spiritualized, and cite Keats's letter to Bailey where Keats writes of an afterlife "having what we call happiness on Earth repeated in a finer tone and so repeated – And yet such a fate can only befall those who delight in sensation rather than hunger as you do after Truth," I believe they miss the point precisely because they are unaware of the hermetic implications.[53] Throughout the letter, Keats has been asserting the power of the Imagination to arrive at a truth, so long as the processes, the compositions and minglings of the imagination that he puts forth in alchemical terms, are followed. Keats is describing to Bailey *a process*, a means to a spiritual truth in which Bailey has expressed some doubt. Once this is recognized, the emphasis in the line quoted above shifts. Keats is not expressing doubt in the truth or dismissing an abstract truth. He is telling Bailey it cannot be arrived at if Bailey does not go about it the proper way – "such a fate can only befall those who delight in sensation rather than hunger *as you do* after Truth."[54] To put it bluntly, Keats appears to be telling Bailey he is going about it the wrong way.

It is not the desire for the truth that Keats argues against. Rather, he is reassuring Bailey that the gradations of sensations and the imagination's interactions are a valid way to reach that truth, and he uses the hermetic arguments stressed by Paracelsus, the Rosicrucians, and the Freemasons to do so. Keats's comments to his brothers one month later further indicate that this is the case. When Keats writes of "Negative Capability," he is discussing the ability of a "Man of Achievement," like a "Man of Genius," who can make an imaginative leap rather than rely solely on "consequitive reasoning."[55] He writes:

... at once it struck me, what quality went to form a Man of Achievement especially in Literature & which Shakespeare possessed so enormously – I mean *Negative Capability*, that is when man is capable of being in uncertainties, Mysteries, doubts, without any

---

50  Keats, *Letters I* 185.

51  Ronald A. Sharp, *Keats, Skepticism, and the Religion of Beauty* (Athens: University of Georgia Press, 1979) 5.

52  Goellnicht, "Keats's Chemical Composition" 150.

53  Goellnicht, *The Poet-Physician: Keats and Medical Science* 65.

54  Italics mine.

55  Keats, letter to George and Tom, 21 and 27 December 1817, *Letters I* 193.

irritable reaching after fact & reason – Coleridge, for instance, would let go by a fine isolated verisimilitude caught from the Penetralium of mystery, from being incapable of remaining content with half knowledge. This pursued through Volumes would perhaps take us no further than this, that with a great poet the sense of Beauty overcomes every other consideration, or rather obliterates all consideration.[56]

Those men who insist upon "fact & reason" miss the truths to be grasped by apprehension of the beautiful and the operations of the imagination that may be caught from the "Penetralium of mystery."

Regardless of whether or not Keats's word "Penetralium" is correct, his language links this letter to his previous thoughts expressed to Bailey. This language also contains hermetic overtones that encourage the interpretation I am suggesting. As noted previously, the Rosicrucian adepts were often warned that they would find themselves in just the state Keats describes of "uncertainties, Mysteries, doubts" through which they were enjoined to persevere until their operations yielded a sudden insight and "the transfiguring ecstasy ... when the adept, after long pain and self-sacrifice of the quest in this world, a world in which opposites are forever quarrelling, [found] his cross – the symbol of that struggle and opposition – suddenly blossom with the rose of love, harmony and beauty."[57]

Furthermore, the same concepts came into play in the rituals of higher degree Freemasonry such those relating to the Royal Arch where initiates deliberately were blindfolded and disorientated to simulate the same state and sent on a "quest" involving alchemical allegory to reach a symbolic inner sanctum of the Masonic Temple in a physical representation of a metaphorical journey to discover the "Mysteries" of Freemasonry and the truths it offered. Keats's "Penetralium" is a variation upon "penetralia" which signifies the inner sanctum of a temple, and it is quite possible he had such connections in mind. His discussion appears in a letter he wrote at exactly the same time he composed his review "Mr. Kean" in the *Champion* in which he asserted "The spiritual is felt when the very letters and prints of charactered language show like the hieroglyphics of beauty; – the mysterious signs of an immortal freemasonry!" and framed the reference with commentary on "unimaginative days ... of sickly safety and comfort," thereby suggesting that the imaginative and spiritual aspects of Freemasonry, like the "Man of Achievement" and the Freemason Kean's performance, could offer the same comfort and physic to men that Keats describes in his letters to Bailey.[58]

By the time Keats again refers to "consequitive reasoning" one month later in his "Pleasure Thermometer" letter to John Taylor in which he requests Taylor insert the famous lines beginning "Wherein lies Happiness?" into Book I of *Endymion*, the associations between the imagination, sensations, beauty, happiness, a spiritualized afterlife, and hermetic concepts have become so consistent, it comes as no surprise to discover Keats explicitly alluding to alchemy. The concepts Keats has been

---

56  Keats, *Letters I* 193–94.

57  Richard Ellmann, *The Identity of Yeats* (London: Faber Press, 1954) 64.

58  Keats, "Mr. Kean," *The Poetical Works & Other Writings of John Keats*, ed. H. Buxton Forman, rev. Maurice Buxton Forman, vol. 5 (New York: Phaeton Press, 1970) 229, 227 and 232 respectively.

testing and refining for months in various letters, following the same process he has recommended to Bailey, have crystallized into a full and assertive expression of "a regular stepping of the Imagination towards a Truth," that he is sure of even though he thinks that to Taylor, "a consequitive Man," his claims must have seemed "a thing almost of mere words."[59]

Keats writes:

> Wherein lies Happiness? In that which becks
> Our ready Minds to fellowship divine;
> A fellowship with essence, till we shine
> Full alchymized and free of space. Behold
> The clear Religion of heaven –

and claims that

> My having written that Argument will perhaps be of the greatest Service to me of any thing I ever did – It set before me at once the gradations of Happiness even like a kind of Pleasure Thermometer – and is my first Step towards the chief Attempt in the Drama – the playing of different Natures with Joy and Sorrow.[60]

Keats's own emphasis here has led scholars to view both this letter and its corresponding passages in *Endymion* as keys to portions of Keats's philosophy, and virtually all agree that the concepts expressed are linked to the previous letters discussed. His "Pleasure Thermometer" lies at the heart of disputes about whether his poem functions as stages of ascent upon a Neo-Platonic ladder as scholars such as de Selincourt and Finney have suggested, as a summation of an aesthetic philosophy in which the highest essence is beauty as Ford and Sharp believe, or even as a chemical analysis of the creative process as Sperry and Goellnicht contend. Keats's choice of words, however, leads to yet another possibility that combines these previous perspectives. His references tie the lines in *Endymion* to the hermetic concepts embodied in Rosicrucian and Masonic philosophies that he has already expressed in the context of his letters. Moreover, when these same lines are examined within the context of those surrounding them in Book I of *Endymion*, the ties become even stronger.

Although Keats refers to the lines beginning "Wherein lies Happiness?" as "a preface … necessary to the Subject," the question and the answer Endymion supplies are embedded within a much longer passage that functions as a response to Peona's reproof of his visions and his reaction to them. Endymion is offering a defense to Peona's questions "Then wherefore sully the entrusted gem of high and noble life with thoughts so sick? Why pierce high-fronted honour to the quick for nothing but a dream?," and the exchange itself appears within the greater context of a discussion upon sickness, health, the imagination and happiness (I.757–60). Keats indicates as much not only in his letter to Taylor but also when, in his 22 November letter to Bailey, he remarks "In a Word, you may know my favorite Speculation by my first

---

59  Keats, letter to John Taylor, 30 January 1818, *Letters I* 218.
60  Keats, *Letters I* 218–19.

Book and the little song I sent in my last."[61] As we have seen, Keats's November letter draws together all these concepts.

In addition, while Keats speaks in his letters about the role imagination plays in providing health and happiness, in the lines surrounding his "Pleasure Thermometer" in *Endymion* he introduces a concept relating sickness to imagination's converse – phantasy. This too, however, corresponds closely to the Paracelsian theories of health that he offers Bailey, all the more so because Paracelsus's formulation of Imagination as medicine and his warnings against phantasy occur in the same passage in the work *Opera Omnia*. Although portions of this have already been cited, the entire passage provides such pertinent insight into Endymion's and Peona's arguments, and thus Keats's, that it is worth reprinting in full. Paracelsus writes:

> Imagination is Creative Power. Medicine uses Imagination fixed. Phantasy is not imagination, but the frontier of folly. He who is born in imagination discovers the latent forces of Nature. Imagination exists in the perfect spirit, while phantasy exists in the body without the perfect spirit. Because Man does not imagine perfectly at all times, arts and sciences are uncertain, though, in fact they are certain and obtained by means of imagination, can give true results. Imagination takes precedence over all. Resolute imagination can accomplish all things.[62]

Just as Paracelsus makes a distinction between the two, Keats does as well. Where Peona chides Endymion for "thoughts so sick" and characterizes his "dreams" as "more slight than the mere nothing that engenders them," while charging him to do more than sigh for love and "be rather in the trumpet's mouth," Endymion counters that his hopes for accomplishment and "thirst for the world's praises," are such that "nothing base, no merely slumberous phantasm," could so divert him (I.758; 755–56; 737; 770–71). In contrast to her understanding of dreams, he offers another, in which dreams may be prophetic and visions born of a love that "might bless the world with benefits unknowingly" are "true" and not the same as those that leave men "fancy-sick" (I.827; 851; 853). In effect, he argues for the imagination.

This distinction between true dreams and visions born of and distilled by the imagination in "perfect spirit," the imagination in its "essence" and "sublime," and those "mere nothings" engendered by phantasy has implications for studies not only of this passage alone but also Keats's poetry in general. Keats differentiates between types of dreams, and the keys to their difference lie in his use of hermetic terminology. Peona groups together "visions, dreams, and fitful whims of sleep" and dismisses them all, thereby evoking a spirited reply from her brother (I.748–49). According to Peona:

---

61  Keats, *Letters I* 184–85.
62  Paracelsus, "Interpretatio alia Totius Astronomiae" 102.

The Morphean fount
Of that fine element that visions, dreams,
And fitful whims of sleep are made of, streams
Into its airy channels with so subtle,
So thin a breathing, not the spider's shuttle,
Circled a million times within the space
Of a swallow's nest-door, could delay a trace,
A tinting of its quality: how light
Must dreams themselves be; seeing they're more slight
Than the mere nothing that engenders them! (I.747–56)

Peona describes the origins of visions and dreams as a kind of "fine element" of Paracelsian "spiritual air," that enters into men "in the form of dreams and prophecies," but she misinterprets the significance.[63] Like those who rely upon "consequitive reasoning," Peona doubts the truth of the imagination; she doubts the efficacy of such things as Adam's dream. Indeed, within the framework of the narrative, she functions as a representative of the point of view Keats has been arguing against in his letters to Bailey and his brothers.

Keats has been discussing various aspects of the imagination debate throughout the fall well into the winter, and Peona's use of the hermetic terminology without a "proper" understanding provides Keats the opportunity to give Endymion precisely the argument he himself has been making at various stages and will make throughout his poetic career. It should not be forgotten that Peona refers to Endymion as a "bard," and "one who through this middle earth should pass / most like a sojourning demi-god, and leave / his name upon the harp-string" (I.723–26).[64] Keats extends this identification between the main character's and his own aspirations and views in his letter to Taylor, when he explicitly calls his formulation for Happiness an "Argument" and one he values as perhaps "the greatest Service to me of any thing I ever did."[65] When Keats's comments are framed in this manner, Endymion's response is Keats's as well and refers not just to Endymion's quest for his goddess's love, but also Keats's quest to use the imagination as a means to help man.

Throughout Endymion's response there are multiple hermetic references, and indeed, these references appear even before he speaks. Upon hearing Peona's questions, Endymion first experiences "a conflicting of shame and ruth," but immediately his posture shifts and

Yet, his eyelids
Widened a little, as when Zephyr bids
A little breeze to creep between the fans
Of careless butterflies: amid his pains
He seem'd to taste a drop of manna-dew

---

63 Pagel 299.

64 Peona does this consistently throughout *Endymion*, but the reference gains particular significance when she rebukes Endymion in Book I lines 723–27 for phantasies and reminds him he is destined for greater things than lovesick poems.

65 Keats, *Letters I* 218.

Full palatable; and a colour grew
Upon his cheek, while thus he lifeful spake. (I.761; 765–68)

Keats's simile strikes me as particularly apt since Peona has suggested one hermetic association with the air, but has discounted it. Here, we are presented with a description of a "little breeze" that counteracts her version and does in fact have many of the same effects as the etherealized form of "spiritual air" prized by Paracelsus and the Rosicrucians.

Keats further compounds the hermetic associations by likening the effect to that of a drop of manna-dew that restores color and life. The elixir sought by the Rosicrucians for healing purposes was often referred to as manna or spiritual dew and a pot of manna also was said to be contained both within the hidden tomb of the Rosicrucian founder Christian Rosenkreutz and the secret vault "discovered" by initiates of the Masonic Royal Arch degrees.[66] These are positive associations that speak to the same sort of healthful effects Keats has already spoken of and which he reiterates to Bailey by citing the beneficial aspects of the "English Muse" in his October letter. Moreover, because we as readers know what Peona does not – that Endymion's visions are true – such symbolism sets the stage for the stream of hermetic allusions that follow.

Endymion asserts "nothing base, no merely slumberous phantasm" could distract him from his aspirations. In this phrase he combines the concept of impurity or "base matter," often referred to in alchemy as "sick," with that of phantasy, thereby stressing that the "voyage" he has determined to embark upon is not "the frontier of folly" that "exists in the body without the perfect spirit" that Paracelsus warns against. Though he acknowledges his present state is one that seems "drifting" and akin to "earthly wrecks," he is also acutely aware his "higher hope is of too wide, too rainbow-large a scope" to give up (I.774–76). His phrasing calls to mind not only the aerial display after a storm, but also the burst of colors signifying a successful alchemical transformation and the use of the rainbow as a symbol in higher degree Masonry such as the Royal Arch degrees where it was referred to at times as the heavenly arch supported by pillars of beauty, wisdom and strength.

In both cases, the rainbow served as a symbol of promise and hope and the mark of achievement after that which was "base" had been made "sublime," and that which was sick had been made well.[67] Thus, Endymion's words suggest not only the perseverance Keats often expresses within a hermetic context in his letters but also the resolute faith he places in the process of sensation and imagination that he describes in similar terms to Bailey as the key to happiness. Moreover, in his fuller verse explanation of the benefits of such a process, Keats, through Endymion, sets forth a clear interchange of ideas that validate and support the Rosicrucian and Masonic conceptions adapted from Paracelsus's teachings.

---

66 See for example, *The Chymical Wedding* (Foxcroft, 1690), eds Adam McLean and Deirdre Green (1984), <http://www.levity.com/alchemy/chymwed1.html> and Piatigorsky 119–62.

67 Explanations of the rainbow as the "Arch of Heaven" may be found in Bernard E. Jones, *Freemason's Guide and Compendium* (London: George G. Harrap & Company, Ltd., 1956) 516.

When Endymion asserts that Happiness lies

> In that which becks
> Our ready minds to fellowship divine,
> A fellowship with essence; till we shine,
> Full alchemiz'd, and free of space. Behold
> The clear religion of heaven!

he expresses one of the primary esoteric goals of both philosophical alchemy and the Mysteries of Freemasonry (I.777–81). His visions inspire in him a love and desire for "fellowship divine" that echoes the desire expressed by both the Rosicrucian adepts and Masonic initiates who first prepared themselves in their hearts and then embarked on personal journeys in stages called "grades" or "degrees" that symbolized their advancement closer to the "spiritual essence" in an attempt to harmonize their own will with that of Nature and the will of the "Divine Absolute."[68] Furthermore, Keats's revision from his fair copy version of "that which becks / Our ready minds to blending pleasurable, / and that delight is the most treasurable / That makes the *richest Alchymy*," emphasizes his deliberate choice to use "Alchymy" in such a way that encompasses its multiple meanings.[69]

Using the same metaphors as those of the secret societies, Endymion describes the end result of "step[s] in the mystical ascension" and the "mystical potential to pass from a partial awareness of mortality to that of perfect regeneration 'in the Mansions of Bliss and in the Presence of the Great *I AM*'."[70] The phrase "till we shine, full alchemiz'd, and free of space" expresses the transformative process as well as the Rosicrucian and Masonic perception of man as both material and cosmic, and their hope that man and his religion, rightly understood, would become like the Masonic Temple – universal in scope and supported by the three great Pillars of Wisdom, Strength, and Beauty.[71] Thus, Endymion's answer combines not only elements of the Platonic Ideal but also the aesthetic aspiration to beauty and the alchemical terms that scholars such as Sperry and Goellnicht believe are a chemical representation of the process by which the imagination creates Beauty.

In addition, because Keats writes to Taylor in his letter that the "alchemiz'd" result is the product of "gradations of Happiness even like a kind of Pleasure Thermometer," Endymion's elaboration of the process to Peona further reinforces the connections I have been discussing. As Goellnicht notes, the chemical phrasing suggests a creative process that "originates in sensations gained from physical objects" and progresses through varying levels of intensity that lead to purer sensations and emotions and culminate in friendship and love.[72] As we have seen, this movement from strictly physical sensations to those encompassing the emotional and ultimately the spiritual is characteristic of both Rosicrucian and Masonic philosophies and

---

68  Piatigorsky 132. See also Silberer's chapter "The Royal Art" 378–416.

69  Italics mine.

70  Piatigorsky 129; 132.

71  The three pillars are introduced in the 1730s Masonic exposure *Masonry Dissected* and appear in virtually every exposure afterwards. Piatigorsky 80–85.

72  Goellnicht, "Keats's Chemical Composition" 154–55.

often was presented as an alchemical process. Furthermore, Keats's language and the illustrative examples he provides encourage just such an interpretation.

The "rose leaf" Endymion tells Peona to feel and the "bronze clarions" he bids her hear call to mind Rosicrucian associations, as does the "airy stress" of music, likened to a wind that "with a sympathetic touch unbinds Eolian magic," leading to "old songs" that "waken from enclouded tombs" and "melodious prophecyings" (I.782–91). References to Apollo and Orpheus add to the general atmosphere of magic and the compounding hermetic associations, since Apollo appears as a central figure in Rosicrucian and Masonic symbology and the Orphic hymns and mysteries were understood as part of the *Hermetica*. And all these mystical elements are linked in Endymion's speech to natural locales, thereby suggesting these are connected to Paracelsus's "latent forces of Nature" waiting to be discovered by those born in the imagination.

What Endymion asks Peona to experience with her physical senses quickly accrues by virtue of these associations into an apprehension of something more ethereal, so that when he asks "Feel we these things?" the question indicates a sense perception beyond merely the physical. Indeed, his own reply confirms this: "That moment we have stept into a sort of oneness, and our state is like a floating spirit's" (I.795–97). The first step in Keats's gradations upwards to the "fellowship divine" is through physical sense experiences that become transformed by the sympathetic imagination into a "oneness" with each object's "essence." The act of perception he describes to Peona is the penetrating power and comprehension of the imagination linked to the Rosicrucian and Masonic ideals discussed in conjunction with Keats's letters. Moreover, the "state" "like a floating spirit's" accordingly resembles those spirits in Rosicrucian and higher degree Freemasonry purported to exist in an intermediate state between man and the divine power as well as the intermediate state in alchemical transformations in which evaporation separates impure matter and draws off the "spirit" for further purification.[73]

Other, higher stages and degrees also exist, as becomes clear when Endymion tells Peona:

> But there are
> Richer entanglements, enthrallments far
> More self-destroying, leading, by degrees,
> To the chief intensity: the crown of these
> Is made of love and friendship, and sits high
> Upon the forehead of humanity.
> All its more ponderous and bulky worth
> Is friendship, whence there ever issues forth

---

73 Keats would have encountered the Rosicrucian doctrine of spirits in many works, including Pope's *Rape of the Lock*, Darwin's *Botanic Garden* and *Temple of Nature*, and numerous gothic novels. Variations on the doctrine were cited by authors such as Barruel as part of "Occult Masonry" and the "Rosicrucian and Scotch Degrees" where such spirits were said to provide "the secrets of the past, present, and to come," as well as insights into Nature (Barruel 120–21). Masonic authors stressed that this was a system of allegory and symbol. Keats later used the doctrine as the basis for his *Song of the Four Fairies*.

A steady splendour; but at the tip-top,
There hangs by unseen film, an orbed drop
Of light, and that is love: its influence,
Thrown in our eyes, genders a novel sense,
At which we start and fret; till in the end,
Melting into its radiance, we blend,
Mingle, and so become a part of it, –
Nor with aught else can our souls interknit
So wingedly: when we combine therewith,
Life's self is nourish'd by its proper pith,
And we are nurtured like a pelican brood. (I.797–815)

Yet again, Keats's terminology both fits the chemical processes of purification and distillation and the alchemical processes that metaphorically describe man's attempts to reach a higher spiritual state. Just as art and the imagination operate upon each other in a cycling of influence, so do the varying degrees of affection and both tend to purify by "self-destroying" "entanglements, enthrallments" that paradoxically also separate out the "disagreeable" or impure. The process described is explicitly alchemical both in the exoteric and esoteric senses. Keats's "self-destroying" "entanglements" match exactly the stages of alchemy in which matter was successively "destroyed" or broken down and purified, separated, and then recombined, in a continuous cycle that led, step by step, to the highest and most potent state in which the elixir could be obtained. Moreover, Keats's version of the elixir "an orbed drop of light that is love" has the same effect as its alchemical counterpart – projected onto man it inspires a change "at which we start and fret" and acts as a catalyst until "we blend, mingle, and so become a part of it."[74]

Keats's conception of the Philosopher's Stone or Elixir as an orb both liquid and light is characteristic of the many designations applied to the ultimate result. The Orb was the common symbol to signify the ultimate unity both physically and psychologically in Rosicrucian texts such as *The Chymical Wedding* where it was also described as liquid and glowing. And in the rituals of Freemasonry the same symbolism appeared, as did a particular stress upon the mystical "Light" that transforms man. This is particularly true in the higher degree rituals such as the Royal Arch that informed initiates that the Royal Arch "is dedicated to enlightening those who are in darkness, and illuminating the Way, the Truth, and the Life."[75] This symbolic Light is presented as acting *upon* the candidates. Given that Keats's conception of the power of love functions in precisely the same manner, it is only appropriate that he make use of the hermetic imagery.

In addition, if we recall again Keats's letters to Bailey and Woodhouse, it becomes clear that Endymion's "degrees" entail a progression similar to that Keats has described in which the most basic senses spark mental as well as emotional responses that, in the "imaginative mind," lead to a greater sympathy with the object

---

74 For a step by step breakdown of the process, see Gareth Roberts, *The Mirror of Alchemy: Alchemical Ideas and Images in Manuscripts and Books from Antiquity to the Seventeenth Century* (Toronto: University of Toronto Press, 1994) 57.

75 Piatigorsky 135.

or person. This, in turn, stimulates the imagination still more so that one such as Keats, of "the poetical character," once moved from "speculations on creations of [his] own brain" finds his own self "anhilated."[76] It begins first with physical sense perceptions that give pleasure such as the softness and scent of a rose leaf brushed against the lips or light music. That pleasure stimulates both the affections and the imagination and leads to stronger "sensations" which bring a sympathy and imaginative insight that draws forth the "essence" of things. The music that delights and "with a sympathetic touch unbinds Eolian magic" also draws forth "old songs," "ghosts of melodious prophecyings" and "bronze clarions" that are the past sense memories of places and part of them still. An imaginative mind such as Endymion's enters into what "he sees or imagines" and "lives for a time in their souls or Essences or ideas" and ostensibly "feels" them just as Endymion suggests "in a sort of oneness ... like a floating spirit."[77] As previously suggested, this too is the process that appears in the Rosicrucian and Masonic texts, and although Keats does not speak to Bailey or Woodhouse about the "richer entanglements ... leading ... to the chief intensity" crowned by love and friendship, Rosicrucian and Masonic texts contain these elements as well.

This union, in which "our souls interknit" and "combine" with love causes a transmutation and, through Endymion, Keats expresses a clear belief that this effect is indeed nourishment to "Life's self," and reinforces both the meaning and the alchemical nuances of it by saying "we are nurtured like a pelican brood." His description matches that found in countless alchemical and Rosicrucian texts such as the well known *Twelve Keys* by Basil Valentine in which adepts were instructed to purify and "raise it [the matter] in its degree, so that it surpass in brilliance all the stars of heaven, and become in its nature as rich in blood, as the pelican when he wounds himself in his breast, so that his young may be well nourished ... and can eat of his blood."[78]

Furthermore, the final mystical aspect of alchemy, the "union" in which contraries were fused, found its allegorical equivalent in the sexual love Endymion appears to suggest in his speech and later realize. As Endymion continues, he claims that "Just so may love, although 'tis understood the mere commingling of passionate breath, produce more than our searching witnesseth," and though he is not sure yet exactly *what*, he does have an intuitive sense that he is correct in this assessment (I.832–33). Because these claims almost immediately follow his description of the "Pleasure Thermometer," and because Keats soon places Endymion, quite literally, in a series of sexual encounters with the divine Cynthia, the implication is that the

---

76 The reference to the "imaginative mind" is in Keats's letter to Bailey, 22 November 1817, *Letters I* 185. The remaining quotes appear in Keats's letter to Woodhouse, 27 October 1818, *Letters I* 386–87.

77 The initial quotes appear in Woodhouse's letter to Taylor reiterating Keats's concept of "the poetical character" *Letters I* 389, but the final two are from Endymion's speech in Book I (796–97).

78 Basil Valentine, *Twelve Keys* (Eisleben: 1599) <http://www.levity.com/alchemy/twelvkey.html>.

"richer entanglements ... leading by degrees, to the chief intensity" also include sexual love, though that love is eventually turned to a higher purpose.

This sexuality inherent in *Endymion* does not, however, pose the problem commentators traditionally have believed it does in terms of a "fellowship divine" once the poem is viewed not only as an allegory but an allegory containing alchemical overtones. In hermetic terms, sexual consummation was viewed as symbolic of both the "essence" and the means by which man must reach that essence through the realities of life. Virtually every alchemical text Keats might have encountered contained descriptions of sexualized unions, often described as marriages, sometimes between a king and queen, other times between a goddess such as Venus and her paramour Adonis, and some texts such as the *Chymical Wedding* made use of aspects of both.[79] Sexual love served as the exoteric metaphor and led quite naturally in these allegories to the more generalized and esoteric assertions that it was through the power of love that a commingling of contraries took place and a transmutation was achieved. The mystical union between man and woman, the human and the divine, and the desirer and desired was understood as symbolic of love as "all strength and power," the "Divine Nature" and "Divine Elixir," and that which "dissolves and changes [all] to itself ... a transmuting and transforming nature" that "restores that which is fallen and degenerated to its primary beauty, excellence and perfection."[80]

Aside from such specifics, the greater allegorical meaning contained within the stages of alchemy Keats employs also suits his design. Although the image of the pelican wounding itself to feed its young may strike readers today as somewhat gruesome, for centuries the same image was often used as an alchemical metaphor for self-sacrifice and transformation of the spiritual self. The self-destroying Keats references represented a process by which the individual will was incrementally "destroyed" so that baser elements might be drawn off, then the self was recombined in successive stages with a broadening sympathy designed to bring the adept into harmony with the world and then the divine. The pelican symbolized the sacrifice required to reach the highest degree, and once there, to offer "loving sacrifice" to the

---

79 The *Chymical Wedding* is divided into days and framed by a dream vision. Throughout the allegorical narrative Cupid plays a role, and on the "Fifth Day" Christian Rosenkreutz describes his discovery of a "sepulcher" with an altar to Venus in which an alchemical process of dissolution is occurring. In a passage with unmistakable sexual overtones, Venus is revealed to him, naked and asleep, and he learns that when the alchemical dissolution is complete she "shall awake and be the mother of a King." The King and Queen also "lie together." Similarly, Silberer's *Hidden Symbolism* opens with Rosicrucian allegory entitled *Geheime Figuren der Rosenkreuzer...* published between 1785 and 1790. Like most allegories of this nature, the story is told as a dream vision and contains several episodes of sexual intercourse between a "bride" and "bridegroom," a "queen" and her "king," and the narrator and a maiden he "loves ardently" (1–15). Significantly, when the sexual unions of the king and queen are complete they reappear wearing crowns of pearls surmounted by brilliant diamonds.

80 Ethan Allen Hitchcock, *Remarks Upon Alchemy and the Alchemists* (Boston, 1857; Whitefish, MT: Kessinger Publishing, 2003) 134–35. Hitchcock lived contemporaneously with Keats and was a well known member of a Rosicrucian society. His emphasis upon love as portion of alchemy's and his own society's philosophies speaks to the perceptions of the "Great Work" at the time.

world without loss of well being. In his study, *Le Symbolisme Hermetique dans ses Rapports avec la Franc-Maconnerie*, Masonic scholar Oswald Wirth stressed just this meaning in the symbolism of the pelican, claiming, "The master [Mason] must make himself loved and he can only succeed by himself loving with all the warmth of a generosity extending even to absolute devotion, even to sacrifice of himself."[81]

In addition, not only the emblem of the pelican but all the alchemical symbolism employed by the Rosicrucian and higher degree Masonic societies represented a progression by degrees to attain greater wisdom of the world and greater self-knowledge that might ultimately aid both the self and mankind. As the pelican suggests, the sympathies and love, in particular, were considered integral to this process. While the mystical aspects of esoteric Rosicrucianism and Masonry focused on the refinement of the self, candidates were taught that it was not enough that they transmute themselves in this process. The humanistic ethos of both societies required that men put their gained wisdom to use in society and project the interior lessons learned outward to benefit the world.

In texts like the *Fama* and *Confessio*, readers were told the end result of such a quest was "a general Reformation" of the world, directed "to the love, help, comfort and strengthening of our Neighbors, and to the restoring of all the diseased," so that "there shall cease all servitude, falsehood, lies, and darkness."[82] Likewise, as Silberer explained in his discussions of alchemy and the "Royal Art" of Freemasonry, once a Master Mason found himself within the radiance of "the Light," "it [was] not enough that he get light from its original source, he must also be bound by endless activity to those whom he is to lead. The necessary bond is sympathy, love."[83] Love was considered the strongest of the sympathies. Thus, the "main work" of esoteric alchemy took place not only in the intellect but also the heart, because it was the heart that spurred man on and made him aware of his bonds both with nature and mankind in general. This was "the special object of alchemy to bring into life and activity; that by whose means, if it could universally prevail, mankind would be constituted into a brotherhood."[84]

Overall, the gradations Keats puts forth in his "Pleasure Thermometer" and the language he uses to describe both it and Endymion's convictions embody hermetic concepts and philosophies associated with the Rosicrucian and Masonic societies, and recognizing the hermetic connotations allows us to resolve several of the critical arguments centering on the passage. The point is often raised that Keats added the passage too late to give it such emphasis, and that Endymion's response to Peona seems out of place, occurring as it does in the first Book, and offering a prescription that Endymion himself seems unable to follow at times in the ensuing narrative. Yet, when we consider that Keats was employing terms, symbolism, and concepts associated with hermetic philosophies even before he began writing *Endymion*, these ideas take on a different hue. Instead, they are the result of a continual process by

---

81  Oswald Wirth, *Le Symbolisme Hermetique dans ses Rapports avec la Franc-Maconnerie* (Paris: n.p., 1909) as quoted by Silberer 412–13.

82  The first two quotes are taken from the *Fama* and the final from the *Confessio*.

83  Silberer 412.

84  Hitchcock 43–44.

which Keats has been refining his speculations in letters and poetry for over a year, and to give such a credo to Endymion is hardly inappropriate when he is viewed as an adept or candidate just embarking on his quest. The goal, its benefits, and the hope of attainment were always held out to adepts, and they embarked upon their work by placing faith in just such a "truth" as Endymion does. At the same time, as Rosicrucian allegories and Masonic rituals made clear, regardless of whether adepts or initiates knew the words, it still remained for them to truly understand the meaning, and this could only be achieved by direct experience.

Keats's own assertions that "axioms in philosophy are not axioms till they are proved upon our pulses," and "we never feel them to the full until we have gone the same steps," bear reference here as well because "the same steps" he conceives of as a gradual enlightenment as man explores the "Chambers" in his "Mansion" of human life are also the "Steps" in wisdom and spiritual understanding referred to in the rituals of the secret societies that constituted the speculative "work" of both the Rosicrucians and Freemasons.[85] Similarly, when we recall Keats's awareness that it is one thing to "know" and quite another to both know and do, as well as his affirmation that arriving at a truth via the imagination is a long, arduous process, even though the "vast idea" may be before a man and "clear / As any thing most true," Endymion's assertions are not at all surprising. They echo those of the poet in *Sleep and Poetry*. That Endymion, like the poet, must go through the process of learning does not invalidate his earliest instincts, and his missteps along the way serve instead to illustrate the very difficulty of the undertaking that Keats stresses in his letters and poetry.

---

85  Keats, letter to Reynolds, 3 May 1818, *Letters I* 279.

# Chapter Five

# Initiation Rites and Trials of Earth

As many critics have suggested, Keats's poetry and letters continually evoke a sense of process. The implicit critical understanding is that Keats has embarked upon a journey in which he hopes to both learn and create. Similarly, the movement within poems themselves often has been characterized as a progression. Many scholars work with a variation of Jack Stillinger's influential theories of flight and return in which the speaker of a poem moves from the real to the ideal, but for one reason or another, cannot remain there. Upon return, however, the speaker discovers that his experience has garnered him knowledge that has changed him in fundamental ways, and his perspective upon life has been irrevocably altered.[1] Typically, this characterization is then expanded by analogy to arrive at conclusions about Keats's poetry as a whole.

Stillinger used his representation to argue that virtually all of Keats's major poems represent attempts on his part to address the imperfect and mutable nature of life and the question of whether or not the limitations of this impermanence could be transcended by visionary imagination. He concluded that Keats's poems reveal a shift in philosophies from imagination as a desired form of escape to a more balanced belief that the escapist tendency could not solve the problem and had to be discarded for a version of the imagination that embraced "experience and process as his own and man's chief good."[2] Drawing upon Stillinger's work, others such as Wolf Hirst and Hermione de Almeida, while accepting the inherent tension between the actual and the ideal in Keats's poetry, rejected the contention that Keats was able to fuse the dichotomies in his work. Instead, Keats's poetry was described as a movement begun in an escapist form of satisfaction followed by disillusionment without a positive, redeeming result. As Wolf Hirst argued, the overall evolution of Keats's poetry was regarded as development "toward a philosophical resignation to the inevitable triumph of mutability over love, beauty, and happiness, and of actuality over a poet's visions."[3]

Many other variations of the basic pattern also exist, ranging from M. H. Abrams's discussions of the *Naturphilosophes'* concepts of journey and return in a spiraling progression of historical and spiritual development, to Charles Patterson's

---

1    Jack Stillinger, "The Hoodwinking of Madeline," *The Hoodwinking of Madeline and Other Essays on Keats's Poems* (Chicago: University of Illinois Press, 1971).

2    Stillinger, *The Hoodwinking of Madeline* 100. This view is most forcefully expressed and clearly delineated in his chapter "Imagination and Reality in the Odes."

3    Wolf Z. Hirst, *John Keats* (Boston: Twayne Publishers, 1981) 158.

use of Joseph Campbell's "monomyth" and the archetype of the hero.[4] Process, however, remains the defining and common element in all these approaches that examine Keats's poetry throughout his career. It is significant, then, that the hermetic philosophies Keats appears to draw upon in his writings also rely substantially upon the same ideas of progression to illustrate not only the role of the imagination in physical and spiritual health but also man's mental and spiritual development.

Hermetic philosophies embodied by the Rosicrucian and Masonic societies encompass portions of all these theories and lend credence to the criticism positing Keats's imagery and metaphors as part and portion of a structural model that repeats the pattern of a character set into motion in some way who arrives by degrees not quite back where he began.[5] Moreover, the quest motif embedded in the allegorical texts of the Rosicrucians and the initiation rituals of higher degree Freemasonry, as well as the alchemical metaphors for process, validate suggestions that Keats's myths are derived from Campbell's "monomyth," in no small measure because they match the storyline in which a hero is called or compelled to embark upon a journey into the unknown where he experiences a "profound initiation with supernatural aid" and then returns to the world, with "new knowledge to bestow a boon upon his fellow men."[6]

For all their similarities, however, the conclusions scholars arrive at when discussing process in Keats's poetry are oftentimes radically different. The difference derives from the varying importance critics attribute to the process itself. It is in this distinction that hermetic philosophies may play their most vital role in Keats's letters and poetry, because in alchemical allegories and the initiation rituals of the secret societies, the *means* by which man hoped to arrive at a higher state and prepared himself to do so were considered just as important as the end result. The nature of this knowledge means that while Keats was working with esoteric concepts, the concepts themselves were understood during the Romantic period as functioning within a humanistic framework. This is a crucial factor when considering the traditional critical interpretations of Keats's poetry as a conflict between real and ideal, mortal and immortal, or earthly and transcendent.[7]

The hermetic framework of Rosicrucian and Masonic philosophies requires a more subtle distinction because these philosophies required that such diverse poles exist in a constant interchange. As Gareth Roberts noted in *The Mirror of Alchemy*, alchemical narratives, usually presented as allegorical romances, were characteristically "vivid, surreal and dream-like," and continually made use of the language of paradox both to express transcendent value and the process by which

---

4    M. H. Abrams, *Natural Supernaturalism: Tradition and Revolution in Romantic Literature* (New York: W. W. Norton & Co., 1971). Charles I. Patterson, Jr., "The Monomyth in the Structure of Keats's *Endymion*," *Keats–Shelley Journal* 31 (1982): 64–81.

5    For example, M. H. Abrams, "The Circuitous Journey: Pilgrims and Prodigals," *Natural Supernaturalism* 141–96. Abrams explicitly delineates the symbolic import of progression and progress in hermetic philosophies and cites alchemy as one of the most frequent and strongest metaphors.

6    Patterson 66–67.

7    Ronald A. Sharp, *Keats, Skepticism, and the Religion of Beauty* (Athens: University of Georgia Press, 1979) 1.

a man might attain it.[8] They were the chosen means of imparting knowledge in Rosicrucian texts and during higher degree Masonic rituals precisely because while actively engaging man's imagination, they also exemplified the perspective that man could not reach a higher spiritual realm unless he engaged himself fully in the material world.

This qualification may seem small, but it has significance when we consider Keats's own struggles to address such issues in his life. As an exoteric representation of the esoteric goals of Rosicrucianism and Freemasonry, alchemical concepts epitomized a perspective that did not reconcile opposites nor reject one aspect for the other. If Keats's poetry is examined from such a perspective, the concept of conflict becomes modified. The division disappears, and the focus becomes one in which characters such as the poet, Endymion, and later Apollo must learn to move *through* the real *to* the ideal, through the mortal to the immortal, and through the earthly to the transcendent. Furthermore, the final philosophical position is not one in which a conflict has been resolved. Rather, it is one in which the seemingly disparate elements have been fused to create something new, something sublime.

Such an approach necessitates that the troubles of the world not be avoided or even "philosophised" away, to use Keats's term.[9] Taken from Keats's extended February to May letter of 1819 to George and Georgianna, this term appears in the midst of passages suffused with hermetic linguistics and ideas, shortly after Keats provides the elemental *Song of Four Fairies: Fire, Air, Earth and Water* where Salamander, Zephyr, Dusketha, and Breama are the sylphs of Rosicrucian lore and paired exactly according to the hermetic doctrines of contraries.[10] Keats illustrates the spirits of the poem as in conflict. Salamander, the spirit of fire, troubles wind and water, and they in turn give aggravation to him, but the "annoyances" of this light-hearted exchange are understood as a portion of the world itself, and the poem leads almost immediately to a more serious, extended version of the same thoughts.

Keats concludes that the philosophizing away of all troubles is an impossibility, because the nature of the world will not allow a "perfectibility" in which man's happiness is divorced from "the worldly elements."[11] He asserts instead that "the inhabitants of the world will correspond to itself," and "the point [of happiness] at which men may arrive is as far as the parallel state in inanimate nature and no further." Yet, the system of correspondences he describes leads him immediately into his speculations about a system of "Soul-making" that does provide for a happiness beyond this life. In fact, he views the imperfect nature of this world as the key to arriving at a perfect bliss offered to the individualized soul in the next. Although

---

8    Gareth Roberts, *The Mirror of Alchemy: Alchemical Ideas and Images in Manuscripts and Books* (Toronto: University of Toronto Press, 1994) 70–71.

9    John Keats, letter to George and Georgianna, 21 April 1819, *The Letters of John Keats, 1814–1821*, ed. Hyder Rollins, vol. 2 (Cambridge, Mass.: Harvard UP, 1958) 101. Hereafter, this work will be referred to as *Letters II*.

10   See Bernard Blackstone's *The Consecrated Urn: An Interpretation of Keats in Terms of Growth and Form* (London: Longmans, Green and Co., 1959) 101–104 for a brief but thorough analysis of this poem.

11   Keats, *Letters II* 101. All quotes in this paragraph are taken from the same portion of Keats's letter and the same page.

Keats initially appears to be denying transcendence, his thoughts lead him directly to what is perhaps one of the most religious of all his speculations. The progression of ideas that appear at first contradictory are in fact hermetic, and ones, moreover, that Keats has been examining in various forms since the beginning of his poetic career.

This approach is nowhere more evident than in Keats's own allegorical romance *Endymion*. Keats argues in *Endymion* that the only way by which a man could enter into "fellowship divine" and become "full alchymized" was by living within society and laying the foundations for his spiritual life in the reality of his daily work for both himself and mankind. This is precisely what Rosicrucian and Masonic rituals and texts taught, and it is also what Endymion learns as he engages in his quest and what the poet of *The Fall of Hyperion* later discovers in his conversation with Moneta. Seen from this perspective, the allegorical nature of poems like *Endymion* and *The Fall of Hyperion* is symbolic of a philosophy Keats was attempting to formulate recognizing that the dreamer who indulges in phantasy and the visionary who tells "truth unto the men of this generation" are "sheer antipodes" (*Fall of Hyperion*, I.200) and that within a man's mind there are but "three steps from feathers to iron," but also offering an alternative to the absolute rejection of a transcendental stance.[12] As in the texts associated with the Rosicrucians and Freemasons, in Keats's poems, man cannot gain wisdom, and he cannot attain a higher state or merge with the sublime, unless he paradoxically learns to reach "Ethereal things" using the "Things real" that constitute the base matter of life.[13]

These thoughts of Keats's appear in yet another letter to Bailey, dated 13 March 1818, where his imagery and linguistics once again parallel those of hermetic philosophies. Keats writes to Bailey that "probably every mental pursuit takes its reality and worth from the ardour of the pursuer – being in itself a nothing – Ethereal things may at least be thus real, divided under three heads." He proceeds to differentiate amongst "Things real – things semireal – and no things" based upon the degree in which the Spirit must "greet" [sic] them to grant them worth and existence. The sonnet *Four Seasons fill the Measure of the year...* follows and approaches the same concept from another perspective in which "beauty" and "fair spring thoughts" are drawn into a man and "dissolv'd" into his "Soul" wherewith they mingle, and then, while avowing he is not a "Reasoner" Keats remarks:

> that every point of thought is the centre of an intellectual world – the two uppermost thoughts in a Man's mind are the two poles of his World he revolves on them and every thing is southward or northward to him through their means – We take but three steps from feathers to iron.[14]

These concepts turn upon similar ones used in Freemasonry where man is told his spirit must greet pursuits of the Lodge and the value is not to be found in the materials themselves but rather the emotions and intellect found in the "Inner Ritual." Similarly, the image of a compass underlies Keats's description of the intellectual world where the south is feathers and the north is iron. As we have seen, in the intellectual lodge

---

12  Keats, *Letters II* 220 and *Letters I* 243, respectively.
13  Keats, *Letters I* 242.
14  Keats, *Letters I* 242–43.

of the Masons "from North to South" and "as high as the Heavens," the North, like iron, represents the unrefined sense and knowledge of reality without wisdom, while the South, like the lightness of feathers, symbolizes "illuminated human intelligence and understanding, which results from the material brain-mind being thoroughly permeated and enlightened by the Spiritual Principle."[15] And, perhaps even more significantly, the man moving through the lodge ritual literally takes "three steps" when he is "raised" from one to the next of the three initial degrees.

The process through which Endymion must journey also illustrates these ideas I have been discussing even as it appears to derive many of its particulars from the myths and initiation rituals surrounding Rosicrucianism and Freemasonry, and the structure of the poem itself reinforces the hermetic concepts. *Endymion* is a hermetic poem in which readers can discern some of Keats's earliest attempts to engage both the processes of metaphysics and the underlying philosophical imperatives commonly attached to the secret societies. It is an exploration of not only what Keats referred to as "a trial of my Powers of Imagination and chiefly of my invention" but also his acquaintance "with the Soundings, the quicksands, & the rocks" surrounding what he called his "Speculations" in which the very act of writing might serve as "a regular stepping of the Imagination towards a Truth."[16] For Keats, the process was as important as the result, and *Endymion* is a study in process. It is not only Endymion who learns as he progresses on his journeys – the poet does as well. Taken in this light, the hermetic imagery and quest motif that permeate the poem become more than ornamentation. Instead, they provide additional meaning and nuance to Keats's developing beliefs, and his continued use of such allusions in the later poems such as *The Fall of Hyperion* and *Lamia* suggests that his philosophy does not fundamentally change, although it does expand and become more sophisticated.

In Masonic terms, Endymion's initial encounters with Cynthia resemble the first stages of a process of initiation; they have infused him with a desire to "see the Light." But, before he can attain his desire, he must learn that his spiritual happiness depends on an interchange with the world and society as well as his goddess. The transformation that brings Endymion to this realization is one he must experience mentally before his physical apotheosis can occur, but the means by which he learns the truths he has so confidently stated to Peona in Book I must be both physical and mental for them to be fully understood and embraced. The physical aspects of his journey take Endymion from the natural world of his home, into the earth, then through the sea and air in each successive book, and this progression of locales follows traditional hermetic allegories. And although its presence has oftentimes been unclear to scholars, the fourth hermetic element of fire is also present, albeit in

---

15  W.L. Wilmshurst, *The Meaning of Masonry. A Philosophical Exposition of the Character of the Craft* (London: Lund, Humphries & Co.; Whitefish, MT: Kessinger Publishing, 2007) 93; 103.

16  Keats, *Letters I* 169–70, 374, and 218–19 respectively. Keats wrote all these phrases in direct reference to his larger aims in *Endymion*. The first appears in a 8 October 1817 letter to Bailey, the second in a 25 September 1818 letter to Hessey, and the third in his 30 January 1818 letter to Taylor.

a metaphorical sense that highlights the fact that Endymion's journey is mental as well as physical.

Many scholars believe that Keats meant to present Endymion as passing through all the elements, but they often have had difficulty discussing the element of fire and have tended to simply dismiss it. This has led others to reject the theory. The settings in each book are drawn so strongly, many have difficulty accepting that fire may be present without a detailed evocation similar to that Keats gives for Endymion's passage through the earth, sea, and then air. Perhaps the most persuasive solution to this problem to date has been provided by Walter H. Evert who has referred readers back to Lempriere's classical dictionary and the varied entries on the deities of light and love in which Hecate's and Cupid's powers were said to extend over heaven and hell as well as the earth and the sea, and Cupid's "divinity was universally acknowledged."[17] The entries provide for not only Cynthia's dominion over heaven, earth, and hell as was commonly understood, but also the sea, and they offer a rationale for Endymion's journeys that combines the themes of love and harmony with the elements. Evert believed Lempriere's descriptions of Cynthia's and Cupid's identities were unique, but a hermetic text provided precedent for Lempriere's. Apuleius's *The Golden Ass* explicitly connected all of these concepts as well as those of the four elements and rites of initiation.[18]

While Apuleius's work is commonly acknowledged as the primary source for Keats's "Ode to Psyche," it proves a likely source for *Endymion* as well. Keats not only appears to have drawn upon the text for his general characterizations, but also some particulars. In Book I, while recounting his visionary dreams, Endymion compares Cynthia to Venus rising from the sea, and his description not only calls to mind Lempriere's description of Hecate or Cynthia but also Apuleius's own in which the Goddess rises from the sea and reveals herself to Lucius after he has petitioned her and then fallen into a magical sleep.[19] She declares herself the

> governesse of all the Elements, the initiall progeny of worlds, chiefe of powers divine, Queene of heaven, the principall of the Gods celestiall, the light of the goddesses: at my will the planets of the ayre, the wholesome winds of the Seas, and the silences of hell be

---

17  Walter H. Evert, *Aesthetic and Myth in the Poetry of Keats* (Princeton: Princeton UP, 1965) 111.

18  Bernard Blackstone does not develop the idea of Apuleius's text as a vital source for *Endymion*, but he does mention Apuleius's name in a footnote in *The Consecrated Urn, an Interpretation of Keats in Terms of Growth and Form* (London: Longmans, Green and Co., 1959) 134. While arguing that Endymion experiences "an initiation through the elements; at each stage the aspirant confronts a new ordeal, advancing by degrees to the point of liberty" and that contraries become combined "within the elements and the aspirant himself," Blackstone noted that Apuleius emphasized passage through the elements as part of the initiation rituals for the cult of Isis. I am indebted to him for putting me on the track of this source.

19  Although he did not develop the idea further, Douglas Bush briefly noted the similarity between Keats's description of Cynthia and that found in *The Golden Ass* in *Mythology and the Romantic Tradition in English Poetry* (Cambridge, Mass.: Harvard UP, 1937) 103.

disposed; my name, my divinity is adored throughout all the world in divers manners, in variable customes and in many names.[20]

Similarly, in the central portion of *The Golden Ass*, the "Oracle of Apollo" describes Cupid, as one who

> flies with wings above in starry skies,
> And doth subdue each thing with firie flight.
> The gods themselves, and powers that seem so wise,
> With mighty Jove, be subject to his might,
> The rivers blacke, and deadly flouds of paine,
> And darkness eke, as thrall to him remaine.[21]

As previously noted, Apuleius's tale was included in the *Hermetica* and the same chapters in which these descriptions appeared were also widely understood during the Romantic period as a basis for Rosicrucian and higher degree Masonic initiation rites. *The Golden Ass*, as its translator Adlington remarked in his Address to the Reader, was designed to instruct via allegorical tales so that readers might, "by the pleasantnesse thereof bee rather induced to the knowledge of their present estate, and thereby transforme themselves into the right and perfect shape of men."[22] And a 1799 "English poetical paraphrase" of Apuleius's tale of Cupid and Psyche declared, "APULEIUS was a Platonist and a Mystic, and ... he is perpetually recurring to the rites and cabbala of the many religious fraternities into which he had been initiated."[23]

In addition, the trials of the characters portrayed in *The Golden Ass* represent a complex mix of sorrow and joy as well as wisdom garnered from experiences both in life and in the more specific context of initiation into a secret society. Lucius tells his readers that:

> Thou shalt understand that I approached neere unto Hell, even to the gates of Proserpina, and after that, I was ravished throughout all the Elements, I returned to my proper place: About midnight I saw the Sun shine, I saw likewise the gods celestiall and gods infernall, before whom I presented my selfe, and worshipped them: Behold now have I told thee,

---

20 Lucius Apuleius, "The Eleventh Booke: The Forty-Eight Chapter," *The Golden Asse* (1566), trans. William Adlington, ed. Martin Guy (1996) <http://eserver.org/books/apuleius/bookes/eleven.html>.

21 Apuleius, "The Fifth Booke: The Twenty-Second Chapter," <http://eserver.org/books/apuleius/bookes/five.html>.

22 William Adlington, "To the Reader," *The Golden Asse* <http://eserver.org/books/apuleius>.

23 As quoted by Elizabeth Imlay, "Freemasonry, the Brontes, and the Hidden text of *Jane Eyre*," *Secret Texts: The Literature of Secret Societies*, eds, Marie Mulvey Roberts and Hugh Ormsby-Lennon (New York: AMS Press, 1995) 216. Sources such as this indicate common knowledge Keats would have access to in which the story was framed by concepts of Neo-Platonism as well as initiation.

which although thou hast heard, yet it is necessarie thou conceale it; this have I declared without offence, for the understanding of the prophane.[24]

*The Golden Ass* focuses upon Lucius's attempts to find and eat roses which are "the cure" for ill magic that has transformed him into an ass, but his adventures parallel an inner progression whereby he learns, as Endymion does, to broaden his sympathies and is "spiritualized" till he becomes a proper priest for the goddess. Thus, *The Golden Ass* contains not only the myth of a mortal who gains immortality through love but also initiation rites figured forth as the allegorical quest of a main character through the four elements, and the underlying theory of correspondences that critics employ when they theorize about the structure of *Endymion* and which Keats himself expresses clearly in his April 1819 letter.

Furthermore, the connection between Cupid's dominion and love provides yet another link not only between the texts but also Endymion's movement through all the elements. Apuleius's description of Cupid and love as "fiery" completes the equation; love is the fire that works on Endymion throughout the four books and propels his transformation. Cupid appears in each of the four books of *Endymion*, and in each he is linked to mystery, light and heat, and love. In Book I, he is a "character'd" cloud in the well in which Endymion sees his love, and the sight of him almost induces Endymion to follow (I.889–90). In Book II, his bow is likened to the fire of lightning, "his quiver is mysterious," and "from forth his eyes / There darts strange light of varied hues and dyes," and Endymion "feels" his gaze "and no more controls / the burning prayer within him," (II.538–46) and in Book III he moves through the revelry in Neptune's hall and in the hymn sung there he is called the "Bright-winged Child," "sweetest essence," and "Dear unseen light in darkness! Eclipser / Of light in light" (III.978–87). Finally, in Book IV, as the Indian maid "in a new voice, but sweet as love," swears "By Cupid's dove" she is transformed into Cynthia and "into her face there came / Light, as reflected from a silver flame" (IV.78–83).

To call love the fire that works upon Endymion becomes more understandable if readers recall the conflation of love, light, and fire in the hermetic symbolism Keats draws upon in the "Pleasure Thermometer" passages. In addition, Cupid's association with flame and light and his close connection to Cynthia throughout the verse narrative provides yet another reason to make this claim. Cynthia, as the goddess of light serves as Apollo's counterpart in *Endymion* and Keats ascribes to her many of the same characteristics he applies to Apollo, including light and fire.

---

24 Apuleius, "The Eleventh Booke: The Forty-Eight Chapter." The similarities did not pass unnoted by authors such as Barruel who highlighted such instances to show that Freemasonry was utterly incompatible with Christianity, proclaimed "The name only has been changed; and the secret has been handed down under the denomination of Free-Masonry," and angrily pointed out the Masonic practice of referring to the uninitiated as "prophane." The Abbé Barruel, *The AntiChristian and Antisocial Conspiracy. An Extract from the French of the Abbé Barruel, to which Is Prefixed Jachin and Boaz, or an Authentic Key to the Door of Free-Masonry Ancient and Modern* (Lancaster: Joseph Ehrenfried, 1812) 140.

As the object of Endymion's love, therefore, she also mingles these with love.[25] As we have seen, Endymion's alchemical declarations that love is an "orbed drop of light," and his arguments throughout the "Pleasure Thermometer" passage as well as those surrounding it, combine these concepts and rely upon fire as a metaphor as well. When Endymion recounts his dreams to Peona, he tells her of "the loveliest moon" that "did soar / So passionately bright, my dazzled soul / Commingling with her argent spheres did roll," and it is this passionate brightness, so like his lover, that he likens to "a paly flame of hope" that keeps him entranced even after Peona bids him to let go of such dreams (I.592–95; 984).

Of course, the metaphor of love as fire and light is common, but its familiarity should not preclude the symbolism I am suggesting, particularly because authors often proudly asserted the universality of such hermetic metaphors appearing in alchemical, Rosicrucian and Masonic texts. Keats would have encountered the association of love and fire in the context of initiation rituals not only in *The Golden Ass* but also Mozart's *Magic Flute* as well as various Masonic exposures. Readers of exposures were told "The most ancient Masonic rituals take into account purification by the four elements," and "in order to contemplate the Queen of Hell [Hecate] – that is, the truth hidden within himself" the initiate was required to pass through flames representative of "circumambient passions" and "allow himself to be penetrated by the beneficent warmth that they emit."[26] In a similar fashion, the same association was also made in various alchemical allegories such as the Rosicrucian *Chymical Wedding*, where spiritual flames figure prominently throughout each stage of the adept Christian Rosenkreutz's journey and the "wedding" itself. There is even an episode in which he secretly witnesses Venus bound in sleep until an alchemical process is completed, and he is pricked by one of Cupid's darts that the deity tempers in flame.[27]

*The Chymical Wedding* provides yet another reason why love should be considered the spiritual fire that tempers and tests the candidate rather than an actual realm of fire. Quite simply, Endymion is a mortal, and like the questers in alchemical allegories, he cannot pass through fire. In terms of plot, the literal path of fire is not open to him, just as it is denied the character Christian Rosenkreutz in *The Chymical Wedding*, when he is told that there exist "four ways, all of which, if you do not sink down in the way, can bring you to [the] royal court," but "by the fourth no man shall reach the place, because it is a consuming way, practicable only for incorruptible bodies."[28] The substitution of the mental for the physical, however, in no way diminishes its effects in *The Chymical Wedding* or *Endymion*.

---

25  Evert presents this argument throughout his chapter "*Endymion.*" Stuart Sperry does as well in *Keats the Poet* (Princeton: Princeton UP, 1973) 88–99.

26  As quoted in Jacques Chailley's *The Magic Flute, Masonic Opera*, trans. Herbert Weinstock (New York: Alfred A. Knopf, 1971) 137–38. The original quote is from Michel Brenet's *Francs-Maçons Parisiens du Grand-Orient de France (fin du XVIII siecle)* 308.

27  "The Fifth Day," *The Chymical Wedding*, (Foxcroft 1690), eds Adam McLean and Deirdre Green (1984), <http://www.levity.com/alchemy/chymwed1.html>.

28  "The Second Day," *The Chymical Wedding*.

Keats's use of the metaphor of fire implies more than the simple "hope" or "burnings" of love in poetic verse when it is considered within the larger context of hermetic philosophies, and Keats's own assertions within *Endymion* support this interpretation. He opens the poem claiming that "human life" encompasses love, hope, and beauty like "an endless fountain of immortal drink, / Pouring unto us from heaven's brink" and these essences "become a cheering light / Unto our souls" that "always must be with us, or we die" (I.23–25; 30–34). As the poem progresses, however, he stresses they also share portion of our existence with

... the war, the deeds,
The disappointment, the anxiety,
Imagination's struggles, far and nigh,
All human; bearing in themselves this good,
That they are still the air, the subtle food,
To make us feel existence, and to shew
How quiet death is. (II.153–59)

These are the different natures of joy and sorrow of which Keats writes in his letter to Taylor, and they are the "Materials" of the world he declares necessary to man's salvation more than a year later in his Vale of Soul-making letter. They are the ways in which "the heart must feel and suffer" if it is to be "the Minds Bible ... the Minds experience ... the teat from which the Mind or intelligence sucks its identity" and the means by which an "Intelligence destined to possess a sense of Identity" becomes a "Soul."[29] Through the heart and the imagination, they are what man must embrace if he wishes to live "a life of any worth ... a continual allegory" both physical and spiritual.[30]

References abound throughout the poem where contraries are twinned in the paradoxical manner characteristic of alchemical allegorical romances, and Endymion "must feel and suffer in a thousand diverse ways": "pleasure is oft a visitant; but pain / Clings cruelly" (I.906–907); love appears as "fairest joys" and "unrest," "tenderest worth" and "seared dearth," "blessings" and "curse," "first heaven, then hell,"(II.366–74) an "unhappy ... felicity" (II.762–63), and "bliss" combined with "pain" (II.773), "joy and grief" (III.702), and "loving and hatred, misery and weal" (IV.12). The fire that burns Endymion, much like the flames that will consume Lamia, is one that will ultimately fuse opposites and force elemental change within the self, and the extent of its dual nature is demonstrated throughout the narrative.

In Book I, although love is "the paly flame of hope," and despite Endymion's claims to Peona of love's power, its immediate result is the exact opposite of what he argues. He confesses to Peona that his visions in which he has experienced immortal love have had terrible consequences. Because of them, nature's beauty has faded and become tainted for him, and he feels as though darkness and disappointment have overtaken his soul.[31] In addition, the effect has not only altered his view of nature but

---

29 Keats, letter to George and Georgianna, 14 February–3 May 1819, *Letters II* 102–103.

30 Keats, *Letters II* 67.

31 Keats, *Endymion* I.691–705.

also his interaction with others. Far from promoting fellowship, the experience has placed him in "fixed trance," and instead of joining the converse of his people, he spends his days "alone and sad," and feels as though mere "human neighbourhood" is like an envenomed sting (I.403; 477; 621–22).

While Endymion has an intuitive, imaginative apprehension of what the outcome of consummation with the divine *should* be, he has not yet gone through the entire process of what Cynthia later refers to as spiritualization. He lacks the experience proved on the pulses to understand that the path does not lie through a rejection of the world and all it represents, but rather the fusion of not only hope and despair but also the natural and spiritual. His initial desire to separate these aspects represents the same danger Lycius encounters in *Lamia*, but Endymion is given the opportunity to pass through the stages of learning and have his immortal love.

From this perspective, Book I, while containing the impetus of love that sets Endymion on his journey, does not contain a form of ascension on his part. Rather, it introduces Endymion's "desire to see the Light" which is first born in the heart. This is an important distinction to make because so many scholars who advance Neo-Platonic or transcendental interpretations feel compelled to make this Book more than what it is – a beginning. That Endymion's true journey and initiatory steps begin in earnest only in the second Book is reinforced by the very structure of the poem itself. While Book I lays out the natural world and its base materials necessary for Endymion's advancement, it is not until Book II, that opens with the declaration "O sovereign power of love! O grief! O balm!," that he begins to fully engage the symbolic elements by passing, literally, into the Earth (II.1).

Endymion plunges into the Earth and thereby follows the pattern of Masonic ritual where the element is described in one authorized eighteenth-century text as "the subterranean domain where germination and seeding develop," and reiterated in inscriptions found in lodges telling candidates "Visit the Interior of the Earth by Following the Right Road and You Will Find the Hidden Stone."[32] In a scene replete with symbolism associated both with the Rosicrucians and Psyche, as well as language recalling his previous encounter with the mystery of "character'd" Cupid, Endymion plucks a rose that blooms like magic and yields "A golden butterfly; upon whose wings / There must be surely character'd strange things" (II.55–62). He follows its flight to a fountain and there he learns from a nymph

> ... that thou must wander far
> In other regions, past the scanty bar
> To mortal steps, before thou canst be ta'en
> From every wasting sigh, from every pain,
> Into the gentle bosom of thy love. (II.123–27)

Like the dreaming sleep that first reveals his love and sets him on his way, the mystical guide he follows through extraordinary natural beauty, and his arrival at the

---

32 Jacques Chailley's translation of Brenet's *Francs-Maçons Parisiens du Grand-Orient de France* 137–39. The concepts and language would have been available to Keats through multiple exposures. Barruel makes multiple references to subterranean passages and caves in his descriptions of higher degree rituals.

fountain, reflect standard plot devices in alchemical allegories and Rosicrucian texts.[33] The rose also is symbolic of initiation in multiple texts – Christian Rosenkreutz, for example, plucks roses, wears them, and offers them to others during his quest, and in *The Golden Ass* Lucius's cure to transform him from ass back to man depends upon his eating roses. The butterfly was a well-known symbol of Psyche and the soul's transformation via initiatory rites.

The warning Endymion receives is common as well. Similar warnings are found throughout Rosicrucian texts such as *The Chymical Wedding*. During his trials, Christian Rosenkreutz is faced with paths representative of the elements and must choose to continue or return homeward but before he makes his choice he reads upon a tablet "beware! You know not with how much danger you commit yourself to this way."[34] As for Masonic rituals, the chorale of *The Magic Flute* warns that the initiate's trials followed a "dangerous route," and the Royal Arch ceremonies place "sojourners" on a "path" representative of "wayfaring upon a plan of impermanence."[35] After passing through "the dark night of the soul" the initiate responds to the "impulse ... issued from the Highest and Primal Light" and is told he must embark upon unknown paths both difficult and dangerous before achieving full awareness of his own nature and bliss in the presence of the beloved "Light."[36] Like those who present themselves for initiation, Endymion must journey deep into "the silent mysteries" before he gains full identity.

In Book II, the hermetic associations continue to compound as well as the emphasis upon love and self-knowledge as a fusion of opposites. When Endymion is just beginning to learn the extent of his quest, he moves through a series of reversals in which the flames of love combine with sense perception and all the elements to propel him forward. As he wanders through the caverns, the mystery and awe almost overwhelm him and, weary, he stops his journey. "Thoughts of self" return him to a sudden sense that he has followed an "elf / Whose flitting lantern, through rude nettle-briar, / Cheats us into a swamp, into a fire, / Into the bosom of a hated thing," but once "he has raught / The goal of consciousness," he becomes aware of "the deadly feel of solitude," and longs again for the "companionship" of the natural world he has left behind (II.275–84). No sooner does he hate the fire of love and

---

33 To cite only two examples of a great many, they correspond to occurrences in *The Chymical Wedding* and the *Geheime Figuren der Rosenkreuzer...* (Altona: 1785, 1788) <http://www.levity.com/alchemy/secret_s.html>.

34 "The Second Day," *The Chymical Wedding*.

35 Alexander Piatigorsky, *Who's Afraid of Freemasons? The Phenomenon of Freemasonry* (London: The Harvill Press, 1997) 131–39.

36 Piatigorsky 131–39. The initiation rites were understood as exploration of mysteries. The lower and higher degrees of Freemasonry were presented to the public as "Lesser Mysteries" and "Greater" or "Grand Mysteries" (Barruel i). "The Lesser Mysteries" taught "the sciences which the [Liberal] Art[s] transmitted." "The Greater Mysteries were essentially spiritual, embracing man's origin, rebirth or regeneration, and his final felicity." John Yarker, "The Mysteries in Relation to Philosophy," *The Arcane Schools: A Review of their Origin and Antiquity; with a History of Freemasonry and its Relation to the Theosophic, Scientific, and Philosophic Mysteries* (Belfast: William Tait, 1909) <http://www.hermetics.org/yarker.html> 119.

resign himself to "an unknown time, surcharg'd with grief," however, then he rebels and places his faith in Cynthia, and finds himself "warming and glowing strong in the belief / of help" (II.292; 299–300).

The "goal of consciousness" Endymion strives for is tied to his opposing views of love for Cynthia who, although Keats does not explicitly designate her as such in the poem, was understood in myth to represent the "Queen of Hell," who also was referred to in the Masonic ritual as "the truth hidden within himself." Characterizing Cynthia as the Queen of all the elements, he petitions her for aid, crying out:

> Within my breast there lives a choking flame –
> O let me cool it the zephyr-boughs among!
> A homeward fever parches up my tongue –
> O let me slake it at the running springs!
> Upon my ear a noisy nothing rings –
> O let me once more hear the linnet's note!
> Before mine eyes thick films and shadows float –
> O let me 'noint them with the heaven's light! (II.317–24)

The series of ills and cures he speaks of combine both fiery pain and solace derived from air, water, earth, and light, and an intuitive, momentary realization similar to the claim Keats makes in his September 1817 letter to Jane Reynolds that

> In truth the great Elements we know of are no mean Comforters – the open Sky sits upon our senses like a sapphire Crown – the Air is our Robe of State – the Earth is our throne and the sea a mighty Minstrell playing before it – able like David's Harp to charm the evil spirit from such Creatures as I am – able like Ariel's to make such a one as you forget almost the tempest-cares of Life.[37]

And, as in his letter where Keats speaks of these comforting "Elements" in the context of "pleasing" himself "in the Idea of [Jane's] Sensations," the concept of sensations also looks forward to his letters to Bailey on the same topic. Keats presents Endymion's prayer as a progression through the senses similar to the progress he suggests to Bailey, and Endymion himself initially recommends to Peona in Book I. It is one, however, that stresses both the pains of love and growing self-consciousness as well as his need for the natural world he rejected in Book I when all of nature seemed blighted after he had tasted immortal joys.[38] His petition reverses his confession to Peona and reflects a growing awareness characteristic of this stage of the initiation ritual.

Walter Evert has argued that Endymion's reacceptance of the natural world "is the first step in his lessoning of how the divine is truly to be apprehended," and in Book II Endymion must learn also that his goal

> … is to be achieved not by direct assault on heaven, from the upper reaches of human experience, but by submission and descent … . The movement is from aspirant being to humble nothingness … the submission to experience [and] … until he has gone such steps,

---

37  Keats, *Letters I* 158.
38  Keats, *Letters I* 158.

Endymion will not understand the first principles of that nature in which his mortality participates and through which alone he may perceive authentic intuitions of more exalted being.[39]

The humility Evert stresses is characteristic of the early stages of initiation, particularly in higher degree rituals such as those of the Royal Arch where the focus is upon a "contemplative interiorization of symbols," like the "fantastic figures" (II.294) Endymion traces with his spear while pondering his lot, and the candidate must endure "a test in humility and obedience" and is often reminded that "he that humbleth himself shall be exalted," even while he is compelled physically to endure the difficult path.[40] The process, too, strives to teach the initiate the first steps by which he may gain "a partial awareness of mortality" that "cannot be absolute but represents the highest point that human nature can reach without Divine Inspiration or Revelation," in hopes that this process of refinement may enable him, after death, to attain the state of "perfect regeneration," in the presence of the Divine.[41]

Endymion's momentary realization does not, however, signal a complete transformation, and his progress through the Earth continues to represent a series of reversals in which he often wishes to still separate the elements of nature and man. Although he has reappraised his rejection of the natural world above, and come one step closer to the refining of his senses to the apprehension of the Divine, his supplication to Cynthia reflects another kind of rejection. Accordingly, his prayer that she "Deliver me from this rapacious deep!," is not fully answered, but he is granted a respite of sorts and one of a hermetic type. Within the confines of the caverns, where symbolically, "germination and seeding" have their roots, a magical germination occurs and lush growth spreads out before him. A "Dew-dropping melody" inspires in him an "elemental passion" that momentarily consumes his conflicting emotions of bliss and misery, and he is led by a heavenly guide to Adonis's bower (II.373; 375).

As Darwin explained in *The Temple of Nature*, Adonis commonly symbolized the cycles of Nature and the processes of birth, life, death, and rebirth.[42] The myth as well as the figure often appeared in hermetic texts and higher degree Masonry where it signified the same as well as the immortality which might be achieved in esoteric processes of self-realization embodied by alchemy. Adonis's and Venus's roses, so closely connected to the myth, as well as various mystery societies in ancient times, also linked their love story to Rosicrucianism, as did the ancient rituals in which Adonis was worshipped with a blend of mourning and celebration. In Keats's poem, the Adonis episode provides Endymion solace and an example of immortality achieved through love. Furthermore, the myth's use in the societies to teach the constant interchange of dichotomies and interaction between the natural and divine suggests it may also function as reinforcement of the process through which Endymion must pass while he follows Venus's command to "still obey the

---

39 Evert 128.
40 Piatigorsky 132–33.
41 Piatigorsky 132–33.
42 Erasmus Darwin, notes, "Canto I," *The Temple of Nature: or the Origin of Society* (New York, 1804).

guiding hand that fends / Thee safely through these wonders for sweet ends" (574–75).[43]

After his encounter with Venus and Adonis, Endymion once again cycles between wonderment and weariness and then finds himself "wayworn; / Abrupt, in middle air, his way ... lost" (II.655–56). However, in the continuing process of submission, he trusts to the experience and "himself he flings, / Committed to the darkness and the gloom: / Down, down, uncertain to what pleasant doom" (II.659–61). The contrast between this and his previous ascent upon a diamond path from Adonis's bower into increasing gloom almost to the height of "a vaulted dome like heaven's," not only emphasizes the uncertainty inherent in the path he must follow but also matches portions of a Rosicrucian ritual described by Barruel. In the ritual, adepts were guided through rooms resembling deep caves and up precipices almost to the summit of the lodge whose ceiling was painted to resemble the heavens and set with a blazing star not unlike the diamond orb Endymion follows.[44] The initiates, like Endymion, had to submit and "plummet down ... through unknown things," in a physical lesson of humility that impressed upon them the confusion and impermanence inherent in life while also encouraging them to trust to their hearts for guidance (II.662–63).

Endymion's trust and acceptance indicate a progression on his part, and as before, this progress is represented by a heightening sense ability and new bowers of lush generative growth in which Endymion finds himself transported. Endymion's senses are becoming refined, so much so that they seem "grown / Ethereal for pleasure," and he delights in fantasies of winning his love before he recalls his humility and declares "No, no, too eagerly my soul deceives / Its powerless self: I know this cannot be" (II.669–70). He asks instead that he might "by some sweet dreaming flee to her entrancements" (II.701–703). His request bears little of his previous agony, however, and though he fears this feeling of "sudden exaltation" will pass to melancholy, his request for dreams is not represented as a total escape, but rather a temporary "soothing foil" (II.680; 705). In effect, he is very gradually learning to integrate the sharp contrasts of his experiences, and that increased ability prepares him for the next level of intensity and the greater sensation of Cynthia's appearance and their lovemaking.

As indicated by Endymion's speech to Peona in Book I, his union with Cynthia is one with strongly hermetic tones. She is his "known Unknown! From whom my being / sips Such darling essence," and to her he is both bliss and pain inextricably mingled (II.739–40; 773). Although Cynthia claims she still fears to break her bonds of secrecy, she tells him that for their shared love she "could fly / With thee into the ken of heavenly powers," promises him "an immortality of passion's thine: / Ere long I will exalt thee to the shine / Of heaven ambrosial," and even offers him

---

43 For discussion of the symbolism of the Adonis myth, Venus, and the rose, see Kenneth Mackenzie's *The Royal Masonic Cyclopaedia, Masonic Classics Series* (1877; Wellingborough: The Aquarian Press, 1987).

44 Barruel 111–12. Barruel describes this ceremony using adjectives designed to call to mind horror and fear, but the similarities of the experience to those of a dream Christian Rosenkreutz has during *The Chymical Wedding* suggest instead the more positive interpretation supplied.

"lispings empyrean" of immortal speech (II.795–96; 808–10). She promises him all that is attainable by "entanglements, enthrallments … self-destroying, leading by degrees, to the chief intensity" of love in whose "radiance, we blend, / Mingle, and so become a part of it" (I.799–800; 810–12), and explicitly recalls his words with her own desire to "melt into thee" and "entwine hoveringly" (II.815–17). This is the esoteric knowledge, fellowship, and union with the Divine that is the goal of the philosophical alchemy practiced by the Rosicrucians and embodied in the initiation rites of higher degree Freemasonry, and it is figured forth in the traditional alchemical metaphor of love-making. At this point, however, these are promises not yet come to fruition, and as in alchemical allegories, this first physical consummation marks not the completed work, but rather another stage in Endymion's progressive spiritualization.

That he has advanced, though, is evidenced by his response upon awakening to find Cynthia gone. His experiences have "temper'd" him and "his soul Eolian tun'd" communes "with melancholy thought" rather than rage from "Love's madness," and his contemplative mood of self-examination as Book II draws to a close leads him to another important realization similar to his reacceptance of the natural world at the Book's opening (II.860-74). The twinned episodes resemble the circuitous return in the catechisms of Masonic rituals in which a candidate is required to re-examine his previous lessons and thoughts, but does so with greater understanding and heightened sympathies.[45] Endymion thinks:

> And now, …
> How long must I remain in jeopardy
> Of blank amazements that amaze no more?
> Now I have tasted her sweet soul to the core
> All other depths are shallows: essences,
> Once spiritual, are like muddy lees,
> Meant but to fertilize my earthly root,
> And make my branches lift a golden fruit
> Into the bloom of heaven … (II.901–909)

This passage has been variously interpreted by scholars, but the usual assessment resembles Evert's when he writes that Endymion "wrongly … estimates the effect of his experience," and again rejects a process intended to impress upon him the necessity of his engagement with the natural world if he ever hopes to attain a higher spiritual state.[46] In this case, however, I believe Endymion has understood the effect of his experience quite well. The language and imagery of the passage derive from hermetic sources, and their symbolism signals Endymion's conscious understanding and readiness to advance to the next stage of ritual.

---

45  Keats would have found this structural element in any exposure of Masonic rituals where it was represented by the movement of candidates in a circular motion as well as up and down through levels. It also appeared in the catechisms candidates recited. Although the base phrases remained the same, as the candidates rose in degrees, their responses became more complex and accrued additional symbolism.

46  Evert 41; Sperry 132.

Blackstone also has analyzed this passage from a hermetic standpoint, and his comments provide some insight. He argues that Endymion's sexual encounter with Cynthia has transformed him and the "essences" he once rated as "spiritual," he now recognizes as part of the processes of the natural world that correspond to the spiritual health in man not because they are literally spiritual themselves, but rather because they nourish the spirit. Furthermore, as Blackstone notes, this recognition represents the traditional hermetic concept of interchange between the materials of Nature and the life of man in which the process of gaining wisdom leads to a spiritual fruition or progression that when directed back into engagement with the world activates still more progression.[47] While Evert based his analysis upon his study of classical myth and Blackstone relied upon *Timaeus* to arrive at his conclusions, both men support an interpretation of a process in which the physical and natural world provide nourishment for the spiritual world, but there is more to Keats's passage than either appears to realize.

It is not only the concepts or even the adjective "golden" in Keats's passage that make his cycle symbolic of hermetic processes. The images of the tree and its fruits are quite literally alchemical and appeared in multiple alchemical and Rosicrucian texts including Paracelsus's *Aurora* where he explained that the spiritual golden tree rising from the "philosophical earth" put forth blossoms to heaven and in time produced fruit.[48] Moreover, they appear in *The Chymical Wedding* in the context of love and in an episode that bears important reference to Keats's use of the Adonis myth symbolizing much the same process. On the "Fifth Day" of the "wedding," Christian Rosenkreutz is led underground by a guide to a vaulted room lit by great gems. Inside he sees a vessel holding a golden tree "which continually dropped fruit into the vessel; and as often as the fruit fell into the vessel, it turned into water, and ran out from there into three small golden vessels standing by." He follows his guide to a room below this vault and there sees Venus, naked but for a light coverlet, and in a sleep so deep he wonders if she is alive until he sees a tablet declaring she will not awake until the fruit of her tree is entirely melted. The heat that causes the tree to grow and the fruit to melt is described as clear flames, but it soon becomes clear that Cupid keeps watch over the flames and they are sustained by love.[49]

When we recall that Endymion's allusions to his own tree representative of spiritual growth rooted in the physical are prefaced not only by his reflections upon his life in general but also his adventures in "earth's deep maw," and "all its

---

47 Blackstone 144–45.

48 Paracelsus, *Paracelsus his Aurora, & Treasure of the Philosophers… Faithfully Englished …*, transc. Dusan Djordjevic Mileusnic (London: Giles Calvert, 1659) <http://www.levity.com/alchemy/paracel3.html>. Paracelsus added that "the philosophers compare their matter to a certain golden tree of seven boughs," and "a certain matter rises out of the philosophical earth, as if it were a thicket of branches and sprouts: like a sponge growing on the earth. They say, therefore, that the fruit of their tree tends towards heaven." The image also appeared in texts such as Michael Maier's *Atalanta Fugiens*, trans. and transc. Clay Holden, Hereward Tilden and Peter Branwin (Oppenheim: 1617) <http://www.levity.com/alchemy/atalanta.html> and the Rosicrucian work the *Geheime Figuren der Rosenkreuzer…* (Altona: 1785, 1788) <http://www.levity.com/alchemy/secret_s.html>.

49 "The Fifth Day," *The Chymical Wedding*.

buried magic, till it flush'd / High with excessive love," the parallels strengthen the likelihood that it is his *understanding* of the use to which he will put both the natural world and her spiritual love that is the crucial experience here. While the love-making is certainly important, it remains only a portion of the entire process, one step to the ultimate end of spiritualization. This perspective is further indicated by the question Endymion poses to himself: "And now ... How long must I remain in jeopardy / Of blank amazements that amaze no more?" It reminds us that his senses have been progressively refined throughout his travels in the earth, and the repetition of the word "Now" immediately following suggests neither reversal nor completion on his part, but rather, a readiness to move forward. He rejects "blank amazements," and he does so because he has understood the lesson. In a combination of all the hermetic associations with the trial of Earth, Endymion signals that he has "arrived at a truth hidden within himself."

Once Endymion's greater self-knowledge and the refinement of his senses are taken into account, the brief episode that follows becomes not only a transition to the trial of water but also a clear demonstration of his increasing abilities. Presented with the natural occurrence of the streams, Endymion bridges the gap between nature and mind in an act of imaginative apprehension when he creates their story of love that parallels his own. Similar to Paracelsus's artists born in the imaginative spirit and Keats's various forms of "the Poet," he enters into the spirit and life of the waters and understands their language and their essence. His final act is one of imaginative sympathy when, like the Rosicrucian "cabalistic rector," he offers prayers for Alpheus and Arethusa to his "gentle Goddess" that she might "soothe" and "assuage" their pains and "make them happy" (II.1015–17).

The act of fellowship with the waters that Endymion experiences also calls to mind a similar passage a few hundred lines previously in which Keats, in a direct address to the reader, describes the same imaginative activity directly following Endymion's and Cynthia's union. He writes:

> Ye who have yearn'd
> With too much passion, will here stay and pity,
> For the mere sake of truth; as 'tis a ditty
> Not of these days, but long ago 'twas told
> By a cavern wind unto a forest old;
> And then the forest told it in a dream
> To a sleeping lake, whose cool and level gleam
> A poet caught as he was journeying
> To Phoebus' shrine; and in it he did fling
> His weary limbs, bathing an hour's space,
> And after, straight in that inspired place
> He sang the story up into the air,
> Giving it universal freedom. (II.827–39)

Here, the passage acts as an interlude to move the reader from the scene of sexual passion to Endymion's response when he awakes and finds his lover gone. It also, however, reminds the reader that Endymion's story is the poet's as well. The process by which Endymion learns to transmute the materials of life to spiritual nourishment, beauty, and fellowship divine is the same as that the poet must follow if, as Keats declares, he is to create "some shape of beauty," that "moves away the pall / From our dark spirits," a lovely tale, that heard or read, will, like the elixir, become "An endless fountain of immortal drink, / Pouring unto us from the heaven's brink" (I.12–13; 21–24).

Both Endymion and the poet must enter into the life of the world around them and the fellowship they experience must be one in which the elements of the natural world and love figure prominently. And, what they create from their imaginative sympathies must not remain only within themselves. Rather, they must give it "freedom" and turn it to the benefit of others. As we have seen, this process is one intimately connected with the goals and philosophies of the Rosicrucians and Freemasons, and one, moreover, that Keats understood very early on in his career and continued to evince throughout his poetry and letters in terms that explicitly call to mind hermetic philosophies.

Like the figure portrayed in "The Poet," "Where's the Poet," "Bards of Passion and Mirth," and other poems, the narrator of *Endymion* and the character Endymion experience the same interchange between the elemental spirits and man. The poet narrator holds "mystic communings" with the elements and

> He passes forth into the charmed air,
>     With talisman to call up spirits rare
> From plant, cave, rock, and fountain. – To his sight
> The husk of natural objects opens quite
>     To the core: and every secret essence there
> Reveals the elements of good and fair;
> Making him see, where Learning hath no light. [50]

The poet in *Endymion* is able to capture their secret essence and the knowledge they may impart to man. He can absorb his story from "cavern wind," "forest," and "lake," and Endymion can comprehend the secret tale told by the magical fountains buried in the grotto, and like the poet, release the story to the air in spoken word, spurred on by "quenchless burnings" of his heart (II.844).

These same concepts find their corollaries in Keats's letters not only to Bailey but also to Haydon in May of 1817 when Keats speaks of "the Sun the Moon the Stars, the Earth and its contents as materials to form greater things – that is to say ethereal things," to Jane Reynolds in September 1817 where he affirms "the great Elements we know of are no mean Comforters," and to his brother Tom in June 1818 when, describing the beauty of natural world surrounding him, Keats writes, "I shall learn poetry here and shall henceforth write more than ever, for the abstract endeavor of being able to add a mite to that mass of beauty which is harvested from these grand materials, by the finest spirits, and put into ethereal existence for the relish of one's fellows."[51] To create poetry and put it into ethereal existence is to complete

---

50 "The Poet," *John Keats: Poems, Transcripts, Letters, &c. Facsimiles of Richard Woodhouse's Scrapbook Materials in the Pierpont Morgan Library*, ed. Jack Stillinger, vol. 4 (New York: Garland Publishing, Inc. 1985) 305.

51 Keats, *Letters I* 143, 158 and 301.

the cyclic exchange between man and the elements symbolized by the golden tree of alchemy and the prayer Endymion offers for Alpheus and Arethusa. In the process of doing so, the poet uses his imaginative abilities to fulfill his duty as a "sage," and "humanist, physician to all men" (*Fall of Hyperion* 189–90).[52]

---

52  Keats, *Letters I* 271.

# Chapter Six

# Trials of Water and Air

The process of interchange elaborated upon in first half of *Endymion* continues throughout the poem in its entirety. It is expressed yet again in the opening passages of Book III, and as before, the relationship between imaginative apprehension and communion with the elements is reiterated in hermetic terms. Keats's words evoke the skills attributed to the Rosicrucian adepts, while also stressing the concepts of reformation espoused by the Rosicrucians and widely related to the higher degree Freemasons. After speaking of arrogant kings, "tiptop nothings" who "lord it o'er their fellow-men," who provide no solace and only "tinsel," and "sear up and singe / Our gold and ripe-eared hopes," Keats writes:

> Are then regalities all gilded masks?
> No, there are throned seats unscalable
> But by a patient wing, a constant spell,
> Or by ethereal things that, unconfin'd,
> Can make a ladder of the eternal wind,
> And poise about in cloudy thunder-tents
> To watch the abysm-birth of elements.
> Aye, 'bove the withering of old-lipp'd Fate
> A thousand Powers keep religious state,
> In water, fiery realm, and airy bourne;
> …
> Yet few of these far majesties, ah, few!
> Have bared their operations to this globe –
> Few, who with gorgeous pageantry enrobe
> Our piece of heaven – whose benevolence
> Shakes hand with our own Ceres; every sense
> Filling with spiritual sweets to plenitude
> As bees gorge full their cells. And, by the feud
> 'Twixt Nothing and Creation, I here swear,
> Eterne Apollo! That thy Sister fair
> Is of all these the gentlier-mightiest.
> …
> O Moon! Old boughs lisp forth a holier din
> The while they feel thine airy fellowship.
> Thou dost bless every where, with silver lip
> Kissing dead things to life. (III.1–57)

The ideas of "tinsel" and "gilded masks" speak not only to the false kings but also the false gold the Rosicrucians condemned in their manifestos. As in those texts, Keats's own turns to the hope of a reformation and the affirmation that there exist "real" regalities to oppose the "nothings" he decries. Likewise, Keats's "ethereal things," and "thousand Powers" that preside over the birth of the elements and "keep religious state, / In water, fiery realm, and airy bourne" are nothing if not the Rosicrucian spirits. Even the "spiritual sweets" that fill the senses "as bees gorge their full cells," draw upon a very common Rosicrucian metaphor of the alchemist as honey bee that itself functioned as symbolic of the soul's individuation and eventual liberation and later served as one of the emblems given to Master Masons upon their initiation.[1] Finally, Cynthia in her role as counterpart to Apollo also fulfills his Rosicrucian, regenerative role by encouraging fellowship and with her blessing, "kissing dead things to life." The conjunction of the sun and moon was an alchemical commonplace, as was the concept of sunlight or even moonlight working upon decomposed or dead materials and generating light with their beneficent touch. Keats might even have encountered these concepts in the third book of Milton's *Paradise Lost*, long recognized as filled with alchemical allusions, where

... with one virtuous touch
The arch-chemic sun so far from us remote
Produces with terrestrial humor mixed
Here in the dark so many precious things ... (III; 608–11).

In addition, Keats's line describing "old boughs" that "lisp forth a holier din," and the many other references to "religious state," "benevolence," "spiritual sweets," consecration and blessing recall previous passages discussed. They further emphasize that the interchange between the "ethereal things" or "far majesties" such as Cynthia and the world of "our own Ceres" includes men such as the poet who may catch the sounds of mystery from the elements and the natural world and release them again to the world. The poet who fills his senses with "spiritual sweets to plentitude" experiences the divinity in nature, and this effects a reformation within his heart, mind, and spirit. In turn, the poet communicates to others, and his poetry provides the physic and solace necessary to treat men who must live in the world of "prevailing tinsel" and "tiptop nothings" he would reform.

   These concepts and their hermetic associations formed the core of the Rosicrucian manifestos that taught readers that "the clear and manifested Light and Truth" of the "Librum Naturae," might be understood through study and might yield "more wonderful secrets ... than heretofore they did attain unto, and did know" and that "the knowledge thereof [should] be manifested and revealed to many" so it would "raise many and divers thoughts in men."[2] This in turn would benefit all mankind and in particular "those which by reason of the course of the world ... are hindered through

---

1   The images and explanations of their symbolism appeared in Rosicrucian texts by Fludd and Maier as well as Masonic *Monitors*. See Lance S. Owens's discussion of the bee and hive symbols in "Joseph Smith and the Kabbalah: The Occult Connection," *Dialogue: A Journal of Mormon Thought* 27.3 (Fall 1994) 134–66: 117–94. As Owens explains, the symbolism was exceptionally common and based upon various allegorical texts such as Porphyry's *Cave of the Nymphs* which Thomas Taylor translated and discussed.

2   *Confessio Fraternitatis* and *Fama Fraternitatis*, respectively, trans. Thomas Vaughan (1652), transcriber, Kevin Day (Sept. 2002), <http://www.levity.com/alchemy/confessi.html> and <http://www.levity.com/alchemy/fama.html>.

all manner of importunities of this our time" and are most in need of guidance to renew wisdom and "all Arts ... so that finally Man might thereby understand his own Nobleness and Worth" to effect "the love, help, comfort and strengthening of our Neighbors."[3] They were also the same philosophies and Mysteries that Barruel objected to so strenuously when he declared higher degree Freemasonry to be based upon a natural religion that promoted the destruction of Christianity and all the monarchies of the world, and the significance of such associations should not be overlooked.

Although critics have long objected to this opening passage and either ignored or puzzled over what seems to be a political diatribe unrelated to the lines that follow it, the two are in fact connected by the popular hermetic knowledge of the Romantic period and the accusations against the secret societies that promoted it. Furthermore, the entire passage, properly understood, binds together Keats's previous conceptions of the poet's duties and Endymion's growing understanding of the same, and creates a transition to the trials Endymion must face under the sea. Having refined his senses and arrived at a greater understanding of both himself and Nature, Endymion must now put his growing abilities to use to regenerate Glaucus and the world of lovers he encounters.

Glaucus's story comprises approximately three-quarters of Book III, and most scholars recognize parallels between his experiences and Endymion's, particularly in terms of their forced separations from their loves and the parts they play in what Sperry terms "humanitarian service." Critics often refer to the episode in which Endymion revives the dead lovers as indicative of Endymion's increasing attitude of sympathy and selfless charity towards others that re-affirms the fellowship with mankind he lost after his earliest encounters with Cynthia. Likewise, the majority also concur that Glaucus's experience with Circe represents a negative encounter not only because of its outcome but also because of his utter immersion in mere physical sensation when he takes her as his lover. Past these general conclusions, however, there appears to be little agreement.

The very lack has led some to suggest the episode is symptomatic of an ambiguity that reflects a growing distrust of the visionary imagination on Keats's part and an increasing conviction that the dichotomies with which he has been struggling throughout the poem cannot be resolved as he claimed in Book I. Several scholars argue that Glaucus's story acts as a warning to Endymion to be more content with the real world.[4] Others offer variations on that theme. Donald Goellnicht, for example, argues that "Glaucus's ailment, like Endymion's, stems from a psychological discontentment," and Wolf Hirst suggests that the episode represents both characters' tendencies to escape in erotic fantasy.[5] And while Walter Evert does not believe the episode functions as a repudiation of the visionary imagination, he does portray Glaucus as one who "foolishly desired more than the simple bounty of nature," and

---

3    The *Confessio* and *Fama*, respectively.

4    See Stuart Sperry, *Keats the Poet* (Princeton: Princeton UP, 1973) 107–10.

5    Donald C. Goellnicht, *The Poet-Physician: Keats and Medical Science* (Pittsburgh: University of Pittsburgh Press, 1984) 184. Wolf Z. Hirst, *John Keats* (Boston: Twayne Publishers 1981) 68–69.

contends that part of Endymion's "lesson" is to learn to accept that simple bounty rather than wish for more.[6]

Many of the disputes about how to interpret Glaucus's story reference his early experience with Circe. Because Glaucus describes his own passion in terms mirroring those used in descriptions of both Adonis and Venus and Cynthia and Endymion, critics often apply the same values to his initial encounters with Circe. They then argue that the deadly outcome is illustrative of Keats's growing rejection of the visionary and his growing awareness that the visionary imagination is a means of escapism rather than inspiration.[7] When both Glaucus's story and his and Endymion's subsequent actions are examined in the context of hermetic concepts, however, the episode functions instead in the same fashion as the tale of Cupid and Psyche that lies at the heart of *The Golden Ass*. Glaucus's story is a parable from which Endymion will learn and a microcosmic representation of the mental and spiritual trials through which Endymion must pass. The end result for Endymion is not rejection of the visionary or the transcendent, but rather, another example of how contraries must be mingled in order to progress in the interchange of sympathies and imagination with Nature, heaven, and fellow man.

Indeed, when the character of Glaucus and the tale he tells are examined more closely, it becomes clear that here, as before, Keats makes a distinction between the visionary and what Paracelsus and the Rosicrucians termed "phantasy" and warned against. While Glaucus's tale does function as a cautionary one, it is not one indicating Endymion should be content with his lot or wary of the visionary imagination. Rather, Glaucus presents Endymion and readers with a story representative of the dangers of "false gold" in the form of what Glaucus correctly identifies as a love for "arbitrary" sense and a "specious heaven," similar to the Paracelsian definition of phantasy as that which exists solely in the body without the spirit (III.459; 476).

Glaucus's passion for the nymph Scylla has much the same initial effect upon him as Endymion's for Cynthia. Like Endymion, he finds his passion leads to agony and grief and his perspective is one of marked subjectivity. In his pain, however, he seeks out Circe and an easier path than the one Endymion takes. Glaucus attempts to find "a shortcut to happiness" or a magical cure.[8] Such selfish motives and quick fixes are precisely those that lead men awry, and as the *Confessio* warns, the end result of endeavors based upon these will always be disastrous, and God will act against such men by driving them into "the wilderness and solitary places," just as Circe drives Glaucus into the isolated depths of the ocean.[9] Glaucus's experience in Circe's bower is designed to illustrate this point. He becomes a "tranced vassal" to a sensuous phantasy of love that takes place in a bower that mimics those in which

---

6    Walter Evert, *Aesthetic and Myth in the Poetry of Keats* (Princeton: Princeton UP, 1965) 142–43. This resembles Jack Stillinger's assessment as well in *The Hoodwinking of Madeline and Other Essays on Keats's Poems* (Chicago: University of Illinois Press, 1971).

7    Evert summarizes many of these points of view in his discussion of the Glaucus–Circe episode 142–45.

8    Hermione De Almeida, *Romantic Medicine and John Keats* (New York: Oxford UP, 1991) 18–21.

9    *The Confessio Fraternitatis*.

Adonis and Endymion met with their lovers, but Glaucus's experience lacks the elements of true, devout love, spirituality, and awareness of the contraries of life necessary to prevent his "love dream" from being more than a phantasy that will quickly turn to a hell (III.460; 440).

Circe's bower, her words, and even her person all initially draw upon traditional images of gold and light and their related hermetic connotations. Circe is "Phoebus' daughter," and Glaucus awakens in "the light of morn" to the sounds of bees, a lyre, and a "sighing voice;" she appears to him "through a screen of roses," and speaks "honey-words" that fall like "dew," and even calls upon Cupid; and she offers him "soothing warmth" if he is "ripe to taste a long love dream" (III.419–40). When he accepts, she cradles him in roses and devises ever new sensual pleasures for him, and he discovers that "She so did breathe ambrosia; so immerse / My fine existence in a golden clime," that "The current of my former life was stemmed" (III.454–58). Lost in the physical, however, he exhibits no trace of the consciousness of the dichotomies of life and love that have been leading Endymion to greater self-awareness. Instead, time "Shed[s] balmy consciousness within that bower," and all progression halts (III.466). While the treasures offered to Glaucus deliberately evoke those which Endymion seeks and Adonis has gained, the result is given as a stark contrast.

Although Glaucus tells Endymion that he gives his tale so that Endymion may "plainly see how far / This fierce temptation went: and thou may'st not / Exclaim, How then, was Scylla quite forgot?," there is good reason to argue that Glaucus's specificity is meant to do more than deflect charges of infidelity (III.449–52). As with all allegorical tales, there is more at work here than the literal reading of such lines, and the temptation Circe offers extends well beyond the mere physical. She offers Glaucus a life in which joy and grief have been separated and the toil and hardships required for fellowship with man and individuation of the soul have been removed. As the hermetic philosophers warn and Keats illustrates throughout his poetry, the desire for just such a state could be enormously powerful.

Given the moral of Glaucus's tale, and the relationship between his and Endymion's roles, its placement near the center of *Endymion* and its length are justified. In some measure, both men went awry on their paths of love and, having learned from their experiences, now both must expiate their wrongs by actions demonstrating love and sympathy for others. This too reflects hermetic philosophies and, more specifically, various aspects of the initiation rites through which Endymion has been progressing. In the hermetic initiation rituals, water is symbolic of rebirth and redemption; "It is a sort of philosophic baptism that washes [the candidate] clean of all stain" and also gives him "assurance" through its purifying powers.[10] Endymion's and Glaucus's actions in the realm of water illustrate this process.

Furthermore, both men perform tasks and possess characteristics reminiscent of the adepts often portrayed in hermetic texts. Glaucus strongly resembles a Rosicrucian adept who, like the character Lucius in *The Golden Ass*, presents an example of the instruction of a foolish youth who gradually attains wisdom through

---

10 As quoted in Jacques Chailley's *The Magic Flute, Masonic Opera*, trans. Herbert Weinstock (New York: Alfred A. Knopf, 1971) 138. The original is in Michel Brenet's *Francs-Maçons Parisiens du Grand-Orient de France (fin du XVIII siecle)* 308.

his trials and studies over many years.[11] When Endymion first encounters Glaucus, he immediately identifies him as a magician of some sort, an old man wrapped in a blue cloak "O'erwrought with symbols by the deepest groans / Of ambitious magic," who has beside him a pearled wand and sits reading a mysterious book (III.198–99). The cloak, covered with symbols of life but described as "ample as the largest winding-sheet," embodies the paradoxes contained within Nature (III.196). Representative of both life and death, it reveals not only "every ocean-form" but also "storm, / And calm, and whispering, and hideous roar," and resembles in many ways the magical book Glaucus possesses as well – both are means by which man may study Nature and, in Rosicrucian terms, "behold the image and pattern of all the world" (III.199–201).[12]

Furthermore, the book itself and the way in which Glaucus obtains it bear striking parallels to Rosicrucian mythology. As explained in various texts such as the Rosicrucian manifestos and gothic novels like Godwin's *St Leon*, the brothers of the fraternity were sworn each to find a man to be his successor upon his death and to pass on such secrets and wisdom as he and the brothers had gathered together over many years. Their store of wisdom could be communicated both orally and through "a book or volume of all that which man can desire, wish, or hope for."[13] Moreover, while readers of the manifestos were informed that the brothers had written many magical and prophetic books, the most important book was understood to be the Book of Nature from which they read all their secrets and merely transcribed them into written form. They avowed that it was Nature that revealed all their "meditations, knowledge and inventions" and would forever contain

> all that, which from the beginning of the world, Man's wisdom, either through God's revelation, or through the service of the angels and spirits, or through the sharpness and depth of understanding, or through long observation, use, and experience, hath found out, invented, brought forth, corrected, and till now hath propagated and transplanted.[14]

The old man who somehow makes his way to Glaucus from the shipwreck and passes on to him the "treasures" of the scroll and wand before slipping beneath the waves to his grave clearly fulfills the first requirement, and as the words Glaucus reads to Endymion indicate, the scroll itself functions in much the same fashion as the book described by the Rosicrucians. Not only does it contain the prophecy of Glaucus's punishment inflicted by Circe but also the means by which he may eventually free himself from her curse of old age and eventual death. As Glaucus tells Endymion the scroll assures him that

---

11  As Adlington explains in his address "To the Reader," "the metamorphosie of Lucius Apuleius may be resembled to youth without discretion, and his reduction to age possessed with wisedome and vertue." Lucius Apuleius, *The Golden Asse* (1566), trans. William Adlington, ed. Martin Guy (1996) <http://eserver.org/books/apuleius>.

12  *The Fama Fraternitatis.*

13  *The Fama Fraternitatis.*

14  *The Confessio Fraternitatis.*

> ... *he shall not die,*
> *These things accomplish'd: – If he utterly*
> *Scans all the depths of magic, and expounds*
> *The meanings of all motions, shapes, and sounds;*
> *If he explores all forms and substances*
> *Straight homeward to their symbol-essences;*
> *He shall not die. Moreover, and in chief,*
> *He must pursue this task of joy and grief*
> *Most piously; – all lovers tempest-tost,*
> *And in the savage overwhelming lost,*
> *He shall deposit side by side, until*
> *Time's creeping shall the dreary space fulfil:*
> *Which done, and all these labours ripened,*
> *A youth, by heavenly power lov'd and led,*
> *Shall stand before him; whom he shall direct*
> *How to consummate all. The youth elect*
> *Must do the thing, or both will be destroy'd.*
> (III.695–711, italics Keats)

Glaucus's tasks, and the hope held out to him, are those of the Rosicrucian adept. Like the adept, he is offered the chance to regain youth and avoid a death imposed upon him by Circe, but only through many years of study, toil, and service to humanity in his "task of joy and grief." He must act "piously" in the service of love, and although he himself will have gained the knowledge of how to "consummate all," the act will nonetheless remain beyond his power and only capable of "the youth elect" chosen "by heavenly power."

The passage draws together many hermetic elements. Throughout *Endymion*, true lovers have been presented as the materials upon which an alchemical reaction may be wrought, and Glaucus's task accords with this symbolism. The vessel in which alchemical operations took place was frequently referred to in allegories as a grave which would later be depicted as a crystalline enclosure and finally as a bridal bed.[15] Like the adept in *The Chymical Wedding* and the questers of other alchemical allegories such as the *Geheime Figuren der Rosenkreuzer*, Glaucus must gather the lovers from death and place them "side by side" in a "fabric crystalline" or "crystal place" where they lay as though within a flask (III.735). This is similar to the sphere in *Geheime Figuren der Rosenkreuzer* "made quite transparent, bright and clear like crystal," and enclosures in *The Chymical Wedding* where in the early stages of the work three pairs of dead lovers are placed within an enclosure resembling a fountain, and later, the king and queen of the alchemical wedding are laid beside each other, then clothed in fabric "like crystal."[16] Likewise, in an allusion that recalls

---

15 Herbert Silberer, *Hidden Symbolism of Alchemy and the Occult Arts*, prev. *Problems of Mysticism and Its Symbolism*, trans. Smith Ely Jelliffe (New York: Dover Publications, Inc., 1971).

16 *Geheime Figuren der Rosenkreuzer aus dem 16ten und 17ten Jahrhundert* (Altona: 1785, 1788) <http://www.levity.com/alchemy/secret_s.html>; *The Chymical Wedding*, "The Sixth Day" (Foxcroft 1690), eds Adam McLean and Deirdre Green (1984) <http://www.levity.com/alchemy/chymwed1.html>.

Endymion's own reference to the golden tree of alchemy, once "all these labours" have "ripened," Glaucus is assured Endymion will appear "by heavenly power lov'd and led." This distinction too matches that made by the Rosicrucian writers who often warned that the consummation and final success in such endeavors ultimately depended upon Divine will and blessings without which the work would be destroyed and come to naught.

Although the lovers themselves are locked in a magical stasis, "at rest from joy and woes" and "in order plac'd; / Such ranges of white feet, and patient lips / All ruddy, – for here death no blossom nips," this too corresponds to descriptions found in various alchemical allegories (III.736–40). Hermione de Almeida reads this tableau negatively and argues Keats has depicted them like "angelic embryos ... immune at once to the ripening of life and death," their decomposition "held at bay because the stimulus of death that triggers it (and presupposes life) is missing."[17] Yet, a more positive interpretation is possible. De Almeida is not entirely correct when she argues that death is absent. Death is a presupposition of the lovers' state and one, moreover, understood to exist in a paradoxical interchange with life in alchemical works. The lovers are locked in a stasis, and isolated from both joy and grief, but Glaucus's prophecy indicates there has been a "ripening," and the end purpose of Glaucus's and Endymion's task will be to revive the lovers and return them to the contraries of life.

In addition, De Almeida's allusion to the lovers as "angelic embryos" proves particularly apt, because they do indeed bear strong resemblance to yet another alchemical possibility – that of the "embryos" of the reconstituted king and queen of *The Chymical Wedding* who, after their deaths, are reformed in the course of the alchemical labors. During the climactic passages of "The Sixth Day" of *The Chymical Wedding*, as the experiment reaches its final stages of transmutation and transformation, they are described as "angelically fair babes" of "unspeakable beauty," but because they have yet to be revived, they do not possess "any natural warmth or sensibility in them," and instead are "dead figures, yet of a lively and natural colour."[18] Their sleep is a transitory state that exists between stages of progression, and Keats consistently applies this allusion not only to the lovers in the crystalline cavern but later, at the close of Book III, to Endymion as well. When Endymion is overcome by vision and imagination and feels as though he will die, he swoons into a death-like sleep, but nereids surround him "in kind strife / To usher back his spirit into life" and carry him "Towards a crystal bower far away" (III.1014–15; 1018). He too, however, is progressing to yet another stage of his initiation. Indeed, having accomplished his tasks in the realm of water and refined his "inward senses" still further, he hears Cynthia's tell him "'*tis done* -- / *Immortal bliss for me too hast thou won*" (III.1023–24, italics Keats).

In addition, the hermetic connotations suggested by Keats's lovers extend beyond their description and encompass their revival as well. While the lovers are protected from the disintegration required in alchemical processes and suggested in the initiation ceremonies of Masonic degrees by the story of the Master Hiram's

---

17  De Almeida 121.
18  "The Sixth Day," *The Chymical Wedding*.

body which separates into pieces upon discovery, the requirement is nonetheless met when Glaucus "tear[s] his scroll in pieces small, / Uttering the while some mumblings funeral" (III.747–48). It is these pieces that Endymion later will scatter over all the lovers to catalyze their renewal. Having completed this step, Glaucus then clothes Endymion in his magical cloak, figuratively and literally passing the mantle to the youth, and after striking the air nine times with his wand, thereby providing the impetus of one of the magical and spiritual numbers of Rosicrucian and Masonic rites, he becomes instructor rather than actor, and the action he prescribes remain hermetic in nature.

Before Endymion can revive the lovers, Glaucus urges "patience," a common command given to adepts, and then tells Endymion to "first undo / This tangled thread, and wind it to a clue. / Ah, gentle! 'tis as weak as spider's skein; / And shouldst though break it –" (III.755–58). The task is a delicate one, but even before Glaucus can finish his caution, Endymion completes the trial, and his skill leads Glaucus to exclaim "What, is it done so clean? / A power overshadows thee!" (III.758–59). Like Glaucus's amazement, the clue Endymion is required to untangle and wind represents more than a simple, random choice on Keats's part. The myth of the labyrinth and Ariadne's thread also were a metaphor for the long and complex labors of the alchemist and at times, "wandering in the labyrinth without Ariadne's thread was used as a warning in an alchemical treatise against taking words in their ordinary significance" rather than their allegorical ones.[19]

Unlike Glaucus, who has spent a thousand years in close study and labor, Endymion possesses skills granted by heaven and this point is further reinforced by his mastery of Cabala beyond even the old sage. Glaucus cannot read the "sign or charactery" hidden in the shell he next presents to the youth, but Endymion reads it easily, and his mastery of the heavenly language embedded like signs in Nature emphasizes the esoteric nature of their acts (III.762). The ease with which Endymion untangles and winds the clue, the destruction of the scroll of written words, and the invisible "charactery" present on the shell all emphasize that these actions are based not merely in a spoken charm but rather in a power present in Nature and the heavens and in man's interactions with both. As we have seen, such a meaning formed an integral part of the hermetic philosophies underpinning the allegories contained in Rosicrucian and Masonic rites.

Even the reference in the prophecy to Endymion as the "elect" evokes hermetic connotations and ones, moreover, that tie the passage to the higher degrees of Freemasonry. "Elect" was a term commonly used in reference to Masonic initiates and existed as the name of one of the higher Masonic degrees. In their exposures, both Robison and Barruel wrote of a degree called "Elect" which was available to men who had passed the third, "official" degree of Master Mason, and both men drew careful connections between the Elect degree and those of the Scotch or Occult degrees including the Knights of the Sun and various Rosicrucian degrees.[20] In an

---

19 Gareth Roberts, *The Mirror of Alchemy: Alchemical Ideas and Images in Manuscripts and Books* (Toronto: University of Toronto Press, 1994) 78.

20 The Abbé Barruel, *The AntiChristian and Antisocial Conspiracy. An Extract from the French of the Abbé Barruel, to which Is Prefixed Jachin and Boaz, or an Authentic Key to the*

interesting correlation to Glaucus's and Endymion's interactions, Barruel claimed one "secret object" of the ceremonies of the degree was "to re-establish religious Equality, and to exhibit all men equally Priests and Pontiffs," and "to recall the brethren to natural religion."[21]

By designating Endymion as the "elect" who will take on Glaucus's mantle as well as the task of magus and sage, Keats provides his character with the same role, and certainly, Endymion's ability to restore life to the lovers, and the terms with which Keats describes the episode possess unmistakable hermetic and religious tones. The pious work of "high employ" Endymion undertakes is likened to the very shriving of hell when Glaucus exclaims, "Oh, brave! / The spite of hell is tumbling to its grave," and readers are told both that "Death felt it to his inwards: 'twas too much: / Death fell a weeping in his charnel-house" (III.783; 759–60; 878–88). And, the reanimation of the lovers is marked by "a noise of harmony," and "sounds divine," and each "felt a high certainty of being blest" (III.791; 800; 795).

Finally, as their reward, Glaucus and Endymion receive an example of the true fellowship that the Rosicrucians and Freemasons claimed as one of the highest treasures of their labors. As Keats writes, "The two deliverers tasted a pure wine / Of happiness" and

Speechless they eyed each other, and about
The fair assembly wander'd to and fro,
Distracted with the richest overflow
Of joy that ever pour'd from heaven. (III.801–806).

This is the happiness lacking in Circe's "specious heaven," and the wine they taste recalls not only the orbed drop Endymion likens to love and fellowship divine in Book I, but also the "endless fountain of immortal drink, / Pouring unto us from the heaven's brink," that is the result of the beauty and "lovely tales" a poet may capture from the imagination and the world and offer as physic to mankind, and even the "wine of Heaven" Keats speaks to Bailey of in his November 1817 letter (I.23–24).

Furthermore, these multiple correlations remind readers that Endymion is both a quester and a bard, and his role is the same as that of the poet-priest-physician which Keats aspires to be. It is no accident Endymion breaks Glaucus's wand against a lyre before he sprinkles the fragments of the scroll upon the lovers. The act reiterates his connections to the poet who writes his tale and stresses the ways in which the entire poem functions on multiple levels of correspondences. From start to end, Book III itself cycles between Keats's own world and those of Glaucus and Endymion, and from Glaucus's tale, to Endymion's quest, to Keats's leap "headlong into the Sea" of poetry. The image of leaping "headlong into the Sea" applies to all three men, but appears in Keats's 8 October 1818 letter to Hessey in which he asserts that:

The Genius of Poetry must work out its own salvation in a man: It cannot be matured by law & precept, but by sensation & watchfulness in itself – That which is creative must create itself – In Endymion, I leaped headlong into the Sea, and thereby have become

---

*Door of Free-Masonry Ancient and Modern* (Lancaster: Joseph Ehrenfried, 1812) 98–102.
    21  Barruel 99.

better acquainted with the Soundings, the quicksands, & the rocks, than if I had stayed upon the green shore, and piped a silly pipe, and took tea & comfortable advice.[22]

When we recall Keats's 1817 letters to Bailey regarding sensation and the search for Truth, and his criticism of Wordsworth's "Gypsies" that the poem seems "to have been written in one of the most comfortable Moods of his life" and thus is not so much a "Speculation" or "search after Truth" as "a kind of sketchy intellectual Landscape," it becomes clear that Keats believes he is engaging in the same process through which Glaucus and Endymion pass and his esoteric goals are the same.[23] All three engage in the hermetic process of learning to refine the sensations and imagination, to accept the alternating natures of joy and sorrow, and to turn the dichotomies of life to self-knowledge that may lead, ultimately, to fellowship, aid to mankind, and fulfillment.

The interrelation of Endymion's and Keats's quests is further emphasized by the opening of Book IV in which, as we have seen, Keats invokes the English Muse in explicitly hermetic terms by designating her as "by the hues / Of heaven on the spiritual air begot," and claims her essence has infused the spirits of the bards and thereby provided nourishment for souls whose "spirit's wings" would otherwise be clipped by the despondencies of mortal life (IV.2–3; 17–22). As he sets the stage for Endymion's progression into the next trial of air and the complete fusion of opposites epitomized by his love for Cynthia in her dual natures as the earthly Indian maid and the ethereal goddess of the moon, Keats once again reminds readers that this union will result in benefits that extend beyond Endymion's realization of his desires. Just as the ethereal spirits that open Book III offer men solace and imaginative physic in the troubled days that Keats describes, the English Muse of Book IV does so as well. And, in yet another example of the ways in which Keats's concepts turn back upon themselves in the poem, the Muse's inspiration will provide Keats with the final elements of Endymion's journey and the resolution of the tale that will in turn illustrate to men the wisdom Endymion has gained and give them the solace of poetry.

The Indian maid and the challenge she represents to Endymion, however, prove to be the most extreme trial of all, and Endymion is hard pressed to achieve the resolution he desires. Her presence sets in motion a test of all Endymion has experienced and learned to this point. In the hermetic initiation ceremonies, Air "is the emblem of human life, the tumult of the passions, the collision of diverse interests, the difficulty of undertakings, [and] the obstacles that are multiplied" and placed in the adept's path.[24] Such a description coincides perfectly with the actions and settings of Book IV which multiply contrasts so quickly and powerfully, even as they mingle opposites, that Endymion is thrown into a state of confusion that forces him to still deeper stages of self-contemplation until at last he suddenly wins the spiritualization and fellowship he set as his goal in Book I. It is Endymion's love

---

22 John Keats, *The Letters of John Keats, 1814–1821*, ed. Hyder Rollins, vol. 1 (Cambridge, Mass.: Harvard UP, 1958) 374. Hereafter, this work will be referred to as *Letters I*.

23 Keats, *Letters I* 172.

24 As quoted in Chailley from *Francs-Maçons Parisiens du Grand-Orient de France* 138.

for the human maiden as well as Cynthia and his realization that he is torn because "For both, for both my love is so immense, / I feel my heart is cut for them in twain," that acts as the final catalyst for his transformation (IV.96–97). While he began his journey with desire for the light and love of an immortal, as his tale draws to an end, he is compelled to come full circle and apply his passions and gained knowledge to mortal life, thereby encompassing both.

This circuitous journey, central to both Neo-Platonic and hermetic texts, as well as the themes of process critics identify in Keats's poetry, is amply demonstrated throughout Book IV of *Endymion* and on multiple levels. Just as Keats the narrator circles back to his overarching themes of poetry as solace and physic for the imagination and soul in his opening address to the reader, the storyline also represents a return. Although Endymion faints at the end of Book III and we are told he is carried to a "crystal bower far away," and in his swoon he hears Cynthia exclaim that he has won her "immortal bliss," he discovers himself not in heaven but back in the natural world he left behind at his journey's beginning. His return indicates that despite his success he still has more to learn, and his final trial soon reveals itself to be a reiteration of all that has passed before. As in Masonic initiation rituals where candidates progressing through the various grades repeatedly found themselves facing challenges similar to those encountered before but of a higher intensity, and were required to repeat the lessons they learned previously but with greater refinements of knowledge, Endymion must do the same.[25]

Immediately following Keats's invocation, Book IV commences with the words of the Indian maid, and they too represent a return of sorts. Back in his own native land, the first words Endymion hears are those of the Indian maid declaring

> Ah, woe is me! That I should fondly part
> From my dear native land! Ah, foolish maid!
> … To one so friendless the clear freshet yields
> A bitter coolness; the ripe grape is sour:
> Yet I would have, great gods! But one short hour
> Of native air – let me but die at home. (IV.30–31; 34–37)

She reiterates not only the emotional state Endymion himself expresses in Book I when, forlorn and in love, he finds the positive aspects of nature have turned negative, but also his desire in Book II once he has achieved the goal of consciousness to return again to the companionship of his "native bowers," even if only to die (II.331). As soon becomes clear, she also longs for love. Her longing and state make her appear a kindred soul to Endymion, who cannot help but feel "a kindred pain, / To see such lovely eyes in swimming search / After some warm delight" (IV.62–64). As she continues to speak, she also describes her own reactions to love in terms with which

---

25  As only one example of many, see the popular Masonic exposure *Jachin and Boaz*, that was reissued almost every year as late as 1813. A. C. F. Jackson, *English Masonic Exposures 1760–1769* (London: Lewis Masonic, Ian Allan Group, 1986). The rituals described for each grade contain highly stylized repetitions of both catechisms and actions and the symbols and actions of the ceremonies accrue greater import as each grade progresses and more "wisdom" is revealed to the candidates.

Endymion sympathizes. She asserts that love has had such an effect upon her "That but for tears my life had fled away," and that

> There is no lightning, no authentic dew
> But in the eye of love: there's not a sound,
> Melodious howsoever, can confound
> The heavens and earth to such a death
> As doth the voice of love: there's not a breath
> Will mingle kindly with the meadow air,
> Till it has panted round, and stolen a share
> Of passion from the heart! (IV.75; 78–85)

In effect, she reiterates the same conception of love Endymion expresses throughout much of the poem. In Book I, Endymion describes his visions to Peona as brought on, in part, by breezes mingled with enchanted scents born of Cynthia's love, and tells Peona his meeting with Cynthia in the heavens was so powerful that he "did give / My eyes at once to death: but 'twas to live" (I.566–68; 664–65). Similarly, after Peona's rebuke, Endymion is revived by a breeze and seeming taste of "manna-dew," and in his reply to her he compounds love with the rising intensity and effects of sensation upon the imagination and illustrates their power with reference to "Eolian magic" and the sounds of past and future life (I.764; 788). These sensations based upon and intensified by love appear again in Book II in Cupid's lightning and when a "Dew-dropping melody, in the Carian's ear" reminds him once more of love till "First heaven, then hell, [are] then forgotten clear, / Vanished in elemental passion" (II.373–75). Finally, they are also evoked in Book III, and again linked to love, life, and death. At the height of the lovers' celebrations in Neptune's palace, Endymion finds himself so overcome by sensation and so "far strayed from mortality," he cannot bear the experience and shuts his eyes only to learn that "Imagination gave a dizzier pain," and cries out "O I shall die! Sweet Venus, be my stay!" and "I die – I hear her voice – I feel my wing" (III.1010–13).

These repetitions that open Book IV provide the impetus and reason for Endymion's sudden love of the maiden, but they also serve a larger purpose that Endymion is unaware of but of which we as readers should take note. Keats's poem is constructed as an allegory and thus contains more than a simplistic plot device in which Endymion's sudden attraction can be explained as like to like. The conclusion of the poem is already understood by any reader familiar with Endymion's myth, and even those unaware of the myth have been informed at Book III's close that Endymion's goddess soon will come to take him to heaven. That Keats not only introduces the Indian maid, but then takes such care to draw parallels between her thoughts and Endymion's own suggests she serves a larger role, and one, moreover, beyond that critics traditionally ascribe to her as a representative of reality.

Just as Keats has been returning to and refining concepts throughout the poem, the poem's conclusion in which the Indian maid is revealed as Cynthia requires we as readers "circle back" as well. While some may object to such non-linear thinking, this was characteristic of hermetic allegories and particularly Rosicrucian Romances. Moreover, although neither we nor Endymion initially are aware that the Indian maid and Cynthia are the same, Keats was, and regardless of how Cynthia presents herself to Endymion, she is not mortal. If Endymion completely rejects the immortal, then he also rejects her. Knowing this, it seems unlikely that her goal as the Indian maiden is to persuade Endymion to give up his desire for fellowship with the divine and his trust in the visionary imagination that have proven so crucial to his quest. Instead, she poses this final test in order to compel him to integrate his desire for fellowship with the divine and his trust in the visionary imagination with his material sensations and human sympathies. To do so she provides him with the same combination that appears in Books II and III of a parable from which he should learn and an experience in which he should prove what he has learned upon his pulses. Thus, she deliberately portrays herself as his kindred soul and offers him a story that appears to parallel his own.

In addition to her function as a mortal love who creates a "collision of diverse interests," she is intent upon making Endymion recall his earlier declarations and experiences, much the same way candidates of the higher Masonic degrees were reminded of the catechisms, experiences, and lessons they had learned in previous degrees. The implicit assumption in those rituals was that the initiates, armed with previous knowledge and experience, would then face fresh challenges by applying what they had learned before in a process of increasing integration and wisdom. That the maiden does indeed act in this fashion is reinforced by the repetition she supplies when she tells Endymion her story in her "Sorrow Song." As scholars have noted, her initial attempt to escape sorrow through a willing self-immersion in sensuality bears close parallels to Glaucus's tale in Book III. There are, however, crucial differences between her song and story and Glaucus's, and appearing as they do after so many clearly evoked similarities, the story and perspective she offers represent a progression in consciousness that tests Endymion's own development. In the final trial by air, her presence challenges Endymion to recognize the validity of his previous claims of love's nature that he voiced as true without full understanding, to accept the contraries he has experienced in his journey as the fruitful state of life and spirituality, and to avoid the tendency and desire to separate these that he exhibited earlier in his quest.

Almost immediately, Endymion sees her and his love for her as a series of opposites. She is both life and death to him, "young angel" and "fairest thief," and like the song she sings and captivates him with, she binds together joy, sorrow, and the beauty of the natural world, leading him to mourn for the loss of "wings wherewith / I was to top the heavens," even as he tells her "Thou art my executioner, and I feel / Loving and hatred, misery and weal, / Will in a few short hours be nothing to me" (IV.108–13). However, even while he acknowledges the existence of these conflicting elements, his first impulse is to reject the very integration he has been working towards throughout the poem. In a moment he forgets all the lessons of the previous books and his own claims of love's power.

Accordingly, she responds to his words with a series of questions beginning with "Why must such desolation betide / As that thou speakest of?" and she highlights the joys also to be found in nature and love (IV.126–31). Her questions demand affirmation of life in contrast to Endymion's sudden "thirst to meet oblivion," and she offers a warning as well, telling Endymion his untoward response may, "like snails," "slime the rose to night" (IV.123–24; 132–33). Her words call to mind past hermetic references to roses in the poem and should not be taken lightly. Endymion's present stance is one that endangers not only his love in general but also his final consummation. Given Endymion's misapprehension, her "Sorrow Song" immediately following is a strong reminder to him of the interchange between humanity and Nature as well as those elemental "Passions" Keats writes to Bailey about when he asserts that "I have the same Idea of all our Passions as of Love they are all in their sublime, creative of essential Beauty – In a Word, you may know my favorite Speculation by my first Book and the little song I sent in my last."[26]

Endymion's stance simply will not do because it denies the necessary mingling of contraries and the vital connections between happiness and sorrow in human life and fulfillment in the spiritualized realms thereafter. Despite all the similarities between them that Endymion recognizes in her laments, the perspective she offers is not the same as his. As the Indian maid, Cynthia argues for an acceptance of the mixed nature of life and the necessity of what Keats in his Vale of Soul-Making letter will refer to as "a World of pains and troubles … where the heart must feel and suffer in a thousand diverse ways" so the mind and heart may interact to create an "Intelligence destined to possess the sense of Identity" or a soul.[27]

In addition, her roundelay stresses anew the import of Glaucus's overall hermetic message to the youth, as well as the differences in her perspective and those illustrated by Glaucus's cautionary tale. Although she tells Endymion that in her eagerness to leave her melancholy behind she "rush'd into folly" and joined Bacchus's train of revelers as they crossed the world immersed in the pleasures of song, dance, and wine, unlike Glaucus, she realizes of her own accord that she cannot subsume herself in the merely sensual without becoming "sick hearted" and "weary," and she actively chooses to leave the revels and "stray away into these forest drear / Alone, without a peer" (IV.269–71). This is in direct contrast to Glaucus's story where he unwittingly discovers Circe torturing her past lovers, and when he attempts to escape her horrors, finds himself maliciously cursed and driven into the solitary wilderness of the sea. What Glaucus only learns afterwards through the long study of Nature and his "task of joy and grief" in the service of love, she understands early on and without the impetus of fear or an enforced curse.

This is an important distinction to make because the Indian maid's perspective reveals a progression in wisdom and self-knowledge that reflects the hermetic philosophies to which Endymion increasingly has been exposed. Whereas Keats gives Circe's sensual pleasure and phantasy of "specious heaven" decidedly negative connotations, he does not condemn Bacchus's train, though he does supply it with a wild energy bordering on the frantic. Indeed, Keats has the Indian maid tell Endymion that Bacchus draws participants from all the world who join joyfully and participate in the mirth and laughter. Furthermore, the Indian maid's experience ties her to the Mystery rites of Bacchus or Dionysus and through those to both Rosicrucianism and

---

26  Keats, *Letters I* 184.

27  John Keats, letter to George and Georgianna, 21 April 1819, *The Letters of John Keats, 1814–1821*, ed. Hyder Rollins, vol. 2 (Cambridge, Mass.: Harvard UP, 1958) 102–103. Hereafter, this work will be referred to as *Letters II*.

Freemasonry, thereby reinforcing the suggestion that Endymion is engaged in an initiation himself.

The myth of Dionysus represents concepts of rebirth and regeneration, and because he was commonly portrayed as having been torn to pieces by the Titans then reconstituted, his myth oftentimes was used as a metaphor for esoteric philosophies and alchemical processes and considered a forerunner to Freemasonry's legend of the Master Hiram. In addition, during the Romantic period, the common view of Dionysian rites as a combination of mourning and celebration, and sensual and spiritual pleasure, as well as ritual embodiments of death and salvation, matched the integrative philosophies espoused by Rosicrucianism and Freemasonry and was frequently adopted to argue for or against the societies. Authors opposed to Freemasonry pointed to the Dionysian mysteries and initiation rites as proof of Masonry's pagan origins and unsavory intent and took care to reference Masonic texts linking the Dionysiacs to the ancient architects of Tyre from which Hiram the builder of Solomon's Temple was said to hail.[28]

The Indian maid's song, linked as it is to these various societies, illustrates the general concepts underlying the esoteric philosophies, and several particulars in her roundelay also encourage such an interpretation. Scholars have put forth various theories to explain the maiden's love laments, with most simply claiming that she has been in some way disappointed in love, but it is important to keep in mind that because the maiden is Cynthia, she has *constructed* this story for Endymion. She is not quite the meek and yielding dove, and there are hints that while love is a catalyst in her story, her experience is meant not to parallel a disappointment like Glaucus's but a compelling vision like Endymion's and the conflicts he has experienced thus far. Her self-referential question "what enamour'd bride, / Cheated by shadowy wooer from the clouds, / But hides and shrouds / Beneath dark palm trees by a river side?," and the way she abruptly ends her account of her Bacchanalian experiences by telling Endymion "And I have told thee all thou mayest hear," suggest there is more at work here (IV.189–92; 272).

Her sudden refusal to reveal any more marks her as an initiate of the Mysteries, and Keats could have found similar statements in virtually any esoteric work. In the final Book of *The Golden Ass*, Lucius is willing to share a great deal about his initiation experience, but just as often, he breaks off when arriving at points he is "forbidden to speake of."[29] Alchemical and Rosicrucian allegories, too, often were interspersed with sudden breaks and shifts in subject as authors claimed they were not able to speak of such topics in greater detail, and Masonic authors were infamous for repeating points of initiation that were commonly known in exposures

---

28 John Robison, *Proofs of a Conspiracy Against All the Religions and Governments of Europe Carried on in the Secret Meetings of Freemasons, Illuminati and Reading Societies* (New York; London, 1798; Whitefish, MT: Kessinger Publishing, 2007) 268–69. Alex Lawrie, *History of Freemasonry* (London: Longman and Rees, 1804) and George Oliver, *Antiquities of Freemasonry* (London: G. and W. B. Whittaker, 1823).

29 Lucius Apuleius, "The Eleventh Booke: The Forty-Eight Chapter," *The Golden Asse* (1566), trans. William Adlington, ed. Martin Guy (1996) <http://eserver.org/books/apuleius/bookes/eleven.html>.

then abruptly and mysteriously declining to speak of such subjects any further. When this detail is combined with that of her "shadowy wooer from the clouds," her story begins to resemble more and more Endymion's, including the possibility that his journey functions as an allegorical representation of an initiation rite.

Indeed, there is a distinct possibility that Keats was drawing upon Apuleius's *The Golden Ass*. The work not only provides the example of Cupid as a shadowy, unseen lover, and the tale of Cupid and Psyche as a metaphor for the trials of initiation, the union of the real and ideal, and the merging of the sensual and spiritual, but also the example of an initiate who has two loves – one mortal and one immortal. Excluding the tale of Cupid and Psyche, many of the most well known episodes in *The Golden Ass* were those surrounding the character Lucius's sexual experiences with the servant girl Photis. Translators such as Thomas Taylor oftentimes argued that Lucius's and Photis's relationship served as an allegory for larger philosophical concepts and interpreted their passion as illustrative of physical love that parallels Lucius's later love for the goddess Isis. Such a possibility is strengthened when one considers that Photis's name means "light," and while Lucius does eventually dedicate himself to his goddess rather than her, he never condemns the sensual love Photis represents, just as the Indian maid's Bacchanalian experiences are not condemned, although she calls her attempt to separate sorrow and joy "folly." In a similar fashion, throughout *The Golden Ass*, Photis's sensuality and their love is represented as joyful and indicative of beauty both physical and Neo-Platonic. Discussions of her physical attributes in Books Two and Three of the work frequently lead to short digressions upon philosophy, and the same descriptions given for Photis are repeated in the final Book when Lucius describes his encounters with Isis and pledges devotion to her.

In her book length study of *The Golden Ass*, Danielle van Mal-Maeder has argued persuasively that Photis should not be interpreted as opposed to Isis, but rather, as Isis's means by which she will impel Lucius to begin his journey of self-discovery, and this too matches the Indian maid's function in Book IV.[30] Furthermore, because authors such as Lempriere oftentimes identified Isis as Cynthia's Egyptian counterpart, the correlations between Lucius's relationships with the human girl and the goddess strongly resemble the dichotomy Keats creates. Finally, as Lempriere also told his readers, Osiris "according to the opinion of some mythologists, is the same as the sun and the adoration which is paid by different nations to an Anubis, a Bacchus, a Dionysus, a Jupiter, a Pan etc. is the same as that which Osiris received in the Egyptian temples."[31] Given such identifications, the Mysteries of Bacchus that the Indian maid declines to elaborate upon also bear a similarity to those of Pan whose hymn Endymion presides over in Book I.

---

30 Photis, as maid to an enchantress, arranges for Lucius to witness her mistress's transformation from a woman to an owl and mistakenly provides Lucius with the wrong magical ointment, thereby occasioning his literal transformation to an ass and beginning his journey of physical, mental, and spiritual transformation. Danielle van Mal-Maeder, *Apuleius Madaurensis Metamorphoses – Livre II – Texte, Introduction et Commentaire*, Groningen Commentaries on Apuleius (Groningen: Egbert Forsten, 2001) 296–99.

31 John Lempriere, *Bibliotheca Classica; Or, A Classical Dictionary Containing a Full Account of All the Proper Names Mentioned in Antient Authors* ... (London, 1788).

Although Bacchus and Pan should not be entirely conflated, if only because the celebrations Keats describes honoring Pan are decidedly more solemn and reverent, it should not be forgotten that Pan is the "Strange ministrant of undescribed sounds / That come a swooning over hollow grounds" and "Dread opener of the mysterious doors / Leading to universal knowledge," or that his hymn includes the plea:

> Be still the unimaginable lodge
> For solitary thinkings; such as dodge
> Conception to the very bourne of heaven,
> Then leave the naked brain: be still the leaven
> That spreading in this dull and clodded earth
> Gives it a touch ethereal – a new birth:
> Be still a symbol of immensity;
> A firmament reflected in a sea;
> And element filling the space between;
> An unknown – (I.285–302).

Keats presents Pan, the son of Hermes, as presiding over all the elements including that of ether, the "element filling the space between," and the "universal knowledge" espoused by hermeticism, and he does so using terms and concepts commonly associated with the Rosicrucians and Freemasons. Pan opens "doors" to a universal knowledge that may be found within his "lodge." He inspires thoughts and visions of mysteries, that although they may be pursued to the "very bourne of heaven," yet require the imaginative apprehension and divine revelation of a higher power to bring them to light, and he provides the catalyzing element, the "leaven," that works upon the Prima Materia of earth to transform it into something "ethereal" and born anew. These same esoteric concepts appear throughout *Endymion*, and as the Shepherd King devoted to Pan and Cynthia, who Lempriere relates to Osiris and Isis, they are the ones Endymion must pay reverence to, even as he struggles through the spiritual processes they represent.

As a result of these many inter-relations, the Indian maid's song and her story of embarking upon a journey into the Mysteries, spurred by love and the absence of her divine beloved, and learning through her trials that sorrow and joy must be mingled, and sensual pleasure must be mixed with imaginative and spiritual apprehension, are deliberately designed to educate Endymion. Essentially, Cynthia in the form of the maiden offers Endymion an allegorical summation of all the previous Books and creates a final trial in which he must choose his path rather than be led. But, the correct choice is not a rejection of the ideal or visionary for the real, nor is it a subordination of the material or physical sensations to a Neo-Platonic conception of beauty. Instead, it is a fusion of the opposites.

Once the Indian maid and her questions and song are placed within the hermetic context of initiation rituals, the events that follow gain a greater coherence. Endymion responds to her by pledging his love, but his response quickly makes it clear that he has not understood the wisdom offered in her song. He declares:

Poor lady, how thus long
Have I been able to endure that voice?
Fair melody! kind Syren! I've no choice;
I must be thy sad servant evermore:
I cannot choose but kneel here and adore.
Alas, I must not think, soft Angel! Shall it be so?
Say, beautifullest, shall I never think?
O thou could'st foster me beyond the brink
Of recollection! Make my watchful care
Close up its bloodshot eyes, nor see despair!
Do gently murder half my soul, and I
Shall feel the other half so utterly!
I'm giddy at that cheek so fair and smooth;
O let it blush so ever! Let it soothe
My madness! Let it mantle rosy-warm
With the tinge of love, panting in safe alarm. –
…
Wilt fall asleep? O let me sip that tear!
And whisper one sweet word that I may know
This is the world – sweet dew blossom! (IV.297–314; 318–20)

As we know from Keats's letters to Bailey, Endymion's own declarations about the power of sensations in Book I, and his experiences through the earth and sea, the maiden's song and the senses it touches should stimulate the imagination and lead to greater speculations as well as a broader sympathy with Nature and heaven. When both sense and imagination operate in their proper spheres, the result is a greater understanding of "human life and its spiritual repetition" born of the self-aware and "complex Mind – one that is imaginative and at the same time careful of its fruits – who would exist partly on sensation partly on thought."[32] Endymion's reaction, however, reveals the opposite result.

He wishes to abandon all speculations in favor of simple physical sense. Far from using his sense perception to engage his imagination as a means to create correspondences between "human life and its spiritual repetition," or using the heart and mind in active interchange with the world to achieve the goal of self-knowledge and individuation of the soul, Endymion abdicates self-knowledge. He declares he has no choice and cannot choose and voices a desire to eliminate both thought and recollection. If Endymion makes a choice at all here, it is to implore her to provide him with the same sort of "specious heaven" he was warned against by Glaucus or with the immersion in mere physical pleasure he derives from a misinterpretation of her song.

After saying he "must not think," he leaves this decision to her. If she, like Circe, says this "shall be so," and will "murder" half his soul by condoning his adjuration of thought or speculation, he will eagerly acquiesce to her wish and close all his senses to everything but her body, her breath, her cheek "rosy-warm / With the tinge of love, panting in safe alarm." Moreover, Endymion, the Shepherd King and bard who should be most able to do the work of a "cabalistic rector," would trade his prayers

---

32 Keats, *Letters I* 184–86.

to Pan and "solitary thinkings; such as dodge / Conception to the very bourne of heaven," that provide "the leaven / That spreading in this dull and clodded earth / Gives it a touch ethereal – a new birth," for adoration of her that she might "foster [him] beyond the brink / Of recollection," and shut his eyes to not only despair but also "watchful care."

No wonder she closes her eyes. No wonder she weeps and does not give him "one sweet word" to affirm that his perspective "is the world." Endymion's madness is phantasy; his understanding is merely corporeal; and his speech marks him not as a man dedicated to the "imaginative spirit" but as "one who is vacuous, though assiduous."[33] Thus, it is only proper that his words are cut off by "a most fearful tone, / Like one repenting in his latest moan" and warning "*Woe! / Woe! Woe to that Endymion! Where is he?*" (IV.320–21; 323–25). With this in mind, the journey through the air that Endymion and the maiden embark upon next is not a reward for his embrace of a mortal love as some scholars have maintained. Instead, it is another phase of his trial providing him the experiences necessary to ultimately integrate "human life, the tumult of the passions," and "the collision of diverse interests," and it is marked by contrasts and reversals.[34]

Endymion's and the maiden's journey is often described in positive terms. They are born upwards "High as eagles. Like two drops of dew / Exhal'd to Phoebus' lips," and multiple scenes describing the wedding preparations in the heavens remind readers Endymion eventually will marry his maiden (IV.347–48). But, Keats also makes it clear that celebrations are not yet in order. The winged steeds bear a "mournful freight," and Endymion still is a "mournful wanderer" (IV.359, 407). When he finally learns his goddess's identity, he experiences only a moment when all the elements of earth, sea, and air, and "pains, and care, and suffering" are consumed by the fire of love before he is thrown into a "state perplexing" likened to Icarus's feelings when he soared too near the sun (IV.433; 439). It is at this point, midway through the final Book, that Endymion experiences "Adam's dream," and wakes to find his visions truth, but what might have been a moment of validation and exaltation results instead in confusion and dismay.

Nonetheless, the scene does not contradict the arguments Keats makes to Bailey in his November letter when he relates "Adam's dream" both to the maiden's "Sorrow song" and the Imagination that enables man to conceive of life as "a Shadow of reality to come."[35] Endymion's words to the Indian maid have made it clear that he has forgotten the principles Keats elaborates upon in his letter and that he himself espouses in Book I and begins to experience in Books II and III. To counteract his reversal and compel him to continue the processes of self-awareness, individuation, and integration so that he can reaffirm his bonds of fellowship with humanity and arrive at the "chief intensity" of love based upon both sensation and spirit, Cynthia

---

33 Paracelsus, *Opera Omnia*, tom. II, 472. A. *De Virtute Imaginativa*, tract II, trans. C. H. Josten, as quoted by Desiree Hirst, *Hidden Riches: Traditional Symbolism from the Renaissance to Blake* (New York: Barnes & Noble, Inc., 1964) 66–67.

34 As quoted by Chailley from *Francs-Maçons Parisiens du Grand-Orient de France* 138.

35 Keats, *Letters I* 184–86.

must create an experience even more intense than her presence as the Indian maid while also re-affirming the truth of Endymion's visionary imagination.

By revealing herself in her mortal and immortal forms, Cynthia forces the awake Endymion to viscerally confront the contraries he has declared irreconcilable, and when both her persons dissolve, she precipitates a psychological crisis similar to those initiates of hermetic rituals were forced to undergo. Masonic exposures often described ceremonies in which candidates were deliberately thrown into just the state of confusion Endymion experiences by a series of sharp contrasts between light and dark, noise and silence, companionship and solitariness, displays of sorrow and mirth, physical dislocations, and even acted scenes designed to evoke fear then grant solace or to force candidates to play roles in physical dramas representative of life and death.[36] All were designed to break down the candidate's previous suppositions and thereby force him to examine himself and his views of life from an alternative perspective. And, all found their corollary in the metaphors and philosophies of esoteric alchemy in which the spiritualization and transformation of the materials, or the mind and heart, could only be achieved through a process of, in Keats's terms, "self-destroyings," that could then lead to purification and regeneration.

The scenes immediately following Endymion's awakening provide ample support that Cynthia's dual presence then disappearance function in just the manner I am suggesting. Because scholars most often interpret these scenes as evidence that Endymion at this juncture chooses the Indian maid instead of Cynthia, and thus the real over the ethereal, it is best to give the scenes almost in full. Keats presents Endymion as "too well awake" and acutely aware of Cynthia and "the panting side / Of his delicious lady" and writes:

His heart leapt up as to its rightful throne,
To that fair shadow'd passion puls'd its way –
Ah, what perplexity! Ah, well a day!
So fond, so beauteous was his bed-fellow,
He could not help but kiss her: then he grew
Awhile forgetful of all beauty save
Yound Phoebe's, golden hair'd; and so 'gan crave
Forgiveness: yet he turn'd once more to look
At the sweet sleeper, – all his soul was shook, –
She press'd his hand in slumber; so once more
He could not help but kiss her and adore,
At this the shadow wept, melting away.
The Latmian started up: "Bright goddess, stay!
Search my most hidden breast! By truth's own tongue,
I have no daedle heart: why is it wrung
To desperation? Is there nought for me,
Upon the bourne of bliss, but misery?"

---

36 Some variations of these appeared in every exposure and differed only in form according to the degree. Barruel and Robison provided instances of all these throughout their discussions of the rituals surrounding the higher degrees, and the multiple exposures detailing the first three grades of Freemasonry did as well.

These words awoke the stranger of dark tresses:
Her dawning love-look rapt Endymion blesses
With 'haviour soft. Sleep yawned from underneath.
"Thou swan of Ganges, let us no more breathe
This murky phantasm!
...
Ah, shouldst thou die from my heart-treachery! –
Yet did she merely weep – her gentle soul
Hath no revenge in it: as it is whole
In tenderness, would I were whole in love!
Can I prize thee, fair maid, all price above,
Even when I feel as true as innocence?
I do, I do. – What is this soul then? Whence
Came it? It does not seem my own, and I
Have no self-passion or identity.
Some fearful end must be: where, where is it?
By Nemesis, I see my spirit flit
Alone about the dark – Forgive me sweet:
Shall we away?" (IV.440–41; 445–49; 452–81)

Neither Endymion's actions nor his words indicate a conscious choice on his part. In each of her forms, Cynthia commands and nearly overwhelms his senses, and at each assertion of her power, Endymion changes his mind. His heart leaps to her ethereal form, but soon enough the panting beautiful, dark-haired and dark-eyed girl at his side draws his attention and a kiss, then the goddess's golden hair and blue eyes, then back to the maiden who physically presses his hand and gains another kiss. At this point, the goddess weeps and begins to melt away, but Endymion immediately cries out for her to stay. It is she who chooses to depart against his will. There is nothing to indicate Endymion would not have continued to vacillate between the two, and the kisses he gives the Indian maiden do not prove greater favor. Quite simply, he kisses the maiden because he can, and past experience indicates he would kiss his goddess as well if he were able.

In addition, Cynthia's weeping also does not indicate Endymion has chosen the Indian maid. In both her forms, she is as well aware as Endymion that he has "no daedle heart," and readers should not forget that she is the guiding hand and heavenly power that compels him on this journey so he will be "spiritualiz'd" (IV.994). She is playing her part, knowing it will force him to a crisis. Furthermore, even though her goddess form departs and Endymion suspects he has lost the goddess, he remains divided and confused. Although he ostensibly addresses the Indian maiden, he more frequently speaks to himself. Having had his visions revealed as truth, he now refers to the spiritual air, the "fragrant exhalations" that bred them, as "murky phantasm" from which he would depart. He suspects she may take revenge, then quickly realizes "her gentle soul / Hath no revenge in it." Painfully aware that he is not "whole in love," he questions how he can possibly love them both and still "feel as true as innocence."

Finally, and most significantly, he recognizes that his soul no longer seems his own, and he has "no self-passion or identity," but in his confusion he fails to realize the state he describes is precisely that he spoke of to Peona when he declared that there exist "Richer entanglements, enthrallments far / More self-destroying" (I.798–99). This is not a man who has discovered a balance or chosen to embrace one alternative over the other; this is a man whose previous assumptions and even sense of self are being broken down, and when the Indian maid fades away as well, they are destroyed.

The "Cave of Quietude" that Endymion's soul retreats to after he has been overwhelmed by events acts as a dramatic representation of the state of his spirit and, like other parts of the poem, it matches elements of hermetic initiation rituals. Masonic initiates were typically isolated during a portion of the ritual in a darkened room, sometimes called a "Cabinet of Reflection," where a candidate engaged in a psychological process of "return upon himself" and in his extremity was supposed to turn to his inner spiritual resources.[37] Barruel, while investing his description with decidedly negative overtones, told readers that during the Rosicrucian rites of Masonry an initiate was "abandoned to himself" in "a deep cave, or rather a precipice, whence a narrow tower rises to the summit of the Lodge, having no avenue to it but by subterraneous passages replete with horror."[38] Similarly, the Cave of Quietude lies at the heart of a "den" "of remotest glooms" (IV.512; 515).

Dark regions are around it, where the tombs
Of buried griefs the spirit sees, but scarce
One hour doth linger weeping, for the pierce
Of new-born woe it feels more inly smart:
And in these regions many a venom'd dart
At random flies; they are the proper home
Of every ill … (IV.516–22)

Yet, within the Cave of Quietude, there is a calm achieved by an absolute mingling of all contraries. It is a stasis not unlike that of the lovers in Book III, frozen in a moment, before the soul must begin its progress again, and as with the hermetic doctrines, its blessing is available not through conscious striving, but rather "on a sudden it is won. / Just when the sufferer begins to burn," just when his certainty of his previous conceptions and life have been destroyed (IV.532–33).[39]

Like the lovers, however, Endymion cannot remain in stasis. Soon enough, his trials begin again, and unfortunately, Endymion still has not completely learned his lesson. His steed returns him to Earth, he discovers the Indian maid, and he promptly declares "Let us ay love each other; let us fare / On forest-fruits, and never, never go / Among the abodes of mortals here below, / Or be by phantoms duped" (IV.626–29). In the next breath, he cries "O destiny! / Into a labyrinth now my soul would fly, / But with thy beauty I will deaden it," then "let our fate stop here" (IV.629–31; 633). Endymion would fly to just the sort of labyrinth of confusion that the alchemical

---

37  Chailley 134; Barruel 111.

38  Barruel 111.

39  Goellnicht has suggested Keats created his Cave of Quietude as a contrast to Pope's Cave of Spleen in *The Rape of the Lock* (*The Poet-Physician* 186). If we accept this contention, it is worthwhile to recall that Pope, a Freemason, places his cave in a poem that employs Rosicrucian machinery throughout and is prefaced by a note on Rosicrucianism.

philosophies warned against, and even the most charitable reader would not be faulted for wondering why Cynthia does not leave him in utter exasperation.

As his speech continues, he repudiates his visions and his quest, claiming despite all evidence to the contrary that he has "lov'd a nothing, nothing seen / Or felt but a great dream!," and that he has been "Presumptuous against love, against the sky, / Against all elements, against the tie / Of mortals each to each," against Nature, and even against the "proper glory" of his own soul (IV.637–54). But, even as he extols the virtues and joys of "one human kiss! / One sigh of real breath" and the living, mortal warmth of the Indian maid, he still avows his love for Cynthia remains and must tell himself "no more of dreaming," and "Still let me speak; / Still let me dive into the joy I seek, – / For yet the past doth prison me" (IV.689–91).

There is no need to trace all the reversals and exclamations of doubt that Keats explicitly calls "fancies vain and crude" with which Endymion hopes to convince himself, because we have seen them before. While Endymion's speech does indicate that he has re-established his bond with Nature, that he no longer rejects mortal love as he did in Book I, and further, that he now loves the Indian maid with more than mere immersion in sense and escapism, he still has not achieved the complete understanding that would enable him to extend his sympathies beyond her to society. She must present one more challenge. In response to his speech, she offers her own, declaring her love for him but also telling him he cannot have her.

While scholars typically pass over this speech, there is reason to take note of it, even if only briefly. The maiden opens her speech declaring, "O that the flutter of this heart had ceas'd, / Or the sweet name of love had passed away. / Young feather'd tyrant!" (IV.728–30). As she continues, she asks Cupid "Art thou not cruel?," claims "Ever have I striven / To think thee kind, but ah, it will not do!," and demands of the "milder powers" "Am I not cruelly wronged?" (IV.736–37; 47–48). This is not the same tender girl whose soul melts and who feels "so faint a kindness, such a meek surrender" for love at the Book's opening, and as her speech draws to a close, her passionate words create an even sharper contrast (IV.71–73). She tells Endymion:

> We might commit
> Ourselves at once to vengeance; we might die;
> We might embrace and die: voluptuous thought!
> Enlarge not to my hunger, or I'm caught
> In trammels of perverse deliciousness. (IV.757–61)

She repudiates her former views, and the "perverse deliciousness" of death she entertains and suggests to Endymion, even if only momentarily, seems drastically out of character for her. Indeed, such thoughts seem better suited to Endymion.

Yet, we cannot simply attribute this sudden shift to inconsistency on Keats's part as he grows weary with the poem. Outside of her song, this passage represents her longest sustained speech, and given her identity, it appears to serve a deliberate purpose. As with other passages in the poem, her speech should be read with both her identities in mind as well as the forgone conclusion that Endymion will achieve his final desires after he has been spiritualized. When this is done, it seems that after so many instances in which she has offered counters to Endymion's incorrect perspective and impulses, Cynthia has now changed her methods. She gives him back many of the same views he has been espousing and virtually invites him to embrace them. Significantly, however, Endymion does not.

The sort of loss that overwhelmed him before and sent him careening between extremes, now leaves him "lovelorn, silent, wan" (IV.764). The Cave of Quietude within the chaos of life, and deeper yet, within the soul, has had its effect upon Endymion. His experience has impressed upon him the value of the interchange between contraries

> Where pale becomes the bloom
> Of health by due; where silence dreariest
> Is most articulate; where hopes infest;
> Where those eyes are the brightest far that keep
> Their lids shut longest in a dreamless sleep. (IV.537–42)

As a result, he progresses beyond his previous state, and his reaction mirrors his previous one when Cynthia pledged her love to him in Book II only to disappear, and he having "felt too much for such harsh jars: / The lyre of his soul Eolian tun'd / Forgot all violence, and but commun'd / With melancholy thought" (II.865–68). Keats is following the patterns of repetition characteristic of alchemical allegories and hermetic initiation rituals. The effect is heightened as Endymion and the maiden wander through nature in quiet thought, just as Endymion wandered through the realm of earth, until they rest beneath a tree upon which Endymion himself once carved a crescent moon and stars in "pious charactery" (IV.790). Endymion and his love have come full circle, though he is now a different man than he once was.

Just how different becomes evident when Peona discovers them and joyfully looks forward to his presence with his new bride at the ceremonies the priest and sages will offer to Cynthia that very night. Peona assumes the life she portrayed for Endymion in Book I will now come true, but then finds herself asking him the same question as before: "What ails thee?" (IV.846). Endymion's reply is calm and measured. He will not return with her and instead will become a hermit. He tells Peona:

> I would have thee my only friend, sweet maid!
> My only visitor! not ignorant though,
> That those deceptions which for pleasure go
> 'Mong men, are pleasures real as real may be:
> But there are higher ones I may not see,
> If impiously an earthly realm I take.
> ...
> Let it content thee, sister, seeing me
> More happy than betides mortality. (IV.849–54; 858–59)

He adds that he does not intend to abandon his kingdom or his duties of fellowship. Unlike when he proposed to the Indian maid that they leave humanity for a selfish love, this time he stipulates that "Through me the shepherd realm shall prosper well; / For to thy tongue will I all health confide" (IV.863–64).

His decision looks back to the pleasures of "richer entanglements" and "enthrallments" in which happiness and the crowning intensity of friendship and love lead to "fellowship divine," "the clear religion of heaven," that is "A fellowship with essence; till we shine, / Full alchemiz'd, and free of space" (I.779–98). It looks forward as well, to Keats's "Vale of Soul-making" in which "earthly Happiness" is to be valued but must correspond to the world and cannot advance beyond it, even as the "*World* or *Elemental space*" of Nature, provides the medium "for the proper action of *Mind and Heart* on each other for the purpose of forming the *Soul* or *Intelligence destined to possess the sense of Identity*," and thus achieve "Salvation."[40] Endymion's decision reflects, at last, a conscious awareness of the necessary correspondences and interchange between the real and the visionary and the value of both.

At this point readers might reasonably expect Cynthia to reveal herself and end Endymion's trials. That she does not may be the result of Keats's expressed intention early on to create a poem of four thousand lines and, as various critics have claimed, his need to fill his final Book with further incidents to reach that goal, but Keats could just as easily have added lines after Endymion's and Cynthia's reunion. The extended descriptions of celebration at the end of Book III and the detailed wedding preparations throughout Book IV amply demonstrate his ability to envision such a finale. Moreover, had Keats added the actual wedding celebration, the many critics who have objected to the poem's abrupt ending might have been at least partially mollified. Keats cannot have been unaware of the effect his ending would have upon readers. Despite this, however, he chose to extend Endymion's trial and end the poem abruptly. The reasons why lie in further parallels between Endymion's quest and hermetic allegories and initiation rituals.

The poem's ending may strike critics as poor writing, but it is entirely in keeping with the tradition of allegorical texts such as *The Chymical Wedding*. The recurring narrative elements illustrating the process of an eternal return and progression, and the oblique, dream-like style designed to emphasize that the stories were allegorical and representative of esoteric philosophies, resulted in texts that suddenly broke off as might a vision. Because the goal was both to reveal the Mysteries only to those with the capacity to understand and to force the reader to examine the narrative from a philosophical perspective, authors deliberately constructed endings that left their audiences, like Peona, wondering.[41]

In addition, as with the hermetic philosophies illustrated in alchemical allegories and Rosicrucian texts, the themes of death and rebirth played a central role in initiation rituals. Adepts who dedicated themselves to the long task of discovering and understanding the wisdom contained in Nature and man so they might "inform the understanding, correct the passions ... guide the will" and "discover the majestic form of divinity," could not complete the process of self-elucidation without the "final step in the mystical ascension" whereby they accepted their mortality and the "mystical potential" to pass from that into a "perfect regeneration 'in the Mansions

---

40  Keats, *Letters II* 101–103.
41  Gareth Roberts, *The Mirror of Alchemy: Alchemical Ideas and Images in Manuscripts and Books* (Toronto: University of Toronto Press, 1994) 71–78.

of Bliss and in the Presence of the Great *I AM*."⁴² This final step is also the one Endymion passes through as he contemplates the natural world surrounding him on his way to what he supposes will be his final meeting with the Indian maid.

In a direct, sympathetic communion with the natural world around him, Endymion marks the fading season and says,

>          Night will strew
> On the damp grass myriads of lingering leaves,
> And with them shall I die; nor much it grieves
> To die, when summer dies on the cold sward.
> Why, I have been a butterfly, a lord
> Of flowers, garlands, love-knots, silly posies,
> Groves, meadows, melodies, and arbour roses;
> My kingdom's at its death, and just it is
> That I should die with it: so in all this
> We miscal grief, bale, sorrow heartbreak, woe,
> What is there to plain of? By Titan's foe
> I am but rightly serv'd. (IV.933–44)

His acceptance of his mortality grants him a sort of "deathful glee" that shades to solemnity only when he reaches the sacred grove where he will say goodbye to the maiden, and it is there that he moves from awareness of mortality to a belief in the mystical potential to pass beyond it as well. He is not merely a flighty "King of the butterflies," and he swears by "dusk religion, pomp of solitude / And the Promethean clay by thief endued" with the spark of the divinity that he has wed himself "to things of light" all his life (IV.952–58). To believe death will be all "Is sure enough to make a mortal man / Grow impious," and Endymion turns his thoughts inward "On things for which no wording can be found" (IV.960–62).

Keats's choice of words, however, recalls his "Hymn to Pan." The echo indicates that Endymion's thoughts have turned to speculations and conceptions, inner and divine knowledge, such as he once prayed to Pan for and such as his gradual process of initiation and increasing sense perception have prepared him to more fully grasp. This is confirmed when Peona and the Indian maid arrive. Fully aware of himself, his role in the world, and his bond with the essential light of love and the heavens, Endymion declares "I would have command, / If it were heaven's will, on our sad fate," and thus wins his salvation (IV.975–76). He finally does what he has not done before; he makes an active choice based on his fully formed self-identity and the complete knowledge he has gained through experience. In response, Cynthia announces "By Cupid's dove," and "by the lily truth" her form represents, "And so thou shalt!" (IV.979–80). She reveals herself to him as the mingling of the dark Indian maiden and the "Light, as reflected from a silver flame," a conjunction of the mortal and immortal that Endymion, now "spiritualiz'd," can see and fully grasp, physically and spiritually (IV.983; 993).

---

42 Thomas Smith Webb, *The Freemason's Monitor or Illustrations of Masonry* (Salem: Cushing & Appleton, 1818) 149; Alexander Piatigorsky, *Who's Afraid of Freemasons? The Phenomenon of Freemasonry* (London: The Harvill Press, 1997) 132.

As a result, like the Rosicrucian and Masonic initiates who strove to gain the quintessence, Endymion experiences "the transfiguring ecstasy" of love, harmony and beauty suddenly won "after long pain and self-sacrifice of the quest in this world, a world in which opposites are forever quarrelling" and vanishes with his bride.[43] And Keats, like those authors before him who figured forth this personal, inner transformation for which allegory and words were merely substitutes for experience, leaves to readers the task of explaining his metaphysics to themselves.[44] Thus, his narrative fulfills the final role of such allegories by keeping the mystery of final consummation intact, as it must be if the souls of men are to understand bliss peculiar each to its own identity and reach understanding based upon their own personal quests for knowledge.

---

43  Richard Ellmann, *The Identity of Yeats* (London: Faber Press, 1954) 64.

44  I paraphrase here Keats's comment to Shelley, "My Imagination is Monastry and I am its Monk – you must explain my metap[hysics] to yourself" (*Letters II* 323).

# Conclusion

# "A Beacon Towards a Little Speculation"

Having completed his trial of invention and test of his powers, Keats put *Endymion* before the public in April 1818, and after a tour of Scotland, soon found himself caring for his brother Tom who was dying of tuberculosis. Although he continued to write verse throughout the year, including the fragment *Hyperion*, it was January of 1819 before he began a period of intense composition and produced the series of poems for which he is most remembered. In the intervening time, reviews of *Endymion* began to appear, oftentimes combined with reviews of his 1817 volume *Poems*.

Several of influence were vitriolic in their tone and stance, such as the one in *Blackwood's Edinburgh Magazine* whose position had been hinted at as early as October 1817 when the magazine published the first of its series on the "Cockney School of Poetry" and included mention of Keats in an attack on "Jacobin" Hunt and his "poor tame dilution of the blasphemies of the *Encylopaedie*."[1] The *Quarterly Review* branded Keats a "disciple," in April 1818, in addition to calling him a "neophyte" of Hunt, the "hierophant" of the "Cockney School."[2] The June 1818 reviewer in the *British Critic* followed suit, again naming Keats "disciple" to his "Master" Hunt and saying "Mr. Keats is not content with a half initiation into the school he has chosen," and *Blackwood's* joined the voices using much the same language in its August 1818 review.[3] By Keats's death in February of 1821, the worst of the reviews had become part of the lore surrounding his death, and soon thereafter, Shelley's narrative in *Adonais* of a young poet destroyed by the vicious tendencies of society joined them.

As scholars have long argued, most of the negative reviews while focusing at times upon style were more often and most obviously ideologically motivated. As a member of Hunt's circle, Keats was considered a radical whose style offered evidence of political and poetic views that were not to be countenanced, and the reviewers made no secret of the fact that their distaste for Keats's poetry sprang from this. Ultimately, Keats's own assessments have proved more persuasive. He was well aware that *Endymion* was at times "slipshod," and in his October 1818 letter to Hessey, Keats wrote that a J. S. in the London *Morning Chronicle* was "perfectly right" when he opined that the poem contained "very many passages

---

1   Z. (John Gibson Lockhart) "On the Cockney School of Poetry, No. I" *Blackwood's Edinburgh Magazine* (October 1817) 50.

2   For the full review, see Lewis M. Schwartz's, *Keats Reviewed by His Contemporaries: A Collection of Notices for the Years 1816–1821* (Metuchen, NJ: The Scarecrow Press, Inc., 1973) 129–33.

3   Schwartz 134 and 137.

indicating haste and carelessness" but also "beauties of the highest order."[4] Roughly two years later, while describing to Shelley some of his philosophies about poetry, he also would remark that at the time he wrote the poem his "mind was like a pack of scattered cards."[5] But, other comments in his letter to Hessey indicating that his leap "headlong into the Sea" of *Endymion* had left him "better acquainted with the Soundings, the quicksands, & the rocks" of Poetry's "salvation" indicate he also believed the experience had served him well despite his refusal to take "comfortable advice" from others about the poem's construction.[6]

Keats's own criticism suggests that while he found fault with *Endymion* based on technical points, he believed the process of writing the poem and using it to explore his ideology or philosophy held real value. His comments implicitly acknowledge a connection in his mind between his explorations of "the Genius of Poetry," "matured ... by sensation & watchfulness in itself," his speculations, and his examination of various philosophical concepts.[7] For Keats, "the Genius of Poetry," is the Paracelsian "Genius," a singular, powerful form of the spirits or "Genii" that serve to "direct, teach, inspire, and instruct men."[8] Keats's Genius is the "the vast idea," the "English Muse," the spirit that presides over the Poet, and the "souls" of poems left behind in the Rosicrucian "Bards of Passion and Mirth," that can guide those "mortals of the little week" who "must sojourn with their cares" (30). He knew his goal, what he hoped his verse might do, but like Paracelsus, who believed, "there are many mansions in God's house and each one will find his mansion according to his learning. We are all learned but not equally, all wise but not equally, all skillful but not equally; he who searches most deeply is most," Keats knew that the "Genius" must "work out its own salvation in a man."[9]

Furthermore, despite multiple reviews taking Keats to task for the supposed obscurity of the poem's content, his decision to use mythology, and his tendency to deal in abstractions, he did not abandon his topics of choice and continued to explore

---

4    John Keats, *The Letters of John Keats, 1814–1821*, ed. Hyder Rollins, vol. 1 (Cambridge, Mass.: Harvard UP, 1958) 374. Hereafter, this work will be referred to as *Letters I*.

5    John Keats, *The Letters of John Keats, 1814–1821*, ed. Hyder Rollins, vol. 2 (Cambridge, Mass.: Harvard UP, 1958) 323. Hereafter, this work will be referred to as *Letters II*.

6    Keats, *Letters I* 374.

7    Keats, *Letters I* 374.

8    Robert Burton, "Digression of Spirits," *The Anatomy of Melancholy... By Democritus Junior...* (Philadelphia: J. W. Moore; New York, J. Wiley, 1850) 115–27. University of Michigan, "Making of America Books" <http://name.umdl.umich.edu/ACM8939.0001.001> 126. Burton is citing Paracelsus's definition of "Genius." The word is not only Keats's but literally Paracelsus's as well.

9    The first quote, so very like Keats's speculations on a "Mansion of Many Apartments" in his May 1818 letter to Reynolds, is Paracelsus's and comes from his prologue to a treatise on the spirits. The final quote in the sentence is from Keats's letter. Paracelsus, prologue, "Liber de Nymphis, Sylphis, Pygmaeis et Salamandris et de Caeteris Spiritibus Theophrasti Hohenheimensis," *Paracelsus: Four Treatises*, trans. and ed. Henry E. Sigerist (Baltimore: Johns Hopkins UP, 1941; 1996) 224–25. Keats, *Letters I* 374.

them throughout his career regardless of critical response.[10] The politically motivated reviewers frequently made use of the language of the secret societies, suggesting they were well aware of the hermetic connotations derived from Rosicrucianism and Freemasonry that Keats's poem contained, and that they were well aware that his adoption of these elements signaled his "Jacobin" sympathies. In addition to the ways they portrayed Keats, the June 1818 review in the *British Critic* and *Blackwood's* "Cockney School of Poetry. No. IV" in August 1818 described both the content and language of *Endymion* as obscurely "phantastic," and the product of one ignorant of mythology who has "stooped to profane and vulgarise every association" he makes to "Apollo, Pan, Nymphs, Muses, *and Mysteries*."[11]

Keats's choice of topic and style placed him on the liberal side of the question in the "set of adepts, of illuminati" that Shelley wanted to create literally and that Hazlitt wrote metaphorically and fondly of in his 1820 recollections, and the conservative reviewers were not the only ones who were aware of this.[12] Even favorable reviews contained mention of these traits. In the 7 June 1818 review in the *Champion*, the writer praised the mystical elements but worried that they would not be appreciated by others.[13] And in the 1 November 1818 issue of the *Examiner*, Hunt reprinted a favorable review that appeared first in the *Chester Guardian* in which the writer made the case that

> ... there is a mountainous part of [poetry] where the atmosphere is too rare for common breathing; in other words, that a very high degree of poetical inspiration exists which cannot be made *popular*. Such we fear is the case with Mr. Keats's *Endymion*, which calls for a knowledge of the more erudite or second sense of classical mythology. Thus, in the Hymn of Pan, we are called to a glance not only of the more pastoral Deity, but to that typification of general nature, the great and mystic Pan, who, as an universal intelligence, formed one of the fine indistinct dreams of antiquity.[14]

The conclusions reviewers drew about the value of Keats's writing may have differed, but both sides highlighted his approach and content, and Keats's continued use of both strongly suggests his own, positive valuation of these. He chose, deliberately, to identify himself with these concepts, to adopt the Rosicrucian stance in "Where's the poet? Show him!," and to explore hermetic speculations for the remainder of his career.

If we take into account Keats's continued use of linguistics, images, and concepts related to hermeticism in later poems I have discussed such as "Mother of Hermes!," "Where's the Poet?," "Bards of Passion and Mirth," "As Hermes took to his feathers

---

10  See Lewis M. Schwartz's, *Keats Reviewed by His Contemporaries: A Collection of Notices for the Years 1816–1821* (Metuchen, NJ: The Scarecrow Press, Inc., 1973).

11  Schwartz 119–27. Italics mine.

12  Hazlitt's "On the Conversation of Authors" was first published in the *London Magazine* in September, 1820. It may be found in *The Best of Hazlitt*, ed. P. P. Howe (London: Methuen, 1947).

13  Recall Hazlitt's comment in "On the Conversation of Authors" that "there is a Freemasonry in all things. You can only speak to be understood, but this you cannot be, except by those who are in the secret."

14  Schwartz 150.

light," *Song of Four Fairies*, and *Lamia*, as well as the use of similar elements in the *Hyperion* and *Fall of Hyperion* fragments, Keats's self-deprecating claim to Shelley that his "mind was like a pack of scattered cards" while writing *Endymion* proves to be apt, but not in the way readers may suppose.

The simile has been cited by critics as proof of Keats's own awareness of the ways in which *Endymion* often seems to digress and his thoughts lose their way in the poetic realm he created for others to wander in. The description also, however, suggests that Keats was working with many different concepts and attempting to gather them together. So many, in fact, that the profusion of incident and description became confusing for many readers, and the light foundation of the mythological story almost could not bear the weight of meaning he constructed upon it. Keats suggested this himself when in his preface to *Endymion* he remarked that he was dissatisfied with the poem, but he believed further revision would not change it because "the foundations are too sandy."[15] And at least one reviewer played upon Keats's choice of words while also acknowledging Keats's greater intent and did so by calling to mind several obvious associations with the Freemasons. In the April 1820 review in Baldwin's *London Magazine*, a "correspondent" wrote:

> It will be seen that here is a rich fund of materials, fitted for almost every variety and degree of poetical power to work upon. And if the young builder before us has not erected from them a regular fabric, which will bear to be examined by a professional surveyor, with his square and rule and plumb-line, – he has at least raised a glittering and fantastic temple, where we may wander about ...[16]

However, Keats's comment about the foundations, in conjunction with his additional remark that elements of "mawkishness" readers might find within the poem derived from a period between youth and adulthood in which "the soul is in a ferment, the character undecided, the way of life uncertain, the ambition thick-sighted," often have been cited by reviewers during Keats's day such as those of *Blackwood's*, the *Quarterly* and the *Champion*, and by scholars of our time, with a different understanding.[17] Many have assumed that Keats was speaking of and criticizing himself, but his reference to "foundations" suggests another, additional meaning, and one more in accordance with his continued use of the very elements for which he was first criticized and his own philosophies on poetry expressed in his letters.

As early as October of 1817 Keats knew the poem's subject was slight and that his intention to "make 4000 Lines of one bare circumstance and fill them with Poetry," was a "great task," and given this, it seems his personal criticism springs not from any over-arching disavowal of the philosophies he put forth in the poem, but rather from his acknowledgement that the mythological story itself might not withstand the task he had set.[18] Furthermore, as he began to compose *Hyperion*, the point of difficulty he himself identified in the poem was with the character Endymion and the

---

15  Preface, *Endymion*, 64.
16  Schwartz 167.
17  Schwartz 128.
18  Keats, letter to Bailey, 8 October 1817, *Letters I* 170.

myth, not himself. In a 23 January 1818 letter to Haydon, Keats compared the two poems and remarked

> the nature of *Hyperion* will lead me to treat it in a more naked and Grecian Manner – and the march of passion and endeavour will be undeviating – and one great contrast between them will be – that the Hero of the written tale being mortal is led on, like Buonaparte, by circumstance; whereas the Apollo in Hyperion being a fore-seeing God will shape his actions like one.[19]

The implication is that the subject itself and the character of Endymion, a young man whose soul was manifestly portrayed as "in a ferment," and whose identity matches precisely the characterization Keats offers in his preface, determined the elements of "mawkishness" in the poem. And, when we recall Keats's comments in his letters upon the necessity of the poet to enter into the essence of the characters and situations he describes, a poem describing the initiation of such a youth and his maturing sympathies and imaginative processes by necessity would contain the very elements to which critics objected.

If Keats had written "*without Judgment*" in *Endymion*, as he told Hessey, he would write "*with judgment* hereafter," and part of that exercise of judgment included choosing incidents and characters who could better match the philosophical concepts he wished to explore.[20] Another portion of that judgment included a continual process of narrowing and confining his scope or sorting the materials available to him so that the sheer variety and profusion did not overwhelm. Rather than abandon his metaphysics, Keats refined and concentrated them, and attempted to follow the same advice he would give Shelley in 1820 by curbing his magnanimity and choosing more carefully the "ore" with which he intended to "load every rift" of his subjects.[21] In his comments to Shelley about *The Cenci*, of which Keats chose to judge "the Poetry, and dramatic effect," Keats urges Shelley to accept this advice, because unlike before, his own mind is now "pick'd up and sorted to a pip," and he seems aware that adding *too much* of philosophy, the "purpose" he writes "a modern work it is said must have," might dilute the effect.[22]

The interpretation I am suggesting of Keats's self-criticism has important implications for analysis of his poetry as a whole because it enables us to see *Endymion* and the later poems as part of a continuum that exists in Keats's process of self-education. This perspective reveals that many of the goals of poetry and the philosophical arguments Keats expresses in his early poetry remain as touchstones in his later works. Their presence is consistent throughout his writings, but they appear more clearly in the later works because Keats has concentrated on fewer concepts and attempted to extract the golden "ore" that will convey the concepts with greater

---

19  Keats, *Letters I* 207.

20  Keats, *Letters I* 374. Italics Keats's.

21  Keats, letter to Shelley, 16 August 1820, *Letters II* 323. This is the same letter I have noted previously in which Keats tells Shelley "you must explain my metap[hysics] to yourself," and which Shelley's allusions to in his *Defense of Poetry* reveal he interpreted in alchemical terms (323).

22  Keats, *Letters II* 322–23.

purity and intensity. By delineating the many hermetic elements in *Endymion*, we become better equipped to recognize their presence in his other writings, and the possibilities for interpretation of poems such as *Hyperion* and *Fall of Hyperion* suddenly expand.

A brief discussion of some of the hermetic parallels present in Keats's poetry and the directions such analysis might take can illustrate my point. The connections are particularly evident when readers take a broader view of Keats's poetry from early to late. As we have seen, Keats's tendency to employ hermetic symbolism connected to Rosicrucianism and Freemasonry appears very early in his career, and at least some of the hermetic concepts had been on Keats's mind prior to his firm decision to write *Endymion*. Now, we can identify those elements more easily and track them in his later works. Keats's *Sleep and Poetry*, for example, which functions almost as a preamble for *Endymion* and contains sketches of the myth within it, also contains hints of the hermetic concepts he would later explore. *Sleep and Poetry* contains many of his earliest hermetic ideas about what poetry *does* and the poet's function in the world and includes several hermetic references we are now familiar with such as Apollo's attributes and the powers of the "spiritual air" or ether so often found in hermetic texts. These elements form a bridge between this poem and the *Hyperion* fragments Keats would compose at the end of his career.

As Evert has argued, "the presiding deity" of *Sleep and Poetry* is undoubtedly Apollo to whom Keats consistently refers both directly and indirectly, and we are now able to link Apollo's skills as the god of healing, poetry, and prophecy, to his mingled role with Hermes, and the human connection to both of the Rosicrucians who, like Apollo and the poet in *The Fall of Hyperion* attempted to be "a sage; / A humanist, physician to all men" (I.189–90).[23] The same physic that Keats claims poetry will offer in *Sleep and Poetry*, and in the opening lines of *Endymion*, where the beauty of poetry becomes a means to offer "a sleep / Full of sweet dreams, and health, and quiet breathing" and "an endless fountain of immortal drink, / Pouring unto us from the heaven's brink" to renew imagination and lift despair, culminates in the lines from *The Fall of Hyperion* and reveals itself to be of the same nature throughout these poems (*Endymion* I.4–5; 23–24).

It is to "Poesy" in *Sleep and Poetry*, and by extension Apollo, that Keats offers "ardent prayer" and asks that poetry might:

Yield from thy sanctuary some clear air,
Smoothed for intoxication ...
... that I may die a death
Of luxury, and my young spirit follow
The morning sun-beams to the great Apollo
Like a fresh sacrifice; or if I can bear
The o'erwhelming sweets, 'twill bring me to the fair
Visions of all places ... (53; 55; 56–63)

---

23  Walter H. Evert, *Aesthetic and Myth in the Poetry of Keats* (Princeton: Princeton UP, 1965) 98.

Poesy's sanctuary exists in Apollo's realm, and although the speaker who partakes of its essence of "clear air" may die, his death is one which exalts his spirit, and in an indication of future intent, if he is strong enough, the speaker, like Endymion and later the narrator of *The Fall of Hyperion* fragments, will gain visions through the medium of the ether and insight beyond the traditional scope of mortal man. If he can survive the tests, he will

> Write on my tablets all that was permitted,
> All that was for our human senses fitted.
> Then the events of this wide world I'd seize
> Like a strong giant, and my spirit teaze
> Till at its shoulders it should proudly see
> Wings to find out an immortality. (*Sleep and Poetry* 79–84)

The immortality he seeks is bound to the poetry he will create, and these lines are prophetic of the narrator's claim in *The Fall of Hyperion* that "Poesy alone can tell her dreams," and "with the divine spell of words alone can save / Imagination" and the initiation into mysteries he experiences and recounts (I.8–10).

The similarity is particularly striking between lines 56–63 in *Sleep and Poetry* quoted above and the position in which the poet-narrator of *The Fall of Hyperion* finds himself, in part because Keats uses in both the hermetic concepts of the spiritual air. At the steps of the altar, surrounded by an intoxicating smoke likened to a breeze that "melts out the frozen incense from all flowers, / And fills the air with so much pleasant health," an incense that spreads "forgetfulness of everything but bliss," the speaker in *The Fall of Hyperion* is given an ultimatum (I.99–100; 103–104). If he cannot survive the "o'erwhelming sweets" and mount the steps, he will physically die. However, he fulfills the hope of the speaker in *Sleep and Poetry* – he survives – and when he invokes Apollo's name to gain Mnemosyne's knowledge he is rewarded with visions of the ancient events of "this wide world" about which he writes (I.310).

In addition, both the passages from *Sleep and Poetry* and *The Fall of Hyperion* bear resemblance to the dramatic transformation Apollo himself experiences as he "die[s] into life" in Book III of *Hyperion* when he reads in Mnemosyne's "silent face" "a wondrous lesson" and cries out:

> Knowledge enormous makes a God of me.
> Names, deeds, gray legends, dire events, rebellions,
> Majesties, Sovran voices, agonies,
> Creations and destroyings, all at once
> Pour into the wide hollows of my brain,
> And deify me, as if some blithe wine
> Or bright elixir peerless I had drunk,
> And so become immortal. (III.130; 111–20)

Apollo's "bright elixir" through which he passes from death to life echoes the "clear air, smoothed for intoxication" that leads Mnemosyne to declare to the poet-narrator of *The Fall of Hyperion* "Thou hast felt / What 'tis to die and live again before thy fated hour" (I.141–43). And, the parallels extend even further when one realizes that in *The Fall of Hyperion*, Keats transfers the act of "reading" Mnemosyne's face from Apollo to the poet-narrator. In effect, Keats conflates Apollo and the poet, and in each case, the intoxication is explicitly linked to knowledge and "the events of this wide world" which provide the necessary visions the poet and Apollo must communicate to others for their benefit.

Thus, the functions of poetry and physic are combined just as they are in Rosicrucian mythology and in Keats's extended exposition of these concepts in *Endymion*, where the immortality Endymion strives for parallels the efforts of the adepts who search for the elixir gained by knowledge of the world, "more wonderful secrets … than heretofore they did attain unto, and did know, or are able to believe or utter," that must "be manifested and revealed to many" so they might benefit all mankind with "the love, help, comfort and strengthening of our Neighbors."[24] In the act of writing "all that was permitted, / All that was for our human senses fitted" Keats's poet-narrator of *The Fall of Hyperion* acts as a humanist and physician and fulfills the same functions (*Sleep and Poetry* 79–80).

Furthermore, he provides a form of knowledge designed to do "some good for the world," and combat the constricted "range / In the present strength of manhood" that fetters the imagination and prevents it from "freely fly[ing] / As she was wont of old" (*Sleep and Poetry* 162–65).[25] Indeed, by the time of *Fall of Hyperion*, the young poet who hopes to do all these things in *Sleep and Poetry* literally does them. He writes all that was permitted, and in doing so, he conflates his earlier poetic self with that of Apollo. The two merge and in the fusion they exemplify yet another symbolic touchstone of Rosicrucian and Masonic philosophies present in not only Keats's poetry but also his letters.

Parallels also exist in the topic of dreams and visions that Keats chose to explore in *Endymion* as well as *The Fall of Hyperion*, and further examination of these may well change our perspectives on Keats's poetry as forms of escape versus forms of engagement with the world. While scholars recognize the importance of sleep and dreaming in Keats's poetry, and they often note Apollo's role in prophecy, they also tend to separate the two and make clear distinctions between dreaming and the visionary state. Yet, when Keats's presentation of the two in *Endymion* and *The Fall of Hyperion* is examined from the standpoint of hermeticism, a new interpretation becomes possible that suggests one should not reject dreams entirely but rather move through dreams to a higher state.

There are significant differences in how Peona and Endymion, and thus Keats, conceives of dreams and visions, and these differences are ones which appear not only in *Endymion* but also much later in *The Fall of Hyperion* which Keats, significantly, subtitles *A Dream*. In an early version which Keats later revised of Peona's scolding response to Endymion's confession of the causes of his discontent, she exclaims:

---

24 The *Confessio Fraternitatis*, trans. Thomas Vaughan (1652), transcriber, Kevin Day (Sept. 2002), <http://www.levity.com/alchemy/rosicros.html>.

25 Keats, *Letters I* 271.

> Is this the cause?
> This all? Yet it is wonderful – exceeding –
> And yet a shallow dream, for ever breeding
> Tempestuous Weather in that very Soul
> That should be twice content, twice smooth, twice whole,
> As is a double Peach.[26]

Her response to Endymion's confession is a parallel to Moneta's later description of the dreamer who is a "fever" of himself, "venoms all his days," and "vexes" the world (*Fall of Hyperion*, I.169; 175; 202). In both cases, however, the poet, embodied first by Endymion, who is a bard, and then by the narrator of *The Fall of Hyperion*, counters the assessment given by Peona and Moneta of dreams as causing sickness. Both passages are marked by characters who appear as though they misunderstand the dreams and the poet's goals and intent. The differences appear to lie in how the dreams and thus the imagination are put to use, and in each case, the poet's response is similar to and echoes the thoughts on the imagination and dreams that Keats expresses in his 1817 letters to Bailey employing hermetic concepts.

The narrator's opening lines of *The Fall of Hyperion* provide the clue as to the differences as well as the similarities. He claims, "Poesy," can both "tell her dreams" and "save / Imagination from the sable charm / And dumb enchantment," and asserts that men may tell their dreams "Since every man whose soul is not a clod / Hath visions, and would speak, if he had lov'd / And been well nurtured in his mother tongue" (I.8–15). In these lines, Poesy is given as that which saves Imagination and visions from simple dumb enchantment – it refines the visions of the Imagination into something more. Furthermore, the speaker indicates later to Moneta that the poet's actions and the poetry he creates serve a familiar, specific purpose. He is "sure not all / Those melodies sung into the world's ear / Are useless: sure a poet is a sage; / A humanist, physician to all men" (I.187–90).

Moneta, however, has mistaken him for one of the "dreamer tribe," and while the dreamers and the poets both feel "the miseries of the world / Are misery, and will not let them rest," she contends the dreamer cannot offer a benefit to the world, in part because although

> Every creature hath its home;
> Every sole man hath days of joy and pain,
> Whether his labours be sublime or low –
> The pain alone; the joy alone; distinct:
> Only the dreamer venoms all his days,
> Bearing more woe than all his sins deserve. (I.171–76)

The dreamer makes distinct the joy and pain, he separates them and venoms his days because he will not admit their mingled existence. Such dreams are "shallow" like those Peona dismisses, and like Peona, Moneta finds more nobility in those who "seek no wonder but the human face; / No music but a happy-noted voice" and have no thought to come to places such as her ruined temple (I.163–65).

---

26  As quoted by Bernard Blackstone, *The Consecrated Urn: An Interpretation of Keats in Terms of Growth and Form* (London: Longmans, Green and Co., 1959) 126.

The poet, though, is the dreamer's "sheer opposite;" he "pours out a balm upon the world," and just as the narrator of the poem believes, he does "labour for the mortal good" (I.200–201; 159). He is the opposite because he knows what Keats tells Taylor in his "Pleasure Thermometer" letter and reiterates in his discussion of the "Vale of Soul-making" – that the "Different Natures" of joy and sorrow must be mixed – and that the dreams of Imagination put to higher use can "guess at heaven" and provide men with a means to link the ethereal and the mortal (*Fall of Hyperion*, I.4). This perception of the Imagination follows closely that which Paracelsus and the Rosicrucians espoused and that Keats expresses throughout *Endymion*. It marks the dreams "Poesy" "tells ... with the fine spell of words" as much more than phantasy (*Fall of Hyperion*, I.8–9).

Although I have provided only a few examples of the repetition of hermetic elements such as the spiritual air and the metaphysics of dreams and visions in Keats's poetry, many others exist, including the mystical initiation motif the poet-narrator of *The Fall of Hyperion* finds himself in when he stands at the foot of the steps in a temple, and like initiates in the secret societies, must surmount those steps before he will be granted access to the Mysteries and knowledge Moneta can provide. These elements appear years after Keats's first expression of them and their corresponding metaphysics in his letters and poetry, and his continued exploration of their ramifications and his insistence on an intermingling of the material and spiritual in both the Imagination and life appears to be remarkably consistent.

What does change is Keats's acknowledgement of the complexity of putting into words and effective poetry the speculations he sensed might provide a better "system of salvation" for mankind.[27] Keats was attempting to use the hermetic concepts and linguistics advanced by the secret societies in order to both examine his own beliefs and more clearly express them in his writings. In the process of writing *Endymion*, however, Keats drew upon so many of the hermetic images and concepts embodying the interchange between the contraries of life and the fusion of the material and spiritual through the mediums of sensation and imagination, that even as he was able to better understand his own speculations, he discovered that how he conveyed his conceptions was too diffuse and scattered. Because of this, the poetry intended to make manifest the constant presence and interaction between the material world and the visionary one and to provide men with a means to move from the real to the visionary, to spark their imaginations and thereby provide physic and inspiration for their souls, could not fulfill its function to Keats's satisfaction.

Nonetheless, this does not mean he abandoned the goal or came to suspect it was a false lure. At the end of his career, Keats still was attempting to create a purer and more potent form to communicate many of the hermetic concepts appearing in *Endymion*, even to the point of creating in *The Fall of Hyperion* a frame in which he, the narrator, experiences the mystical trials, dreams and vision states experienced by Endymion and later Apollo in *Hyperion*. His willingness to place himself within the same context as his previous characters strongly suggests Keats had not lost his faith in the potential value of his speculations. That he left both *Hyperion* and *The Fall of Hyperion* unfinished may attest instead to an awareness that these poems, like

---

27  Keats, *Letters II*, 103.

*Endymion* before them, might also require too much "circumstance" that would dilute the effect of the poetry and the philosophical concepts it was meant to embody.

Recognizing the hermetic elements with which *Endymion* is infused allows us to fully accept the poem as the first extended attempt that Keats claimed it was, complete with its faults, without creating a division between his earliest and latest writings. His use of hermetic language, style, and content in his letters and poetry provides us with insight into the progression of his own thought processes, the philosophical questions he posed, and the means by which he attempted to convey his beliefs throughout his poetic career. Instead of the sudden and divisive break in style, content, or even ideology sometimes argued in Keats scholarship, there appears a progression of self-knowledge, wisdom, and awareness of the world and man's life within it that Keats expressed as one of his goals and continually struggled to achieve. We can acknowledge that our differences in interpretation oftentimes may derive from the multiplicity inherent in the concepts Keats was exploring and the varying ways in which he presented those concepts as he examined them more fully and considered the poetic forms they might take.

In a letter to Reynolds dated May of 1818, Keats described human life as a "Mansion of Many Apartments" we all must explore.[28] He believed that as we grow in self-knowledge we find ourselves in a "Chamber of Maiden-Thought" and become "intoxicated with the light and the atmosphere."[29] But, the "breathing" of this "atmosphere" leads to a "tremendous sharpening [of] one's vision into the heart and nature of Man," and "We feel 'the burden of the Mystery'" he would later describe in *Ode on a Grecian Urn* as that which can "tease us out of thought" (44).[30] He believed knowledge and poetry could ease this burden and help us continue "to make discoveries, and shed a light" in the darkening chambers of the mind, despite the "Misery and Heartbreak, Pain, Sickness and oppression" of the world.[31] At the same time, however, as his letters and poetry suggest, Keats knew that the salvation and physic poetry and self-knowledge offered were inextricably bound to darker elements of the "Mystery" and the political and social realities of the world. The joyful intoxication could not be separated from the sorrow, and both played a role in not only the happiness of men on Earth but also the individuation of the soul required for happiness thereafter.

The task Keats set for himself, to express these thoughts in poetry and not only spur men on in the Chamber of Maiden-Thought but also provide the sublime material men needed to refine their imaginations and their sense of the beautiful essence of life around them, was enormously difficult. The dichotomies inherent in the philosophies Keats appears to have espoused required he adopt thought processes capable of accepting a fusion of opposites and discard the impulses of consecutive reasoning that demanded one perspective could not reasonably co-exist with another. Moreover, this mode of thought included another, equally difficult one embodied by the "Negative Capability" Keats strove for that, like mysticism, allowed for

---

28  Keats, *Letters I* 280.
29  Keats, *Letters I* 281.
30  Keats, *Letters I* 281.
31  Keats, *Letters I* 281.

"uncertainties, Mysteries [and] doubts" as a means to truth. Given the nature of his task and his mode of thought, the hermeticism present in Keats's writings places him firmly within a rich and longstanding tradition.

If his letters and poetry have appeared to many readers to present irreconcilable contradictions, it may be because the very nature of the tradition he draws upon necessitated that authors embody those contradictions in their texts and thereby impel readers to shift their own ways of thinking and perceiving the world around them. Just as Keats's tale of Endymion's initiation recounts this process, the means by which Keats communicates the tale requires that readers follow many of the same steps. In doing so, it serves as an early example of the poetry Keats attempted to create that would aid men on their own quests in the chambers of the Mansion of Life and in the Vale of Soul-making. *Endymion* speaks to the imaginative senses Keats would try to evoke in later poems such as *Lamia* and *The Fall of Hyperion* so that the beauties of poetry might provide physic to readers. Similarly, it also presages the way these poems offer both engagement with reality and the hope for something more transcendent, but do so within a design that unsettles previously held reader assumptions and presents such marked contrasts that readers feel compelled to engage in their own speculations.

If, in the extremity of his final illness, delirious from fever and the lack of oxygen from his destroyed lungs, and near starvation, Keats relinquished his speculations and his hopes, the writings of his entire career still attest to the value he believed they held and his attempts to make that value a present force in his society. As he once avowed to his brother George, his speculations and writings represented a process that included both poetry and philosophy, imagination and science, material and spiritual awareness, a "straining at particles of light in the midst of a great darkness," and he wrote "with no Agony but that of ignorance; with no thirst of any thing but knowledge when pushed to the point though the first steps to it were through my human passions" and "with my Mind – and perhaps I must confess a little bit of my heart."[32] To allow Keats's writings this wider range is no fault.

---

32  Keats, *Letters II* 80–81.

# Bibliography

*A Full Report of the Proceedings of the Meeting, Convened by the Hampden Club, which Took Place at the Freemason's Tavern, Great Queen-Street, Lincoln's Inn Fields, on Saturday, the 15th June, 1816, upon the Subject of Parliamentary Reform*. London: William Hone, 1816.

Abrams, M. H. "Keats's Poems: The Material Dimensions." *The Persistence of Poetry: Bicentennial Essays on Keats*. Eds. Robert M. Ryan and Ronald A. Sharp. Amherst: University of Massachusetts Press, 1998.

——. *Natural Supernaturalism: Tradition and Revolution in Romantic Literature*. New York: W. W. Norton & Co., 1971.

Addison, Joseph. "No. 574." *The Spectator*. Ed. Donald F. Bond. Vol. 4. Oxford: Clarendon Press, 1965. 561–65.

Adlington, William. "To the Reader." *The Golden Asse*. 1566. Ed. Martin Guy. 1996. <http://eserver.org/books/apuleius>.

Anderson, James. *The Constitutions of the Free-Masons Containing the History, Charges, Regulations, &c. of that Most Ancient and Right Worshipful Fraternity*. London 1723. Philadelphia: Benjamin Franklin, 1734. *An Online Electronic Edition*. Ed. Paul Royster. University of Nebraska Lincoln Libraries: <http://digitalcommons.unl.edu/libraryscience/25>.

Apuleius, Lucius. *The Golden Asse*. Trans. William Adlington. 1566. Ed. Martin Guy (1996): <http://eserver.org/books/apuleius>.

Baigent, Michael. "Freemasonry, Hermetic Thought and the Royal Society of London." *Ars Quatuor Coronatum: Transactions of the Quatuor Coronati Lodge No. 2076* 109 (1996): 154–87.

Barrett, Francis. *The Magus, or Celestial Intelligencer*. 2 vols. London: 1801. <http://www.sacred-texts.com/grim/magus/>.

Barruel, The Abbé. *Mémoires Pour Servir à l'Histoire du Jacobinisme, The AntiChristian and Antisocial Conspiracy. An Extract from the French of Abbe Barruel to which is Prefixed Jachin & Boaz; or An Authentic Key to the Door of Free-Masonry, Ancient and Modern*. London: 1798.

Barruel, The Abbé. *The AntiChristian and Antisocial Conspiracy. An Extract from the French of the Abbé Barruel, to which Is Prefixed Jachin and Boaz, or an Authentic Key to the Door of Free-Masonry Ancient and Modern*. Lancaster: Joseph Ehrenfried, 1812.

Bate, W. Jackson. *John Keats*. Cambridge, Mass.: The Belknap Press of Harvard University, 1963.

Blackstone, Bernard. *The Consecrated Urn, an Interpretation of Keats in Terms of Growth and Form*. London: Longmans, Green and Co., 1959.

Bond, Donald F., ed. *The Spectator*. 4 vols. Oxford: Clarendon Press, 1965.

Bradley, Joshua. *Some of the Beauties of Freemasonry*. London: 1816.

Brewster, Sir David. *History of Free-Masonry*. Edinburgh: 1804.

Brooks, E. L. "'The Poet' an Error in the Keats Canon?" *Modern Language Notes* 67.7 (Nov. 1952): 450–54.

Brotemarkle, Diane. *Imagination and Myths in John Keats's Poetry*. San Francisco: Mellen Research UP, 1993.

Browne, John. *The Masonic Master-Key through the three degrees, by way of polyglot. Under the sanction of the Craft in general, containing the exact mode of working, initiation, passing and raising to the sublime Degree of a Master. Also, the several duties of the Master, officers, and Brethren while in the Lodge, with every requisite to render the accomplished Mason an explanation of all the hieroglyphics*. London: 1802.

——. *The Master Key through all the Degrees of a Freemason's Lodge, to which is added, Eullogiums and Illustrations upon Freemasonry*. London: 1798.

Buchen, I. H. "Frankenstein and Alchemy of Creation and Evolution." *Wordsworth Circle* 8 (1977): 103–112.

Budgell, Eustace. "No. 379." *The Spectator*. Ed. Donald F. Bond. Vol. 3. Oxford: Clarendon Press, 1965. 422–25.

Burland, C. A. *The Art of the Alchemists*. London: Weidenfeld & Nicolson, 1967.

Burton, Robert. *The anatomy of melancholy, what it is, with all the kinds, causes, symptoms, prognostics, and several cures of it. In three partitions. With their several sections, members, and subsections, philosophically, medically, historically opened and cut up. By Democritus Junior [pseud.]. With a satirical preface, conducing to the following discourse*. Philadelphia: J. W. Moore; New York, J. Wiley, 1850. <http://name.umdl.umich.edu/ACM8939.0001.001>.

Bush, Douglas. *Mythology and the Romantic Tradition in English Poetry*. Cambridge, Mass.: Harvard UP, 1937.

Butler, Marilyn. Appendices B and C. *Frankenstein, Or, the Modern Prometheus, the 1818 Text*, by Mary Wollstonecraft Shelley. Oxford: Oxford UP, 1993: 198–251.

——. Introduction. *Frankenstein, Or, the Modern Prometheus, the 1818 Text*. Ed. Marilyn Butler. Oxford: Oxford UP, 1993.

——. "Myth and Mythmaking in the Shelley Circle." *ELH* 49.1 (Spring 1982): 50–72.

Canning, George and John Hookham Frere. "The Loves of the Triangles." *Poetry of the Anti-Jacobin*. London: Wright, 1799: 108–12.

Calcott. *Calcott's Masonry with Considerable Additions and Improvements, Containing Some Original Matter Never Before Printed*. Philadelphia: Robert DeSilver, 1817.

Chailley, Jacques. *The Magic Flute, Masonic Opera*. Trans. Herbert Weinstock. New York: Alfred A. Knopf, 1971.

Chayes, Irene. "Coleridge, Metempsychosis, and 'Almost all the followers of Fenelon'." *ELH* 24.4 (Dec. 1958): 290–315.

Coleridge, Samuel Taylor. "The Plot Discovered." *The Collected Works of Samuel Taylor Coleridge: Lectures 1795 on Politics and Religion*. Eds. Lewis Patton and Peter Mann. Princeton: Princeton UP, 1971.

——. "To Mr. Justice Fletcher, Letter II." *The Collected Works of Samuel Taylor Coleridge: Essays on His Times in The Morning Post and Courier*. Ed. David V. Erdman. Vol. 2. Princeton: Princeton UP, 1978.

Colvin, Sir Sidney. *John Keats: His Life and Poetry, His Friends, Critics and After-Fame*. 1917. New York: Octagon Books, 1970.

Coneybeare, F. C. "Preface." *Philostratus The Life of Apollonius of Tyana*. Ed. and trans. F. C. Coneybeare. 1912. Cambridge, Mass: Loeb Classical Library, Harvard UP, 1969.

*The Confessio Fraternitatis*. Ed. Thomas Vaughan (1652). Transc. Kevin Day (Sept. 2002): <http://www.levity.com/alchemy/rosicros.html>.

Cox, Jeffrey N. *Poetry and Politics in the Cockney School: Shelley, Keats, Hunt, and Their Circle*. Cambridge: Cambridge UP, 1998.

*The Chymical Wedding*. Foxcroft: 1690. Ed. Adam McLean and Deirdre Green (1984): <http://www.levity.com/alchemy/chymwed1.html>.

Da Costa, Hippolyto Joseph. *Sketch for the History of the Dionysian Artificers: A Fragment*. Red. J. B. Hare. London: Sherwood, Neely, and Jones, 1820. <http://www.sacred-texts.com/cla/dart/dart00.htm>.

Darwin, Erasmus. *The Botanic Garden*. London: 1791.

——. *Temple of Nature, or the Origin of Society, a Poem, with Philosophical Notes*. London: 1803

Davies, Paul. *Romanticism and Esoteric Tradition: Studies in Imagination*. Hudson, NY: Lindisfarne Books, 1998.

De Almeida, Hermione. *Romantic Medicine and John Keats*. New York: Oxford UP, 1991.

——, ed. *Critical Essays on John Keats*. Boston: G. K. Hall & Co., 1990.

De Quincey, Thomas. "Historico-Critical Inquiry into the Origins of the Rosicrucians and the Free-Masons." *De Quincey's Collected Writings: Tales and Prose Phantasies*. Ed. David Masson. Edinburgh: Adam & Charles Black, 1897. 384–448.

——. "Secret Societies." *De Quincey's Collected Writings: Historical Essays and Researches*. Ed. David Masson. London: Adam & Charles Black, 1897. 173–249.

Dermott, Laurence. *Ahiman Rezon*. 1756. Bloomington, IL: Masonic Book Club, 1973.

"The Divine Pymander in XVII Books." *The Corpus Hermeticum*. Trans. John Everard.

London: 1650. <http://www.levity.com/alchemy/corpherm.html>.

Dobbs, B. J. T. *The Janus Face of Genius: The Role of Alchemy in Newton's Thought*. Cambridge: Cambridge UP, 1991.

——. *The Foundations of Netwon's Alchemy or the Hunting of the Green Lyon*. Cambridge: Cambridge UP, 1975.

Duncan, Edgar Hill. "The Natural History of Metals and Minerals in the Universe of Milton's Paradise Lost." *Osiris* 11 (1954): 386–421.

Dyer, Gary R. "Peacock and the 'Philosophical Gas' of the Illuminati." *Secret Texts: The Literature of Secret Societies*. Eds. Marie Mulvey Roberts and Hugh Ormsby-Lennon. New York: AMS Press, 1995. 188–209.

Ellmann, Richard. *The Identity of Yeats*. London: Faber Press, 1954.

Evert, Walter H. *Aesthetic and Myth in the Poetry of Keats*. Princeton: Princeton UP, 1965.

*The Fama Fraternitatis*. Ed. Thomas Vaughan (1652). Transc. Kevin Day (Sept. 2002): <http://www.levity.com/alchemy/rosicros.html>.

Fellows, John. *The Mysteries of Freemasonry, or an exposition of the Religious Dogmas and Customs of the Ancient Egyptians, etc.* London: Reeves and Turner, 1866.

Figulus, Benedictus. "The Book of the Revelation of Hermes, interpreted by Theophrastus Paracelsus, concerning the Supreme Secret of the World." *A Golden and Blessed Casket of Nature's Marvels*. Frankfurt: 1608; London: 1893. <http://www.levity.com/alchemy/paracel2.html>.

Finney, Claude Lee. *The Evolution of Keats's Poetry*. 2 vols. Cambridge: Harvard UP, 1936.

Firminger, W. K. "The Romance of Robison and Barruel." *Ars Quatuor Coronatum: Transactions of the Quatuor Coronati Lodge No. 2076* 50 (1937): 31–69.

Ford, Newell F. *The Prefigurative Imagination of John Keats*. Stanford: Stanford UP, 1951.

Fraser, Alexander. *An Account of the Proceedings at the Festival of the Society of Freemasons at Their Hall, the 27th of January 1813*. London: 1813.

*Free-Mason's Review*. London: 1796–98.

*Geheime Figuren der Rosenkreuzer, aus dem 16ten und 17ten Jahrhundert. Erstes Heft. Aus emem alten Mscpt. zum erstenmal ans Licht gestelit* (Altona: 1785, 1788): <http://www.levity.com/alchemy/secret_s.html>.

Gittings, Robert. *John Keats*. Boston: Little, Brown, 1968.

Goellnicht, Donald C. *The Poet-Physician: Keats and Medical Science*. Pittsburgh: University of Pittsburgh Press, 1984.

——. "Keats's Chemical Composition." *Critical Essays on John Keats*. Ed. Hermione de Almeida. Boston: G. K. Hall & Co., 1990. 143–56.

Gradman, Barry. *Metamorphosis in Keats*. New York: New York UP, 1980.

Gray, Ronald D. *Goethe the Alchemist*. Cambridge: Cambridge UP, 1952.

Gross, Jonathon. "Byron, Freemasonry, and the Carbonari." *Freemasonry in Enlightenment Europe*. Ed. William Weisberger. New York: Columbia UP, 2002. 347–74.

Hazlitt, William. "On the Conversation of Authors." *The Best of Hazlitt*. Ed. P. P. Howe. London: Methuen, 1947.

Hinckley, Edward B. "On First Looking into Swedenborg's Philosophy: A New Keats Circle Letter." *Keats–Shelley Journal* 9.1 (Winter 1960): 15–25.

Hirst, Desiree. *Hidden Riches: Traditional Symbolism from the Renaissance to Blake*. New York: Barnes & Noble, Inc. 1964.

Hirst, Wolf Z. *John Keats*. Boston: Twayne Publishers 1981.

Hitchcock, Ethan Allen. *Remarks Upon Alchemy and the Alchemists*. 1857. Whitefish, MT: Kessinger Publishing, 2003.

Holmyard, E. J. *Alchemy*. 1957. Baltimore: Penguin Books, 1968.

Hunt, Leigh. *The Religion of the Heart. A Manual of Faith and Duty*. London: 1853.

Hutchinson, William. *Spirit of Freemasonry*. London: J. Wilkie and W. Goldsmith, 1775. New York: Bell Publishing Co., 1982.

Iamblichus. "Reply of Abammon, the Teacher to The Letter of Porphyry to Anebo, Introduction." *Theurgia or The Egyptian Mysteries, Reply of Abammon, the Teacher to The Letter of Porphyry to Anebo Together with Solutions of the Questions Therein Contained*. Trans. Alexander Wilder. London: William Rider & Son Ltd., New York: The Metaphysical Publishing Co. 1911. <http://www.esotericarchives.com/oracle/iambl_th.htm#chap1>.

Imlay, Elizabeth. "Freemasonry, the Brontes, and the Hidden text of Jane Eyre." *Secret Texts: The Literature of Secret Societies*. Eds. Marie Mulvey Roberts and Hugh Ormsby-Lennon. New York: AMS Press, 1995. 210–27.

Jackson, A. C. F. *English Masonic Exposures 1760–1769*. London: Lewis Masonic, 1986.

———. "Rosicrucianism and Its Effect on Craft Masonry." *Ars Quatuor Coronatum: Transactions of the Quatuor Coronati Lodge No. 2076* 97 (1984): 115–41.

Jones, Bernard E. *Freemasons' Guide and Compendium*. Revised ed. 1956. London: George G. Harrap & Company Ltd., 1971.

Jones, James L. *Adam's Dream: Mythic Consciousness in Keats and Yeats*. Athens: University of Georgia Press: 1975.

Keats, John. "Mr. Kean." *The Poetical Works & Other Writings of John Keats*. Ed. H. Buxton Forman. Rev. Maurice Buxton Forman. Vol. 5. New York: Phaeton Press, 1970.

Keats, John. *John Keats: Complete Poems*. Ed. Jack Stillinger. 1978. Cambridge, Mass.: The Belknap Press of Harvard UP, 1982.

Keats, John. *The Letters of John Keats, 1814–1821*. Ed. Hyder Rollins. 2 vols. Cambridge, Mass.: Harvard UP, 1958.

Keen, Paul. *The Crisis of Literature in the 1790s: Print Culture and the Public Sphere*. Cambridge: Cambridge UP, 1999.

Kitson, Peter J. "Beyond the Enlightenment." *A Companion to Romanticism*. Ed. Duncan Wu. Oxford: Blackwell Publishers, Ltd., 1998.

Knight, G. Wilson. *The Starlit Dome, Studies in the Poetry of Vision*. 1943. New York: Barnes & Noble, 1960.

Laplace-Sinatra, Michael. "'A Natural Piety': Leigh Hunt's The Religion of the Heart." *The Allen Review* 19 (1997) <http://www.oxford.op.org/allen/hunt.htm>.

Lawrie, Alex. *History of Freemasonry*. London: Longman and Rees, 1804.

Lempriere, John. *Bibliotheca Classica; Or, A Classical Dictionary Containing a Full Account of All the Proper Names Mentioned in Antient Authors*. London, 1788.

Lessing, Gotthold Ephraim. *Lessing's Masonic Dialogues*. 1778. Trans. *The Builder* 1915–1929. Ed. Robin L. Carr. Bloomington, IL: The Masonic Book Club, 1991.

Levinson, Marjorie. *Keats's Life of Allegory: The Origins of a Style*. Cambridge: Cambridge UP, 1988.

Linden, Stanton J. "Alchemy and Eschatology in Seventeenth-century Poetry." *Ambix* 31 (Nov. 1984): 102–24.

———. "Alchemical Art and the Renaissance Emblem." *Secret Texts: The Literature of Secret Societies*. Eds. Marie Mulvey Roberts and Hugh Ormsby Lennon. New York: AMS Press, 1995. 7–23.

——. *Darke Hierogliphicks: Alchemy in English Literature from Chaucer to the Restoration.* Lexington, Kentucky: The University of Kentucky Press, 1996.

Lockhart, John Gibson. "On the Cockney School of Poetry, No. I." *Blackwood's Edinburgh Magazine*: October 1817.

Lowell, Amy. *John Keats.* 2 vols. Boston: Houghton Mifflin Co., 1925.

Mackenzie, Kenneth. *The Royal Masonic Cyclopaedia.* 1877. *Masonic Classics Series.* Wellingborough: The Aquarian Press, 1987.

Magee, Glenn Alexander. *Hegel and the Hermetic Tradition.* Ithaca: Cornell UP, 2001.

Maier, Michael. *Atalanta Fugiens.* Oppenheim: 1617. Trans. and transc. Clay Holden, Hereward Tilden and Peter Branwin. <http://www.levity.com/alchemy/atalanta.html>.

Mal-Maeder, Danielle van. *Apuleius Madaurensis Metamorphoses – Livre II – Texte, Introduction et Commentaire.* Groningen Commentaries on Apuleius. Groningen: Egbert Forsten, 2001.

McCalman, Iain. "Newgate in Revolution: Radical Enthusiasm and Romantic Counterculture." *Eighteenth-Century Life* 22.1 (1998): 95–110.

Mellor, Anne K. *Mary Shelley: Her Life, Her Fiction, Her Monsters.* New York: Routledge, 1989.

Money, John. "The Masonic Moment; Or, Ritual, Replica, and Credit: John Wilkes, the Macaroni Parson, and the Making of the Middle-Class Mind." *The Journal of British Studies* 32.4 (Oct. 1993): 358–95.

Moretti, Franco. "Graphs, Maps, Trees: Abstract Models for Literary History." *New Left Review* 24 (November/December 2003): <http://www.newleftreview.net/Issue24.asp?Article=05>.

Morford, Mark, Robert J. Lenar and Michael Sham. *Classical Mythology.* 7th edn Oxford: Oxford UP, 2002.

Motion, Andrew. *Keats.* New York: Farrar, Straus and Giroux, 1998.

Oliver, George. *Antiquities of Freemasonry.* London: G. and W. B. Whittaker, 1823.

Ormsby-Lennon, Hugh. "Nature's Mystic Book: Renaissance Arcanum into Restoration Cant." *Secret Texts: The Literature of Secret Societies.* Eds. Marie Mulvey Roberts and Hugh Ormsby-Lennon. New York: AMS Press, 1995.

Owens, Lance S. "Joseph Smith and the Kabbalah: The Occult Connection." *Dialogue: A Journal of Mormon Thought* 27.3 (Fall 1994): 117–94.

Pagel, Walter. *Paracelsus: An Introduction to Philosophical Medicine in the Era of the Renaissance.* Basel: Karger, 1958.

Paine, Thomas. *Writings of Thomas Paine.* Ed. Moncure Daniels Conway. Vol. 4. New York: G. P. Putnam's Sons, 1896.

Paracelsus, Theophrastus Philippus Aureolus Bombastus von. "Interpretatio alia Totius Astronomiae." *The Life and Soul of Paracelsus.* Trans. John Hargrave. Ed. John Hargrave. London: Victor Gollancz, Ltd., 1951.

——. *Paracelsus: Essential Readings.* Trans. Nicholas Goodrick-Clarke. Ed. Nicholas Goodrick-Clarke. Wellingborough: Crucible, Thorsons Publishing Group, 1990.

——. *Paracelsus: Four Treatises*. Trans. C. Lilian Temkin, George Rosen, Gregory Zilboorg, and Henry E. Sigerist. Ed. Henry E. Sigerist. 1941. Baltimore: Johns Hopkins UP, 1996.

——. *Paracelsus his Aurora, & Treasure of the Philosophers. As also The Water-Stone of The Wise Men; Describing the matter of, and manner how to attain the universal Tincture. Faithfully Englished. And Published by J.H. Oxon*. Transc. Dusan Djordjevic Mileusnic. London: Giles Calvert, 1659. <http://www.levity. com/alchemy/paracel3.html>.

——. *Paracelsus: Selected Writings*. Trans. Norbert Guterman. Ed. Jolande Jacobi. Bolligen Series 28. 1951. Princeton: Princeton UP, 1979.

Patterson, Jr., Charles I. "The Monomyth in the Structure of Keats's *Endymion*." *Keats–Shelley Journal* 31 (1982): 64–81.

Pausanias. *Pausanias: The Description of Greece*. Trans. Thomas Taylor. London: 1794.

Peck, Walter E. "Shelley and the Abbé Barruel." *PMLA* 36 (1921): 347–53.

Perkins, David. *The Quest for Permanence: The Symbolism of Wordsworth, Shelley and Keats*. Cambridge, Mass.: Harvard UP, 1965.

Piatigorsky, Alexander. *Who's Afraid of Freemasons? The Phenomenon of Freemasonry*. London: The Harvill Press, 1997.

Pirie, David B. "Old Saints and Young Lovers: Keats's Eve of St. Mark and Popular Culture." *Keats: Bicentenary Readings*. Ed. Michael O'Neill. Edinburgh: Edinburgh UP, 1997.

Prescott, Andrew. "The Devil's Freemason": Richard Carlile and his Manual of Freemasonry." Lecture, Sheffield Masonic Study Circle. Sheffield, 30 November 2000. <http://www.shef.ac.uk/~crf/papers/devil.htm>.

——. "Freemasonry and Its Inheritance." Lecture, Meeting of the Masonic Museums and Libraries Group. Sheffield, England, 30 September 2000. *The Centre for Research into Freemasonry*. <http://www.shef.ac.uk/%7Ecrf/papers/museum. htm>.

——. "An Introductory Bibliography of English Language Works on the History of Freemasonry." *The Centre for Research into Freemasonry*. Ed. Andrew Prescott. The University of Sheffield: <http://freemasonry.dept.shef.ac.uk/index. php?q=bibl>.

Preston, William. *Illustrations of Masonry*. 1772. The Universal Masonic Library. Louisville: American Masonic Publishing Association, 1858.

Priestman, Martin. *Romantic Atheism: Poetry and Freethought, 1780–1830*. Cambridge: Cambridge UP, 1999.

——. "Temples and Mysteries in Romantic Infidel Writing." *Romanticism on the Net* 25 (Feb. 2002): <http://users.ox.ac.uk/~scat0385/25priestman.html>.

Primer, Irwin. "Erasmus Darwin's Temple of Nature: Progress, Evolution, and the Eleusinian Mysteries." *Journal of the History of Ideas* 25.1 (Jan.–Mar. 1964): 58–76.

Rix, Robert. "William Blake and the Radical Swedenborgians." *Esoterica* 5 (2003): <http://www.esoteric.msu.edu/VolumeV/Blake.htm>.

Roberts, Gareth. *The Mirror of Alchemy: Alchemical Ideas and Images in Manuscripts and Books from Antiquity to the Seventeenth Century*. Toronto: University of Toronto Press, 1994.

Roberts, John M. *The Mythology of the Secret Societies*. London: Secker & Warburg, 1972.

Roberts, Marie Mulvey. "Science, Magic, and Masonry: Swifts Secret Texts." *Secret Texts: The Literature of Secret Societies*. Eds. Marie Mulvey Roberts and Hugh Ormsby-Lennon. New York: AMS Press, 1995. 97–113.

Roberts, Maureen B. *The Diamond Path: Individuation as Soul-making in the Works of John Keats*, 1997 (April 2003): <http://www.cgjungpage.org/articles/robertm4.html>.

Robison, John. *Proofs of a Conspiracy against all Religions and Governments of Europe, Carried on in the Secret Meetings of Freemasons, Illuminati, and Reading Societies*. Edinburgh: n.p., 1797. New York: George Forman, 1798. Whitefish, MT: Kessinger Publishing, 2007.

Roe, Nicholas. *John Keats and the Culture of Dissent*. Oxford: Oxford UP, 1997.

——, ed. *Keats and History*. Cambridge: Cambridge UP, 1995.

Rollins, Hyder, ed. *The Keats Circle Letters and Papers 1816–1878*. 2nd edn 2 vols. Cambridge, Mass.: Harvard UP, 1965.

Ross, Robert N. "'To Charm Thy Curious Eye': Erasmus Darwin's Poetry at the Vestibule of Knowledge." *Journal of the History of Ideas* 32.3 (July–Sept. 1971): 379–94.

Ryan, Robert M. *Keats: The Religious Sense*. Princeton: Princeton UP, 1973.

——. *The Romantic Reformation: English Politics in English Literature, 1789–1824*. Cambridge: Cambridge UP, 1997.

Schwartz, Lewis M. *Keats Reviewed by His Contemporaries: A Collection of Notices for the Years 1816–1821*. Metuchen, NJ: The Scarecrow Press, Inc., 1973.

Sendivogius, Michael. "Part Two, Concerning Sulphur, Concerning Elementary Fire." *New Chemical Light*. Transc. Jerry Bujas. <http://www.levity.com/alchemy/newchem3.html>.

Sharp, Ronald A. *Keats, Skepticism, and the Religion of Beauty*. Athens: University of Georgia Press, 1979.

Shelley, Mary Wollstonecraft. *Frankenstein, Or, the Modern Prometheus, the 1818 Text*. Ed. Marilyn Butler. Oxford: Oxford UP, 1993.

Shelley, Percy Bysshe. *The Letters of Percy Bysshe Shelley*. Ed. Frederick L. Jones. 2 vols. Oxford: Clarendon Press, 1964.

Silberer, Herbert. *Hidden Symbolism of Alchemy and the Occult Arts*. Prev. *Problems of Mysticism and Its Symbolism*. Trans. Smith Ely Jelliffe. New York: Dover Publications, Inc., 1971.

Smith, S. N. "The So-Called 'Exposures' of Freemasonry of the Mid-Eighteenth Century." *Ars Quatuor Coronatum: Transactions of the Quatuor Coronati Lodge No. 2076* 56.1 (1943): 10–11.

Spence, Joseph. *Polymetis*. London: 1747. New York: Garland Publishing, Inc., 1976.

Sperry, Stuart M. *Keats the Poet*. Princeton: Princeton UP, 1973.

Stallknecht, Newton P. *Strange Seas of Thought: Studies in William Wordsworth's Philosophy*. Bloomington: Indiana University Press, 1958.

Steele, Mabel A. E. "The Authorship of 'The Poet' and Other Sonnets: Selections from a 19th Century Manuscript Anthology." *Keats–Shelley Journal* 5 (Winter 1956): 69–80.

Stevenson, David. *The Origins of Freemasonry: Scotland's Century, 1590–1710*. Cambridge: Cambridge UP, 1994.

Stewart, Trevor. "A Basic Historico-Chronological Model of the Western Hermetic Tradition." (21 March 2003): <http://sric-canada.org/stewartintro.html>.

Stillinger, Jack, ed. *John Keats: Complete Poems*. Cambridge, Mass.: The Belknap Press of Harvard UP, 1978.

——, ed. *John Keats: Poems, Transcripts, Letters, &c. Facsimiles of Richard Woodhouse's Scrapbook Materials in the Pierpont Morgan Library*, Vol. 4. New York: Garland Publishing, Inc., 1985.

——. *The Hoodwinking of Madeline and Other Essays on Keats's Poems*. Chicago: University of Illinois Press, 1971.

——. *Reading The Eve of St. Agnes: The Multiples of Complex Literary Transaction*. New York: Oxford UP, 1999.

Taylor, Thomas. *Thomas Taylor the Platonist: Selected Writings*. Eds. Kathleen Raine and George Mills Harper. Princeton: Princeton UP, 1969.

Thorpe, Clarence D. *John Keats: Complete Poems and Selected Letters*. New York: Odyssey Press, 1935.

——. *The Mind of John Keats*. New York: Oxford UP, 1926.

Valentine, Basil. *His Triumphant Chariot of Antimony, with Annotations of Theodore Kirkringus*. Transc. Ben Fairweather. (London: 1678): <http://www.levity.com/alchemy/antimony.html>.

——. *Twelve Keys*. Eisleben: 1599. <http://www.levity.com/alchemy/twelvkey.html>.

Van Gorden, John H. *Biblical Characters in Freemasonry*. Lexington, Mass.: The Masonic Book Club, 1980.

Vaughan, Thomas. Preface. *The Fame and Confession of the Fraternity of R: C: commonly, of the Rosie Cross. With a præface annexed thereto, and a short declaration of their physicall work. By Eugenius Philalethes*. London: J. M. for Giles Calvert, 1652. Transc. Kevin Day. <http://www.levity.com/alchemy/vaughanp.html>.

——. *Magia Adamica: or the antiquitie of magic, and the descent thereof from Adam downwards, proved. Whereunto is added a full discoverie of the true coelum terræ* (London: T.W. for H.B, 1650): <http://www.levity.com/alchemy/vaughan1.html>.

Waite, Arthur Edward. "The Pictorial Symbols of Alchemy." *Occult Review* 8.5 (Nov. 1908): <http://www.adepti.com/docs/ps2.pdf>.

Ward, Aileen. *PQ* 34 (1955): 177–88.

Wasserman, Earl. "Keats's Sonnet 'The Poet'." *Modern Language Notes* 67.7 (Nov. 1952): 454–56.

Webb, Thomas Smith. *The Freemason's Monitor or Illustrations of Masonry*. Salem: Cushing & Appleton, 1818.

Wells, Roy A. *Royal Arch Matters*. London: Lewis Masonic, 1984.

——. *Some Royal Arch Terms Examined.* London: Lewis Masonic, 1978.

Wilkes, John. *The Late John Wilkes' Catechism of a Ministerial Member; Taken from an Original Manuscript in Mr. Wilkes' Handwriting, never before printed, and adapted to the present Occasion. With Permission.* London: Printed for one of the Candidates for the Office of Printer to the King's Most Excellent Majesty, and Sold by William Hone, 1817.

Wilmshurst, W. L. *The Meaning of Masonry. A Philosophical Exposition of the Character of the Craft.* London: Lund, Humphries & Co., 1922. Whitefish, MT: Kessinger Publishing, 2007.

Wirth, Oswald. *Le Symbolisme Hermetique dans ses Rapports avec la Franc-Maconnerie.* Paris: n.p., 1909.

Woodford, Rev. A. F. A. "Freemasonry and Hermeticism." *Ars Quatuor Coronatorum: Being the Transactions of the Lodge Quatuor Coronati, No. 2076* 1 (1886): 28–34.

Yarker, John. *The Arcane Schools: A Review of their Origin and Antiquity; with a History of Freemasonry and its Relation to the Theosophic, Scientific, and Philosophic Mysteries.* Belfast: William Tait, 1909. <http://www.hermetics.org/yarker.html>.

Yates, Francis. *Giordano Bruno and the Hermetic Tradition.* Chicago: University of Chicago Press, 1964.

——. *The Occult Philosophy in the Elizabethan Age.* London: Routledge & Kegan Paul, 1979.

——. *The Rosicrucian Enlightenment.* Saint Albans: Paladin, 1975.

# Index